Communications
in Computer and Information Science   **1085**

Commenced Publication in 2007
Founding and Former Series Editors:
Phoebe Chen, Alfredo Cuzzocrea, Xiaoyong Du, Orhun Kara, Ting Liu,
Krishna M. Sivalingam, Dominik Ślęzak, Takashi Washio, Xiaokang Yang,
and Junsong Yuan

More information about this series at http://www.springer.com/series/7899

Christian Attiogbé · Flavio Ferrarotti ·
Sofian Maabout (Eds.)

New Trends in Model and Data Engineering

MEDI 2019 International Workshops
DETECT, DSSGA, TRIDENT
Toulouse, France, October 28–31, 2019
Proceedings

 Springer

Editors
Christian Attiogbé 🔟
University of Nantes
Nantes, France

Flavio Ferrarotti 🔟
Software Competence Center Hagenberg
Hagenberg, Austria

Sofian Maabout 🔟
University of Bordeaux
Bordeaux, France

ISSN 1865-0929   ISSN 1865-0937   (electronic)
Communications in Computer and Information Science
ISBN 978-3-030-32212-0   ISBN 978-3-030-32213-7   (eBook)
https://doi.org/10.1007/978-3-030-32213-7

This Springer imprint is published by the registered company Springer Nature Switzerland AG
The registered company address is: Gewerbestrasse 11, 6330 Cham, Switzerland

Preface

This volume is formed by the joint proceedings of the scientific workshops that were held in conjunction with the 9th International Conference on Model and Data Engineering (MEDI 2019), which took place in Toulouse, France, October 28–31, 2019.

Papers from the following workshops were selected for inclusion in the proceedings:

- The Workshop on Modeling, Verification and Testing of Dependable Critical Systems (DETECT)
- The Workshop on Data Science for Social Good in Africa (DSSGA)
- The Workshop on securiTy and pRivacy in moDEls aNd DaTa (TRIDENT)

Together they represent a wide range of topics that fall into the main areas of the MEDI 2019 conference.

Following an open call, workshop proposals were evaluated and selected by the MEDI workshop chairs Christian Attiogbé, Flavio Ferrarotti, and Sofian Maabout. Each selected workshop was managed by its own chairs and had its own Program Committee. An introduction to the selected workshops is presented in the next pages. The joint proceedings include 16 papers which were carefully selected from a total of 34 submissions.

We would like to thank the chairs of the DETECT, DSSGA, and TRIDENT workshops for their excellent work. We would also like to thank the Program Committee members of the workshops for their timely expertise in carefully reviewing the submissions. Finally, we acknowledge the support of the INP - ENSEEIHT school for hosting the workshops.

For readers of this volume, we hope you will find it both interesting and informative. We also hope it will inspire and embolden you to greater achievements and to look further into the challenges that still lie ahead in our digital society.

August 2019

Christian Attiogbé
Flavio Ferrarotti
Sofian Maabout

Contents

Workshop on Security and Privacy in Models and Data

Workshop on Modeling, Verification and Testing of Dependable Critical Systems

Workshop on Modeling, Verification and Testing of Dependable Critical Systems (DETECT)

Workshop Description

Critical systems are emerging fields of research and human safety is dependent upon the precise operation of these systems. The area of critical systems represents an intersection of several systems based on dependability properties like availability, reliability, safety, security, maintainability, etc. These systems are studied in several fields, such as railway, aviation, medical devices, etc.

Critical systems are more and more used in different domains and under several forms (e.g., cyber-physical systems, embedded systems, real-time systems), and have become more complex since they can be networked and composed of heterogeneous subsystems. Due to their heterogeneity and variability, critical systems require the expertise of modeling, verification, and testing areas to ensure their dependability and safety. The DETECT workshop is mainly based on the model-based system engineering paradigm and it aims to create a common community from academia and industry to share best practices, tools, and methodologies, taking into account the functional and non-functional aspects (including, but not limited to: scheduling, performance, security, safety, etc.).

The workshop would like to gather a wide range of stakeholders and its main objective is to provide the scientific community with a dedicated forum for discussing and representing their experience, and reporting state-of-the-art and/or in-progress research related to the model-based verification and testing of dependable critical systems.

For this workshop, contributions are devoted to modeling, verification, and testing of dependable critical systems. Specifically, the relevant topics include, but are not limited to:

- Formal specification and verification of dependable and critical systems
- Domain specific modeling languages, ontologies, methods, and frameworks
- System evaluation of functional and non-functional properties (scheduling, performance, security, safety, etc.)
- Methodologies and tools for CPS and RTES design
- Model-based testing of dependable critical systems
- Test models of dependable critical systems
- Data engineering facilities and requirement engineering techniques for ensuring dependability of critical systems
- Realistic case studies, applications, and experimentation

This volume contains the papers selected for presentation at the workshop. The acceptance rate was 37%. Indeed, DETECT 2019 received 16 papers from 8 countries (Algeria, France, Morocco, the Netherlands, Portugal, Taiwan, Tunisia and the United Kingdom). The Program Committee selected six full papers. Each paper was reviewed by at least three reviewers and was discussed afterwards by the reviewers and the Program Committee chairs.

Organization

DETECT Chairs

Yassine Ouhammou	ISAE-ENSMA, University of Poitiers, Futuroscope, France
Abderrhaim Ait Wakrime	IRT Railenium, France

International Program Committee

Abderrahim Ait Wakrime	IRT Railenium, France
Youness Bazhar	ASML, The Netherlands
Jamal Bentahar	Concordia University, Canada
Alessandro Biondi	Scuola Superiore Sant'Anna, Italy
Rachida Dssouli	Concordia University, Canada
Mamoun Filali-Amine	IRIT, France
Mohamed Ghazel	Ifsttar, France
Abdelouahed Gherbi	ETS Montreal, Canada
Paul Gibson	Télécom SudParis, France
Emmanuel Grolleau	LIAS/ISAE-ENSMA, France
Geoff Hamilton	Dublin City University, Ireland
Jameleddine Hassine	KFUPM, KSA, Saudi Arabia
Rafik Henia	Thales, France
Slim Kallel	University of Sfax, Tunisia
Yassine Ouhammou	LIAS/ISAE-ENSMA, France
Mehrdad Saadatmand	RISE SICS Vasteraas, Sweden
Colin Snook	University of Southampton, UK
Laurent Voisin	Systerel, France

Semantic-Driven Architecture for Autonomic Management of Cyber-Physical Systems (CPS) for Industry 4.0

Ernesto Exposito$^{(\boxtimes)}$ (iD)

Univ Pau & Pays Adour, E2S UPPA, LIUPPA, EA3000, 64600 Anglet, France
ernesto.exposito@univ-pau.fr

Abstract. Today we are living a new industrial revolution, which has its origin in the vertiginous deployment of ICT technologies that have been pervasively deployed at all levels of the modern society. This new industrial revolution, known as Industry 4.0, evolves within the context of a totally connected Cyber-Physic world in which organizations face immeasurable challenges related to the proper exploitation of ICT technologies to create and innovate in order to develop the intelligent products and services of tomorrow's society. This paper introduces a semantic-driven architecture intended to design, develop and manage Industry 4.0 systems by incrementally integrating monitoring, analysis, planning and management capabilities within autonomic processes able to coordinate and orchestrate Cyber-Physical Systems (CPS). This approach is also intended to cope with the integrability and interoperability challenges of the heterogeneous actors of the Internet of Everything (people, things, data and services) involved in the CPS of the Industry 4.0.

Keywords: Semantic-driven architecture · Cyber-Physical Systems · Industry 4.0 · Autonomic Computing

1 Introduction

The 18th century witness the advent of the first industrial revolution that was mainly characterized by the introduction of mechanical capabilities in the manufacturing processes based on power generated by steam engines. Mass production lines based on electrical energy are at the origin of the second industrial revolution towards the 20th century. These first two revolutions were mainly based on advances related to energy sources. In contrast, the third industrial revolution that began in the 1970s had its main origin in the arrival of the computer and the programming capabilities offered to automate manufacturing processes.

Today we are living a new industrial revolution named Industry 4.0, that is directly related to the accelerated advances enabled and promoted by information and communication technologies (ICT). A key element that allows us to

C. Attiogbé et al. (Eds.): MEDI 2019 Workshops, CCIS 1085, pp. 5–17, 2019.
https://doi.org/10.1007/978-3-030-32213-7_1

understand this new revolution is the fact that we live in an increasingly connected world (i.e. connected humans, things, systems and data). In this context, all organizations, including absolutely all industrial or service sectors, are faced to tremendous challenges on how to exploit this full-connected paradigm. These challenges can be grouped into two main types: how to define adequate strategies to exploit the huge amounts of generated data and how to define and integrate the required action plans in order to provide smart products and services of the Industry 4.0 era.

To meet these challenges, organizations of this new digital revolution need to adopt and efficiently apply a rich and complex set of new technologies, including the Internet of Things, social networks, cloud computing, big data or artificial intelligence, among others. However, the transition from a traditional organization to a 4.0 era organization is a very complex process to achieve and requires an appropriate methodology and a concrete reference architecture allowing to respond to the challenges mentioned above.

A significant number of works have been interested in proposing solutions to meet the challenges of designing and developing solutions for the Industry 4.0. In particular, important initiatives coordinated by government agencies and private organizations from countries with the most developed economies (USA, Germany, China and Japan) have been established in order to propose reference architectures that will enable a smooth transition from traditional organizations to the 4th Industrial Revolution, as well as to foster a favorable environment for innovation and creativity for new companies and emerging markets.

However, these initiatives and their reference architectures have different foundations and orientations which, despite fulfilling their role as a guideline and roadmap, do not encourage interoperability and the reuse of common efforts. This paper is interested in identifying the key and common aspects of these different abstract reference architectures in order to propose a concrete reference architecture, based on a semantic-driven architecture (SDA) approach and able to respond to the main challenges of the cyber-physical systems of Industry 4.0: integration, interoperability and process management for the development and operations of intelligent products and services.

This paper is structured as follows: the next section describes the background and explicitly defines the challenges of organizations of the 4th industrial revolution. The third section introduces the reference architectures developed by major global initiatives. The fourth section presents our proposal for a semantic-driven architecture intended to design, develop and manage Industry 4.0 systems by incrementally integrating monitoring, analysis, planning and management capabilities within autonomic and cognitive processes able to coordinate and orchestrate Cyber-Physical Systems (CPS). Finally, the conclusions and perspectives of this work are presented.

2   Background and Challenges Statement

Industrial revolutions have been mainly induced by energy or technological discoveries that have had far reaching economic, political, social and human impacts. The first industrial revolution was recognized as such towards the middle of the 18th century and was characterized by a major transformation in production processes, from manual operations to mechanized operations thanks to the power generated by steam engines [1–3]. Towards the end of the 19th century, the second industrial revolution appeared, again driven by a new source of energy: the electricity. This revolution was characterized by the massification of production and also by a transformation in the role played by human beings, who instead of having global knowledge or skills, should specialize, thus optimizing processes thanks to the division of labor. The third revolution, which began in the 1970s, had a different origin: it is not due to the emergence of new sources of energy, but to technological advances related to the information and communication technologies (ICT) [4]. Indeed, the automation of several production processes was boosted by the computer and its programming capabilities.

Today we are living a new industrial revolution, which has its origin in the vertiginous and accelerated deployment of ICT technologies [5]. This new industrial revolution, called Industry 4.0, takes place within the context of a fully connected world and extends beyond industrial processes automation to include the design, development and operations of intelligent products and services of tomorrow's society. Huge challenges are ahead for existing and future societies of any scale, which must embrace these vast technological advances in order to innovate and develop future markets for products and services. These challenges can be grouped into two main types: how to define adequate strategies to exploit the huge amounts of data obtained from a fully connected world and how to define and integrate agile and context-aware action plans within the smart products and services required by the Industry 4.0.

In order to guide organizations in meeting these challenges, this article proposes to examine this phenomenon through three facets: contextualization of the connected world paradigm, strategies for processing the collected data to yield information and knowledge, and capacity to develop decision models and actions strategies for delivering intelligent products and services.

2.1 Fully Connected World Paradigm

For some years now, the boundaries between the physical world and the computing space have been narrowing drastically and we have been approaching at an accelerated pace towards a Fully Connected World (FCW). Initially, it was the "things" that began to get connected giving birth to the concept of Internet of Things (IoT) and the enormous opportunities envisioned [6–8]. In the same vein, the idea of connecting machines and allowing communication between them gave rise to the concept of machine-to-machine (M2M) [9]. In order to foster interoperability, the concept of Web of Things (WoT) was proposed to encompass open protocols and facilitate access to the connected things [10].

The approach of interconnecting things or machines was opportunely extended by Cisco in 2013 to identify new markets and innovations opportunities leading to the fully connected world: The Internet of Everything (IoE) or the intelligent connection of people, things, data and process [11]. This vision has been naturally associated with other definitions such as the Internet of Data (IoD), Internet of Services (IoS) and Internet of People (IoP) [12–14].

2.2 Data, Information and Knowledge Challenge

In the FCW paradigm, the amount of collectable data grows exponentially and the need for its processing, very often in real time, is essential to produce meaningful information and in particular to create new knowledge. Existing solutions in the area of Business Intelligence (BI), Analytics or Artificial Intelligence (AI) have been successfully applied for years on the basis of data gathered from traditional information systems in order to support strategic decision making [15]. However, the quantity, heterogeneity and frequency of the potentially collectable data under the FCW paradigm of the Industry 4.0, reveal new challenges that will lead important innovations in the area of Big Data [16,17].

2.3 Acting upon a Fully Connected World Challenge

The second major challenge of the fourth industrial revolution is represented by the need to design intelligent systems capable of making the right decisions so that they can act on their environment, with or without human intervention, in order to adapt the offered products and services, while minimizing costs and maximizing customer satisfaction.

Several works have converged in proposing the Cyber-Physical Systems (CPS) as the adequate solution to offer this type of intelligent control through the dynamic and goal-oriented coordination of physical and computational entities [18,19].

However, despite the fact that this solution seems to be the most adapted to respond to the needs of intelligent control of products and services stated for Industry 4.0, today there are still a significant number of unknowns in this regard: there is no clear definition of what a CPS should offer as an automated or semi-automated control service, there is no reference implementation architecture, the interaction interfaces with the coordinated entities have not been standardized, among others [20].

In addition, the complexity related to the coexistence of multiple CPSs able of cooperating or collaborating within the framework of Cyber Systems of Systems (CPSoS) on the basis of the exchange of resources and services and in order to achieve common and/or individual objectives has not been fully addressed.

3 Architectures of Reference

In order to lead traditional organizations in their transition to the 4th Industrial Revolution as well as to create an enabling environment for innovation and creativity for emerging businesses and markets, several initiatives have been initiated worldwide and several architectures of reference have been promoted.

3.1   Industry 4.0 Initiatives

The most significant initiatives have been accompanied by government agencies and private organizations from countries in the most developed economies [5,21].

One of the most significant initiatives is the one presented by the German industry under the name Industrie 4.0. This initiative is aimed at identifying and guiding the use of technologies able to revolutionize the manufacturing industry [22]. To achieve this and to establish a common understanding of this technological revolution, the Reference Architectural Model Industrie 4.0 (RAMI4.0) has been proposed. This is one of the reference architectures that has had the biggest impact worldwide and will be part of our study.

The second most important initiative is represented by the Industrial Internet Consortium (IIC), created by the most important US companies in the area of telecommunications and new technologies [23]. This initiative has proposed the Industrial Internet Reference Architecture (IIRA). This second reference architecture has been developed independently from the RAMI 4.0 architecture and consequently there are important differences between the dimensions of interest as well as the architectural features of both propositions. In our work we are interested in identifying and bringing together the main advantages provided by both reference architectures.

Among the large number of existing initiatives, we can also identify those launched on the Asian continent under the name Made in China 2025 [24] and the Japanese Industrial Value Chain Initiative (IVI) [5]. Both initiatives promote collaboration and common understanding of technologies capable of accelerating the modernization of the industries of the future.

Due to the impact obtained and the vast potentialities identified, this study will concentrate on the main reference architectures, namely RAMI 4.0 and IIRA.

3.2   Industry 4.0 Reference Architectures

As previously indicated, the RAMI 4.0 and IIRA architectures seek to promote a knowledge-sharing paradigm of Industry 4.0, in order to guide organizations in their transition and in particular to advise on the use of the ICT advances. The common point of the two initiatives lies in projecting organizations towards a more intelligent world. Both propose a systemic vision aimed at building complex, connected and intelligent systems. The main difference is that RAMI 4.0 extends this vision to encompass the entire value chain and product lifecycle, while IIRA retains a more concrete vision of the ICT world.

Industrial Internet Reference Architecture (IIRA). The IIRA proposes a standards-based open architecture for the Industrial Internet of Things (IIoT). IIRA defines 4 viewpoints: Business (stakeholders and business vision), Usage (expected IIoT system usage), Functional (functional components of the IIoT system) and Implementation (technologies involved to implement the functional components). In particular, the functional view is decomposed into five functional domains: control domain (closed-loop control involving sensing, control and actuation), operations domain (management and maintenance), information domain (data collection and analysis), application domain (application use-case oriented functions), business domain (business goals-oriented functions). These functional domains are analyzed within two dimensions: the system characteristics to be guaranteed and the system-wide crosscutting functions.

Additionally, IIRA proposes two concerns related to the multilayered viewpoints architecture: the scope of applicability (diversity of industrial sectors) and system lifecycle process (IIoT system conception, design and implementation). The Fig. 1 summarizes the IIRA reference architecture.

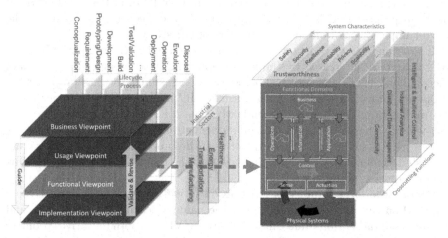

Fig. 1. Industrial Internet Reference Architecture (IIRA).

Reference Architectural Model Industrie 4.0 (RAMI4.0). The RAMI reference architecture is based on tree axis including: the hierarchy levels dimension (from the product to the enterprise and connected world), the life cycle and value stream dimension (product conception and production) and the layered dimension (properties and system structures). The Fig. 2 presents the RAMI 4.0 reference architecture.

The first axis represents the hierarchy levels dimension that clearly characterizes the Industry 4.0 revolution. The highest level represents the connected world, the lower level the smart products and the intermediate levels the smart factory involving field and control devices as well as the stations, work centers and the whole factory.

The second axis targets the main goal of the industry: the whole product lifecycle. It distinguishes two phases. The first is the type phase, where the plans for the development to the maintenance of the product is conceived from the original idea. The second is the instance phase, where each product (the instance) is really produced and maintained.

Finally, the third axis proposes a 6 layered dimension including: asset (representing the physical things of the real world), integration (enabling cyber-physical transition), communication (enabling access to the information), information (collection and processing of relevant data), functional (asset's functionalities), business (organization goals and business processes).

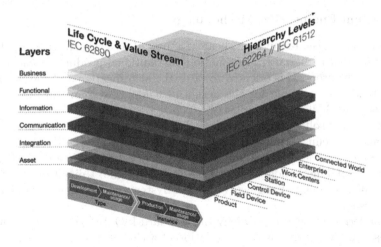

Fig. 2. Reference Architectural Model Industrie 4.0 (RAMI4.0).

4 Semantic-Driven Architecture for Autonomic CPS

Based on the challenges identified for the solution carriers of the 4th industry revolution as well as on the main reference architectures promoted by international initiatives, this section presents a series of proposals in order to guide the design and development of solutions for Industry 4.0. Although the community mainly privileges the manufacturing processes for the elaboration of intelligent products, our proposal also extends to the area of intelligent services.

In both reference architectures previously described a systemic vision aimed at building complex, connected and intelligent systems is proposed. Although the IIRA architecture privileges the term Industrial Internet of Things (IIoT), it could be generalized that both reference architectures are oriented towards the development of a type of intelligent system that can be represented by the Cyber Physical Systems. Indeed, Industry 4.0 systems are characterized by being composed of physical and computational entities that interact intelligently in order to achieve specific objectives, such as for example the intelligent products and services targeted by the Industry 4.0.

In order to ensure that the objective of common understanding and integration of new technologies in the framework of the Industry 4.0 can be guaranteed in a tangible way, it is necessary to extract the key elements of these reference architectures, in particular to guide the design and development of Cyber Physical Systems.

This proposal includes the identification of a suitable methodology as well as the proposal of a generic and concrete architectural framework, based on semantic models and resulting from the reference architectures previously presented.

4.1   System Engineering Methodology

Conscious of the need to guide the bearers of new ideas as well as those in charge of carrying out the digital transformation of traditional production and service companies, our proposal is oriented towards the identification and specialization of a methodology suitable for the design of complex systems and capable of integrating the challenges of Industry 4.0.

In the area of software engineering and systems engineering, several methodologies and modeling frameworks have been proposed for the development of complex systems. For reasons of limited space, this section will not go into details about traditional methodologies, such as (Rational/Agile) Unified Process based on the Unified Modeling Language (UML) or Systems engineering methodologies based on SysML.

We preferred to introduce briefly the standard ISO/IEC/IEEE 42010 which proposes a methodology for the description of architectures in the area of software and system engineering [25]. This standard promotes a methodology for the creation, analysis and development of systems based on the use of descriptions of architectures. To this end, the standard proposes a core ontology for architecture descriptions. Figure 3, presents this core ontology.

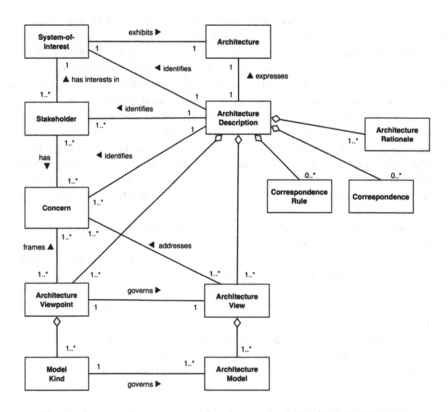

Fig. 3. Core ontology proposed by the standard ISO/IEC/IEEE 42010.

One of the key elements of this core ontology are the architecture viewpoints and views, which are components of models capable of capturing the structural and behavioral foundations of a system architecture.

4.2   Semantic-Driven Architecture

Our architecture is based on the core ontology of the ISO/IEC/IEEE 42010 standard and proposes the definition of 5 viewpoints aimed at integrating the structural and behavioral architectural views of the Industry 4.0 CPS: connection, communication, coordination, cooperation and collaboration viewpoints (see Table 1).

Based on the Semantic-Driven Architecture (SDA) recommendation proposed by the OMG and in particular the Distributed Ontology, Modeling, and Specification Language (DOL) [27], the ontology providing the semantic basis for the architecture of CPS is presented in the Fig. 4. At the connection layer, the fully connected world (IoE) represented by the IoD, IoT, IoS and IoP actors are integrated in order to be part of a CPS. At the communication layer, the required interoperability services are provided in order guarantee the uniform access to the IoE actors (i.e. interoperable actors). At the coordination layers, the required operation processes (based on BPMN, CMMN and DMN specifications) can be designed and implemented in order to obtain concrete instances of CPSs, able to provide the expected product and services. At the cooperation layer, two or more CPSs (CPSoS) would be able to share resources or services, in order to achieve individual goals. Finally, at the collaboration layer, two or more cooperative CPSs (CPSoS) would be able to work together in order to achieve common goals.

Based on the semantic structure previously presented, the integration, interoperability and coordination of the CPSs can be guaranteed for operational processes of production and services. Additionally, the intelligent management of these processes, as well as the self-management capabilities that are required to implement smart CPS can be provided through the Autonomic Computing framework proposed by IBM [26]. An autonomic CPS (A-CPS) must implement autonomic processes for self-* functions based on monitoring, analyzing, planning and executing (MAPE) activities sharing a common knowledge base.

- Monitoring: retrieves state information of the IoE actors via the sensor interface. Relevant information is filtered and stored in the knowledge base.
- Analyzing: compares the observed data from the expected values (symptoms) in order to detect an undesirable state (diagnosis).
- Planning: selects or elaborates strategies aimed at preventing or correcting an undesirable state or intended to achieve the targeted goals (treatment).
- Executing: executes the tuning actions on the IoE via the effector interface and traces this information in the knowledge base for future analysis and planning (treatment results).

The knowledge base is required in order to implement autonomic process based on observed values, the identification of symptoms and diagnosis and the

Table 1. Viewpoints for a CPS layered reference architecture.

Viewpoint (Stakeholders)	Concern	Description	
Connection (IT Network integrator)	IoE entities sharing a common medium or channel	Network Integrability	End devices and access networks (Things and People)
			Internet
			Data centers (Data, People and Services)
Communication (IT Services integrator)	IoE entities able to understand each other by exchanging messages via a common medium or channel	Middleware Integrability	Object/Procedure oriented (ORB / RPC)
			Message/Event oriented (MOM / EDA)
			Service/Micro-service oriented (SOA / MSA)
		Interoperability	Syntactic
			Semantic
			Cross-domains and Open standards
		Communication modes	Synchronous/ Asynchronous
			IN-only, IN-OUT, OUT-IN, OUT-only
			Request/Reply
			Publish/Subscribe
			Push/Pull
Coordination (Business process designer)	IoE entities work together following the orders or the instructions of a coordinator	Intra-system orchestration (CPS)	Service orchestration within a business domain
Cooperation (CPS Orchestrator)	CPS entities work together to achieve individual goals	Inter-systems choreography (CPSoS)	Service choreography among several business domains
Collaboration (CPS Choreographer)	CPS entities work together to achieve a common global goal	Inter-systems orchestration (CPSoS)	Service orchestration among several business domains

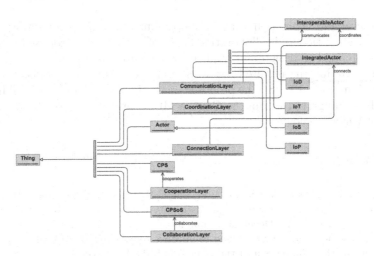

Fig. 4. Structural ontology of the CPS viewpoints.

execution of remedial treatments. The results observed from the treatment need to be captured in order to reconfigure the behavior if required. The behavioral ontology presented in Fig. 5, illustrates the basic entities and relationships enabling the implementation of autonomic process in order to add the self-management capabilities to the CPS.

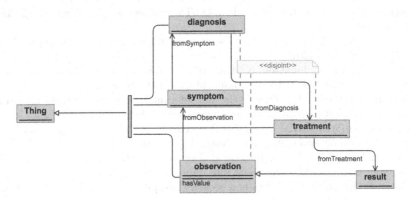

Fig. 5. Behavioral ontology of autonomic CPS (A-CPS).

5   Conclusions and Perspectives

This research work has proposed a well-adapted methodology and a generic architectural framework aimed at facilitating the design and implementation of Autonomic Cyber Physical Systems (A-CPS) for the Industry 4.0. This architecture followed a multi-viewpoints approach and introduced the foundations of the structural and behavioral semantics of the integration, interoperation, coordination, cooperation and collaboration layers of A-CPS. The proposed semantic model is intended to design and implement the autonomic properties by incrementally including the required monitoring, analysis (diagnosis), planning and execution functions A-CPS. The proposed methodology and architectural framework will be integrated within the Capella MBSE opensource tool based on the ARCADIA methodology.

References

1. Li, X., Li, D., Wan, J., Vasilakos, A.V., Lai, C.F., Wang, S.: A review of industrial wireless networks in the context of industry 4.0. Wireless Netw. **23**(1), 23–41 (2017)
2. Huber, A., Weiss, A.: Developing human-robot interaction for an industry 4.0 robot: how industry workers helped to improve remote-hri to physical-hri. In: Proceedings of the Companion of the 2017 ACM/IEEE International Conference on Human-Robot Interaction, pp. 137–138. ACM (2017)
3. Xu, L.D., Xu, E.L., Li, L.: Industry 4.0: state of the art and future trends. Int. J. Prod. Res. **56**(8), 2941–2962 (2018)
4. Liao, Y., Deschamps, F., Loures, E.F.R., Ramos, L.F.P.: Past present and future of industry 4.0-a systematic literature review and research agenda proposal. Int. J. Prod. Res. **55**(12), 3609–3629 (2017)
5. Zhong, R.Y., Xu, X., Klotz, E., Newman, S.T.: Intelligent manufacturing in the context of industry 4.0: a review. Engineering **3**(5), 616–630 (2017)
6. Ashton, K., et al.: That 'internet of things' thing. RFID J. **22**(7), 97–114 (2009)
7. Gershenfeld, N., Krikorian, R., Cohen, D.: The internet of things. Sci. Am. **291**(4), 76–81 (2004)
8. Atzori, L., Iera, A., Morabito, G.: The internet of things: a survey. Comput. Netw. **54**(15), 2787–2805 (2010)
9. Wu, G., Talwar, S., Johnsson, K., Himayat, N., Johnson, K.D.: M2m: from mobile to embedded internet. IEEE Commun. Mag. **49**(4), 36–43 (2011)
10. Guinard, D., Trifa, V.: Towards the web of things: web mashups for embedded devices. In: Workshop on Mashups, Enterprise Mashups and Lightweight Composition on the Web (MEM 2009). In: Proceedings of WWW (International World Wide Web Conferences), vol. 15, Madrid, Spain (2009)
11. Bradley, J., Barbier, J., Handler, D.: Embracing the internet of everything to capture your share of $14.4 trillion. White Paper, Cisco (2013)
12. Weber, R.H.: Internet of things-new security and privacy challenges. Comput. Law Secur. Rev. **26**(1), 23–30 (2010)
13. Schroth, C., Janner, T.: Web 2.0 and soa: converging concepts enabling the internet of services. IT Prof. **9**(3), 36–41 (2007)
14. Conti, M., Passarella, A., Das, S.K.: The internet of people (iop): a new wave in pervasive mobile computing. Pervasive Mob. Comput. **41**, 1–27 (2017)
15. Bordeleau, F.E., Mosconi, E., Santa-Eulalia, L.A.: Business intelligence in industry 4.0: state of the art and research opportunities. In: Proceedings of the 51st Hawaii International Conference on System Sciences (2018)
16. Lee, J., Kao, H.A., Yang, S.: Service innovation and smart analytics for industry 4.0 and big data environment. Procedia CIRP **16**, 3–8 (2014)

17. Wang, S., Wan, J., Zhang, D., Li, D., Zhang, C.: Towards smart factory for industry 4.0: a self-organized multi-agent system with big data based feedback and coordination. Comput. Netw. **101**, 158–168 (2016)
18. Rajkumar, R., Lee, I., Sha, L., Stankovic, J.: Cyber-physical systems: the next computing revolution. In: Design Automation Conference, pp. 731–736. IEEE (2010)
19. Tan, Y., Goddard, S., Pérez, L.C.: A prototype architecture for cyber-physical systems. ACM Sigbed Rev. **5**(1), 26 (2008)
20. Lee, E.A.: Cyber physical systems: design challenges. In: 2008 11th IEEE International Symposium on Object and Component-Oriented Real-Time Distributed Computing (ISORC), pp. 363–369. IEEE (2008)
21. Wang, Y., Towara, T., Anderl, R.: Topological approach for mapping technologies in reference architectural model industrie 4.0 (rami 4.0). In: Proceedings of the World Congress on Engineering and Computer Science. vol. 2 (2017)
22. Kagermann, H., Helbig, J., Hellinger, A., Wahlster, W.: Recommendations for implementing the strategic initiative INDUSTRIE 4.0: securing the future of German manufacturing industry; final report of the Industrie 4.0 Working Group. Forschungsunion (2013)
23. Lin, S., et al.: The industrial internet of things volume G1: reference architecture. Ind. Internet Consortium 10–46 (2017)
24. Li, L.: China's manufacturing locus in 2025: with a comparison of "made-in-china 2025" and "industry 4.0". Technol. Forecast. Soc. Change **135**, 66–74 (2018)
25. ISO: ISO/IEC 42010 systems and software engineering - architectural description (2011)
26. Kephart, J.O., Chess, D.M.: The vision of autonomic computing. Computer **1**, 41–50 (2003)
27. Object Management Groupe: Distributed Ontology, Modelling, and Specification Language (DOL) (2018)

Domain-Specific Scenarios
for Refinement-Based Methods

Colin Snook(✉), Thai Son Hoang, Dana Dghaym, and Michael Butler

ECS, University of Southampton, Southampton, UK
{cfs,t.s.hoang,d.dghaym,mjb}@ecs.soton.ac.uk

Abstract. Formal methods use abstraction and rigorously verified refinement to manage the design of complex systems, ensuring that they satisfy important invariant properties. However, formal verification is not sufficient: models must also be tested to ensure that they behave according to the informal requirements and validated by domain experts who may not be expert in formal modelling. This can be satisfied by scenarios that complement the requirements specification. The model can be animated to check that the scenario is feasible in the model and that the model reaches states expected in the scenario. However, there are two problems with this approach. (1) The provided scenarios are at the most concrete level corresponding to the full requirements and cannot be used until all the refinements have been completed in the model. (2) The natural language used to describe the scenarios is often verbose, ambiguous and therefore difficult to understand; especially if the modeller is not a domain expert. In this paper we propose a method of abstracting scenarios from concrete ones so that they can be used to test early refinements of the model. We also show by example how a precise and concise domain specific language can be used for writing these abstract scenarios in a style that can be easily understood by the domain expert (for validation purposes) as well as the modeller (for behavioural verification). We base our approach on the Cucumber framework for scenarios and the Event-B modelling language and tool set. We illustrate the proposed methods on the ERTMS/ETCS Hybrid Level 3 specification for railway controls (The example model and scenario scripts supporting this paper are openly available at https://doi.org/10.5258/SOTON/D1026).

Keywords: Event-B · Cucumber · Validation · Domain specific language

1 Introduction

Abstraction and refinement play a vital role in analysing the complexity of critical systems via formal modelling. Abstraction allows key properties to be established which are then proven to be maintained as system details are gradually introduced in a series of refinements. However, domain requirements are often written in natural language [3] which can be verbose and ambiguous leading

© Springer Nature Switzerland AG 2019
C. Attiogbé et al. (Eds.): MEDI 2019 Workshops, CCIS 1085, pp. 18–31, 2019.
https://doi.org/10.1007/978-3-030-32213-7_2

to potential misinterpretation by formal modelling engineers. Hence, model verification is insufficient; validation of the model by domain experts is equally important to ensure that it is a true representation of the system in mind. In previous work [9] we proposed a behaviour driven approach to formal modelling that allows domain experts to drive the formal modelling using scenarios. The model is animated to check that the scenario is feasible and reaches the states expected in the scenario. In this paper we propose the use of a Domain Specific Language (DSL) that can be understood both by domain expert and model engineer and is precise enough to provide a repeatable validation/acceptance test of the formal systems model. Furthermore, we propose a technique of synthesising abstract scenarios from more concrete ones, so that the abstract refinements of the model can be checked at an intermediate stage rather than waiting until the final details have been incorporated. We illustrate the approach using the European Rail Traffic Management System (ERTMS)/European Train Control System (ETCS), Hybrid Level 3 (HL3) specification [7] for which we have previously developed a formal model presented in [4].

The paper is structured as follows: Sect. 2 provides background on the Event-B formal modelling language, Cucumber framework for scenarios and the HL3 case study. Section 3 introduces the example scenario (from [7]) that we use for illustrating our proposed method. Section 4 illustrates a possible DSL for scenarios of the HL3 model. Section 5 shows how we would describe the example scenario in our DSL. Section 6 presents abstract versions of the concrete scenario to illustrate how these can be systematically deduced to match the refinements in the model. Section 8 describes future work and Sect. 9 concludes.

2   Background

2.1   Event-B

Event-B [1] is a formal method for system development. An Event-B model contains two parts: *contexts* and *machines*. Contexts contain *carrier sets* s, *constants* c, and *axioms* $A(c)$ that constrain the carrier sets and constants. Note that the model may be underspecified, e.g., the value of the sets and constants can be any value satisfying the axioms. Machines contain *variables* v, *invariants* $I(v)$ that constrain the variables, and *events*. An event comprises a guard denoting its enabling-condition and an action describing how the variables are modified when the event is executed. In general, an event e has the following form, where t are the event parameters, $G(t, v)$ is the guard of the event, and $v := E(t, v)$ is the action of the event.

$$\text{any t where } G(t,v) \text{ then } v := E(t,v) \text{ end}$$

Actions in Event-B are, in the most general cases, non-deterministic [8], e.g., of the form (v is assigned any element from the set $E(v)$) or $v :| P(v,v')$ (v is assigned any value satisfying the before-after predicate $P(v,v')$). A special event called INITIALISATION without parameters and guards is used to put the system into the initial state.

A machine in Event-B corresponds to a transition system where *variables* represent the state and *events* specify the transitions. Event-B uses a mathematical language that is based on set theory and predicate logic.

Contexts can be *extended* by adding new carrier sets, constants, axioms, and theorems. Machines can be *refined* by adding and modifying variables, invariants, events. In this paper, we do not focus on context extension and machine refinement.

Event-B is supported by the Rodin Platform (Rodin) [2], an extensible open source toolkit which includes facilities for modelling, verifying the consistency of models using theorem proving and model checking techniques, and validating models with simulation-based approaches.

2.2   Cucumber for Event-B

The Behaviour-Driven Development (BDD) principle aims for pure domain oriented feature description without any technical knowledge. In particular, BDD aims for understandable tests which can be executed on the specifications of a system. BDD is important for communication between the business stakeholders and the software developers. Gherkin/Cucumber [10] is one of the various frameworks supporting BDD.

Gherkin [10, Chapter 3] is a language that defines lightweight structures for describing the expected behaviour in a plain text, readable by both stakeholders and developers, which is still automatically executable.

Each Gherkin scenario consists of steps starting with one of the keywords: Given, When, Then, And or But.

- Keyword Given is used for writing test preconditions that describe how to put the system under test in a known state. This should happen without any user interaction. It is good practice to check whether the system reached the specified state.
- Keyword When is used to describe the tested interaction including the provided input. This is the stimulus triggering the execution.
- Keyword Then is used to test postconditions that describe the expected output. Only the observable outcome should be compared, not the internal system state. The test fails if the real observation differs from the expected results.
- Keywords And and But can be used for additional test constructs.

In [9], we described our specialisation of Cucumber for Event-B with the purpose of automatically executing of scenarios for Event-B models. Cucumber [10] is a framework for executing acceptance tests written in Gherkin language and provides Gherkin language parser, test automation as well as report generation. We provide Cucumber step definitions for Event-B in [5] allowing us to execute the Gherkin scenarios directly on the Event-B models. The Cucumber step definitions for Event-B allow to execute an event with some constraints on the parameters, or to check if an event is enabled/disabled in the current state, or to check if the current state satisfies some constraint.

2.3   Hybrid ERTMS/ETCS Level 3 Basics

The train separation function of ERTMS/ETCS Level 3 relies entirely on the condition that the system knows at all times the position, length, and integrity status of the train [7]. Each train needs to be fitted with a Train Integrity Monitoring System (TIMS) to report its position and integrity status to the system. Due to the limitation of GSM-R communication, these pre-conditions for Level 3 operation are not satisfied as the train may disconnect from the system because of poor communication. The HL3 concept is brought up to solve the disconnect issue by using a limited implementation of track-side train detection. Trains that are disconnected from the HL3 are still visible using track-side train detection. Thus trains which are not confirming integrity can still be authorized to run on the line.

Figure 1 shows the HL3 system conventions. The track line is divided into Trackside Train Detection (TTD) sections according to the track-side equipment. If no train is shown on the TTD section, the TTD section is considered as *free*. Otherwise, it is considered as *occupied*. This large physical section is then split into as many Virtual Sub-Section (VSS) as required for the intended performance. These VSS are fixed virtual blocks to avoid train collision. The occupation status of the VSS is determined using both TTD status information and position reports of the train. The VSS is considered as *free* when the track-side is certain that no train is located on the VSS while it is considered as *occupied* when some integer train is located on this VSS while the track-side is certain that no other vehicle is located on the same VSS. Status *unknown* and *ambiguous* are used to indicate the states under the scenario with disconnected trains. A VSS is considered as *unknown* when there is no certainty if it is free. And a VSS is considered as *ambiguous* when it is known to be *occupied* but it is unsure whether there is another train on the same VSS. The track-side detection equipment can improve the system performance by providing a faster release of VSS when the TTD is *free* on the basis of train position reports. A train on a track with an established safe radio connection to the track-side is considered as a connected train. The *train location* defines the track-side view of the VSS that is currently occupied by a connecting train, whose granularity is one VSS. The front and rear end of the train location is considered independently from each other. Each train has an estimated front end, while the rear end is derived from the estimated front end and the safe train length through train integrity confirmation. It takes time for a train to stop after it applies brakes. The estimated front end and rear end are extended to the max safe front end and min safe rear end with an additional safety margin to guarantee the safety properties of the system. When the track-side receives the report that the max safe front end of the train has entered a VSS, it considers the train to be located on this VSS. A train that allows the track-side to release VSS in the rear of the train based on its position reports is defined as integer train [7]. However, when modelling the HL3 system in Event-B is complicated as the events in Event-B models can be difficult to validate due to the complexity of conditions that are challenging to explain to domain experts. Fischer and Dghaym propose to

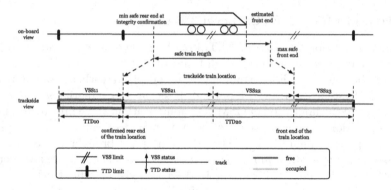

Fig. 1. Hybrid ERTMS/ETCS Level 3 system conventions [7]

create test cases on Event-B models using a Cucumber framework, which defines lightweight structures for describing the expected behaviour readable by both domain experts and modelers [6]. Based on their definition for the concrete scenarios, we define approaches to map concrete scenarios to abstract scenarios and refine the abstract scenarios to concrete scenarios.

3   Example Scenario

In this section, we use Scenario 4: Start of Mission/End of Mission in [7] to illustrate our approach to generation of abstract scenarios. In this scenario, there are eight numbered steps. However, since most steps contain a sequence of actions and consequent state changes, we break the steps down further into sub-steps[1]. We also note that the associated diagram (Fig. 2) shows, for each step, more details about the expected state, than is given in the text. We have included some (but for brevity, not all) of this state in the scenario. Hence, the sub-steps given in *italic* are derived from the diagram rather than the original text of [7].

1. (a) Train 1 is standing on VSS 11
   (b) with desk closed and no communication session.
   (c) All VSS in TTD 10 are "unknown".
   (d) *TTD 10 is occupied and TTD20 is free.*
2. (a) Train 1 performs the Start of Mission procedure.
   (b) Integrity is confirmed.
   (c) Because train 1 reports its position on VSS 11,
   (d) this VSS becomes "ambiguous".
3. (a) Train 1 receives an OS MA until end of VSS 12
   (b) and moves to VSS 12
   (c) which becomes "ambiguous".

---

[1] Note that we have adapted step 3 slightly compared to the specification because our model does not support granting Full Supervision Movement Authority (FS MA) containing VSS that are not free.

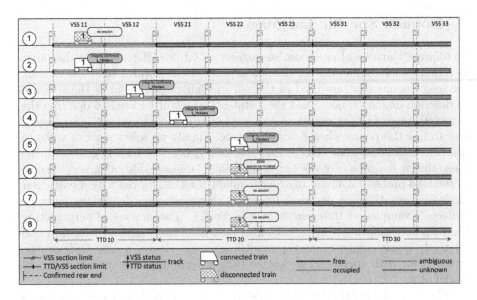

Fig. 2. Start of Mission/End of Mission [7]

   (d) VSS 11 goes to "unknown".
   (e) Train 1 receives an FS MA until end of VSS 22
4. (a) Train 1 moves to VSS 21
   (b) which becomes occupied
   (c) and all VSS in TTD 10 become "free", VSS 11 and VSS 12.
   (d) *TTD 10 is free and TTD20 is occupied.*
5. (a) Train 1 continues to VSS 22
   (b) which becomes "occupied".
   (c) VSS 21 becomes "free";
6. Train 1 performs the End of Mission (EOM) procedure.
7. (a) Due to the EoM procedure VSS 22 goes to "unknown"
   (b) and the disconnect propagation timer of VSS 22 is started.
8. (a) The disconnect propagation timer of VSS 22 expires.
   (b) All remaining VSS in TTD 20 go to "unknown".

This example scenario is useful for understanding the specification but it still contains ambiguities that are revealed when considering a formally precise model. For example trains do not usually move to a new section in one atomic step; it is not stated when position reports are sent or what information they contain. In addition, the use of natural language is not always consistent; in order to animate the scenario in a repeatable way with tool support, we need a more consistent syntax. We also need more abstract versions of the scenario if we wish to validate the initial stages of our model.

4   Domain Specific Language

To improve clarity and precision, we suggest a DSL for HL3 scenarios that aims to retain understandability for domain experts of the natural language version. We select nouns that are used in the natural language version of the scenario to describe domain objects and their state. These will be used to describe the expected state of the model. We select a set of adjectives to provide a consistent way to link the nouns when describing state. Finally we select a set of verbs to describe transitions that change the state of objects The DSL is generic in the sense that it is agnostic of the target modelling language, although very specific to the HL3 problem domain. In order to adapt the DSL for use with a particular modelling notation (in our case Event-B) cucumber step definitions must be written. Examples of these are shown in Sect. 7. The process of constructing the DSL and adapting it using cucumber step definitions is straightforward and relatively quick compared to the modelling stage. Hence, a new DSL can be invented for each specification domain before beginning to construct a formal model of it.

The kind of formal refinement modelling that we wish to support is based on abstract representation of state. In each refinement further distinction of the state values are added, either by replacing a state variable with an alternative one that gives finer detail, or by adding a completely new variable. As state details are added, the transition events that change state are elaborated to deal with the new values. In many cases completely new transitions are revealed. As the model refinement process is state driven, so is our DSL for scenario abstraction/refinement. Therefore in the DSL we add alternative names for state values so that the scenario can be adapted to abstract levels by re-phrasing clauses when the state is modelled more abstractly.

Nouns

```
 1  <train> = <label>
 2  <section> = TTDx
 3  <sub-section> = <section>.VSSy
 4  <ma>   = <abstract ma> | <concrete ma>
 5  <abstract ma> = MA until <sub-section>
 6  <concrete ma> = FSMA until <sub-section> | OSMA until <sub-section>
 7  <timer> = <sub-section>.DisconnectTimer | <sub-section>.ShadowTimer | <sub-section>.
        GhostTimer
 8  <section state> = FREE | OCCUPIED
 9  <sub-section sate> = <abstract sub-section state> | <concrete sub-section state>
10  <abstract sub-section state> = AVAILABLE | UNAVAILABLE
11  <concrete sub-section state> = FREE| OCCUPIED | AMBIGUOUS | UNKNOWN
```

Adjectives

1 <train> stood at <sub-section>
2 <train> connected | disconnected
3 <train> in mission | no mission
4 <train> is integral | is split
5 <train> has <ma>
6 <section> is <section state>
7 <sub-section> is <sub-section state>

Verbs

1   <train> enters | leaves <sub-section>
2   <train> connects | disconnects
3   <train> starts mission | ends mission
4   <train> splits | couples
5   <train> receives <ma>
6   <timer> starts
7   <timer> expires
8   <train> reports position
9   <train> reports position as integral
10 <train> reports position as split

5   Concrete Scenario Using DSL

With reference to the scenario steps listed in Sect. 3, we first illustrate how the natural language scenario of the specification can be expressed in our domain specific language (Fig. 3). In the Sect. 6 we will show how to extract abstract scenarios that fit with our refinement levels.

Steps 1a, 1b, 1c and 1d give the initial starting state which becomes a Given clause in our language (Lines 1–6). Note that the track state is included as Given rather than checked by a Then clause because it does not necessarily follow from the train state. Step 2a is an action that, in our model, requires two distinct events which we conjoin in a When clause (Line 7) where Train1 *starts mission* and *connects*. Steps 2b and 2c, are performed in a single atomic reporting event in our model, giving another When clause (Line 8). Step 2d gives an expected consequence concerning the state of a

```
1   Given Train1 stood at VSS11
2     And Train1 disconnected
3     And TTD10.VSS11 is UNKNOWN
4     And TTD10.VSS12 is UNKNOWN
5     And TTD10 is OCCUPIED
6     And TTD20 is FREE
7   When Train1 starts mission and Train1 connects
8   When Train1 reports position as integral
9     Then VSS11 is AMBIGUOUS
10  When Train1 receives OSMA until VSS12
11  When Train1 enters VSS12
12  When Train1 leaves VSS11
13  When Train1 reports position as integral
14    Then VSS12 is AMBIGUOUS
15    And VSS11 is UNKNOWN
16  When Train1 receives FSMA until VSS22
17  When Train1 enters VSS21
18  When Train1 leaves VSS12
19  When Train1 reports position as integral
20    Then TTD10.VSS11 is FREE
21    And TTD10.VSS12 is FREE
22    And TTD10.VSS21 is OCCUPIED
23    And TTD10 is OCCUPIED
24    And TTD20 is FREE
25  When Train1 enters VSS22
26  When Train1 leaves VSS21
27  When Train1 reports position as integral
28    Then TTD20.VSS21 is FREE
29    And TTD20.VSS22 is OCCUPIED
30  When Train1 disconnects and Train1 ends mission
31    Then TTD20.VSS22 is UNKNOWN
32    Then VSS22.disconnect_propagation_timer starts
33  When VSS22.disconnect_propagation_timer expires
34    Then VSS21 is UNKNOWN
35    And VSS23 is UNKNOWN
```

Fig. 3. Concrete scenario using DSL

VSS, which we check with a Then clause (Line 9). Step 3a grants an On Sight Movement Authority (OS MA) up to VSS 12, to the train (Line 10). Step 3b is somewhat ambiguous since trains can span more than one sub-section and therefore enter and leave them in distinct events which are not normally simultaneous. We interpret Step 3b as two consecutive steps; enter the new VSS 12

(Line 11) and then leave the previous VSS 11 (Line 12). Also, we assume that the train then reports its new position as VSS 12 (Line 13), since otherwise the Virtual Block Detector (VBD) would not know to update the VSS states as indicated in Steps 3c and 3d. Step 3 is a good example of why a more precise domain specific language is needed for describing scenarios. A similar process of interpretation is followed in the remaining steps.

6   Abstract Scenarios

In order to obtain scenarios that can be used to validate our abstract models, we deduce correspondingly abstract scenarios from the concrete one that has been translated into our DSL in Sect. 5. To do this, we consider the data refinement of the model including superposition of new data. The process systematically reduces the concrete scenario by omitting any irrelevant details and only retaining clauses that relate to the data representations used in that refinement level. Note that data representation may vary in refinement levels which affects the Cucumber step definition used to convert the scenarios into a form that can be used to animate the model.

```
1  Given Train1 stood at VSS11
2  When Train1 enters VSS12
3     Then Train1 stood at VSS11,VSS12
4  When Train1 leaves VSS11
5     Then Train1 stood at VSS12
6  When Train1 enters VSS21
7     Then Train1 stood at VSS12,VSS21
8  When Train1 leaves VSS12
9     Then Train1 stood at VSS21
10 When Train1 enters VSS22
11    Then Train1 stood at VSS21,VSS22
12 When Train1 leaves VSS21
13    Then Train1 stood at VSS22
```

(a) Movement on VSS

```
1  Given Train1 stood at TTD10.VSS11
2     And Train1 is disconnected
3     And TTD10 is OCCUPIED
4     And TTD20 is FREE
5  When Train1 connects
6     Then Train1 connected
7  When Train1 enters TTD10.VSS12
8  When Train1 leaves TTD10.VSS11
9  When Train1 enters TTD10.VSS21
10    Then TTD20 is OCCUPIED
11 When Train1 leaves TTD10.VSS12
12    Then TTD10 is FREE
13 When Train1 enters TTD10.VSS22
14 When Train1 leaves TTD10.VSS21
15 When Train1 disconnects
16    Then Train1 disconnected
```

(b) Movement on VSS

Fig. 4. Abstract scenarios

Once a state has been checked at a particular refinement level it does not need to be checked at subsequent levels because the proof of refinement ensure this. Any Then clauses of the previous level are omitted and only if the state data representation is refined to add more detail is it necessary to add new Then clauses. In our case the concrete scenario derived from the specification has the correct final Then clauses to match our most concrete model refinement. In general the starting specification scenario could contain excess state checks that are already dealt with in earlier refinement levels. The number of Then clauses to add, is somewhat subjective; one could for example check that nothing else has changed state after each When clause. In the examples we have avoided this and adopt the same

```
1  Given Train1 stood at TTD10.VSS11
2    And Train1 disconnected
3    And TTD10 is OCCUPIED
4    And TTD20 is FREE
5  When Train1 starts mission and Train1 connects
6    Then Train1 in mission
7  When Train1 receives MA until TTD10.VSS12
8    Then Train1 has MA until TTD10.VSS12
9  When Train1 enters TTD10.VSS12
10 When Train1 leaves TTD10.VSS11
11 When Train1 receives MA until TTD20.VSS22
12   Then Train1 has MA until TTD20.VSS12
13 When Train1 enters TTD20.VSS21
14 When Train1 leaves TTD10.VSS12
15 When Train1 enters TTD20.VSS22
16 When Train1 leaves TTD20.VSS21
17 When Train1 disconnects and Train1 ends mission
18   Then Train1 no mission
```

Fig. 5. Missions and generic MA

policy as the given scenario of the specification which is to only check for expected changes in state. In the rest of this section, we present how the specification scenario is abstracted at the different level of refinement according to our development.

```
1  Given Train1 stood at TTD10.VSS11
2    And Train1 disconnected
3    And TTD10.VSS11 is UNAVAILABLE
4    And TTD10.VSS12 is UNAVAILABLE
5    And TTD10 is OCCUPIED
6    And TTD20 is FREE
7  When Train1 starts mission and Train1 connects
8  When Train1 reports position as integral
9  When Train1 receives OSMA until TTD10.VSS12
10   Then Train1 has OSMA until TTD10.VSS12
11 When Train1 enters TTD10.VSS12
12 When Train1 leaves TTD10.VSS11
13 When Train1 receives FSMA until TTD20.VSS22
14   Then Train1 has FSMA until TTD20.VSS22
15 When Train1 enters TTD20.VSS21
16 When Train1 leaves TTD10.VSS12
17 When Train1 reports position as integral
18   Then TTD10.VSS11 is AVAILABLE
19   And TTD10.VSS12 is AVAILABLE
20   And TTD10.VSS21 is UNAVAILABLE
21 When Train1 enters TTD20.VSS22
22 When Train1 leaves TTD20.VSS21
23 When Train1 reports position as integral
24   Then TTD10.VSS21 is AVAILABLE
25   And TTD10.VSS22 is UNAVAILABLE
26 When Train1 disconnects and Train1 ends mission
```

Fig. 6. Position reports, VSS availability and integrity

Movement on VSS. Our most abstract model contains no other state except for the position of trains on VSS and hence, for its scenario, we pick only the clauses that are related to train movement and add Then clauses that check the train's position after each movement (Fig. 4a).

Radio Communication and TTD. In our first and second refinements we add radio communication and status of TTD. Here we have combined them into one scenario for brevity. We add Then clauses to check train connection and TTD state after any When clause that should affect this (Fig. 4b).

Introduce Missions and Generic Movement Authority. Our next model refinement introduces movement authority but does not distinguish between Full Supervision Movement Authority (FS MA) and OS MA modes. In the scenario we must use the generic form of the DSL syntax which was introduced for this purpose. Note that we still split the granting of Movement Authority (MA) into two When clauses so that the state check is an abstract version of the order that will later be enforced in a refinement. The refinement also introduces the start of mission and end of mission procedures (Fig. 5).

Introduce Position Reports, VSS Availability, Integrity and Distinguish Between FS and OS MA. In this refinement, we refine MA to distinguish between FS MA and OS MA and introduce position and integrity reporting of trains which, in conjunction with TTD status, determines abstract VSS status. Notice that we replace the more abstract MA checks with OS MA and FS MA ones. At this stage, VSS status is bi-state instead of the final four states of the concrete scenario (Fig. 6).

Introduce Timers. This refinement introduces propagation timers that expand the unavailable area of VSS in case a non-communicative train moves. When the propagation timer expires, the adjacent VSS in the TTD become unavailable. Notice that the scenario is not like a refinement; we can add checks of old variables when further steps of the scenario should affect this. In the previous scenario we did not specify the state of these VSS, hence leaving room to add them now without introducing a contradiction.

```
 1  Given Train1 stood at TTD10.VSS11
 2    And Train1 disconnected
 3    And TTD10.VSS11 is UNAVAILABLE
 4    And TTD10.VSS12 is UNAVAILABLE
 5    And TTD10 is OCCUPIED
 6    And TTD20 is FREE
 7  When Train1 starts mission and Train1 connects
 8  When Train1 reports position as integral
 9  When Train1 receives OSMA until TTD10.VSS12
10  When Train1 enters TTD10.VSS12
11  When Train1 leaves TTD10.VSS11
12  When Train1 receives FSMA until TTD20.VSS22
13  When Train1 enters TTD20.VSS21
14  When Train1 leaves TTD10.VSS12
15  When Train1 reports position as integral
16  When Train1 enters TTD20.VSS22
17  When Train1 leaves TTD20.VSS21
18  When Train1 reports position as integral
19  When Train1 disconnects
20  When Train1 ends mission
21    Then TTD20.VSS22.disconnect_propagation_timer starts
22  When TTD20.VSS22.disconnect_propagation_timer expires
23    Then TTD20.VSS21 is UNAVAILABLE
24    And TTD20.VSS23 is UNAVAILABLE
```

Introduce VSS State. In this refinement of the scenario we introduce the full VSS states of the specification. That is, available is replaced by free and not available is replaced by ambiguous, occupied or unknown as appropriate This refinement brings us back to the full concrete scenario that was described in Sect. 4.

7 Tool Support

In this section, we show examples of specifying step definitions that link the domain specific scenarios with our model at different levels of refinement. Our step definitions are built on top of the Cucumber for Event-B.

We start with our most abstract model which has events for trains to enter or leave a VSS. The signature of the event to move the rear of a train is as follows

```
1 event ENV_rear_leave_section
2 any
3   tr // The train
4   vss // The VSS from that the train moves
5 where ... then ... end
```

In order to link the above event with the Gherkin commands, e.g., When Train1 leaves VSS11, we define the following step definition.

```
1 When(~/^${id} enters ${id}$/) {
2   String train, String vss ->
3   fireEvent("ENV_rear_leave_section", "tr = " + train + " & " + "vss = " + vss)
4 }
```

Here fireEvent is a library method from Cucumber for Event-B to fire an event in the model with possible additional constraints on the event's parameters. In the step definition above, the information about the train ID and the VSS is extracted using pattern matching and subsequently used to build the parameter constraint accordingly.

In the same model, we have a variable occupiedBy $\in$ VSS $\leftrightarrow\!\!\!\!\rightarrow$ train to keep track of information about occupation of VSS by trains. We can use this to specify the step definition for commands, such as, Then Train1 stood at VSS11,VSS12, as follows

```
1 Then(~/^${id} stood at ${id_list}$/) {
2   String train, String vss_set ->
3   assert true == isFormula("occupiedBy ~[{" + train + "}]", "{" + vss_set + "}"
      )
4 }
```

Here isFormula is a library method from Cucumber for Event-B to compare the evaluation of a formula (e.g., occupiedBy$\sim$[{TRAIN1}]) and the expected result (e.g., {VSS11, VSS12}).

Step definitions might need to change according to refinements of the model. For example, when we introduce TTD information, event ENV_rear_leave_section is split into two events: ENV_last_train_leave_ttd (when the TTD will be freed) and ENV_rear_leave_section otherwise. We introduce an alternative step definition, which selects whichever case is enabled, to reflect this refinement:

```
1  When(~/^${id} leaves ${id}$/) {
2    String train, String vss ->
3    String formula = "tr = " + train + " & " + "vss = " + vss
4    if (isEventEnabled("ENV_rear_leave_section", formula))
5      fireEvent("ENV_rear_leave_section", formula)
6    else if (isEventEnabled("ENV_last_train_leave_ttd", formula))
7      fireEvent("ENV_last_train_leave_ttd", formula)
8  }
```

8   Future Work

We have previously used natural language descriptions of scenarios manually converted ad-hoc into cucumber and executed with model animation tools. The use of a DSL and abstract scenarios is a new proposal that requires further investigation and development. In future work we will continue to develop scenarios from the HL3 case study and investigate tool automation of the abstractions based on the refinements from the model. We will employ the scenario-based modelling techniques in other domains such as aerospace to test its generality. Our eventual aim is to utilise the scenarios in a 'kind of' continuous integration development environment for formal modelling. Our future project commitments include model transformation from Event-B systems models to semi-formal component models and the use of precise and abstract scenarios could be utilised to validate and verify this transformation stage by co-simulation of scenarios in both models.

9   Conclusion

One of the strengths of formal methods lies in efficient, generic verification (using theorem provers) which obviates the need for test cases and hence instantiation with objects. However, to leverage this strength we need to convince domain experts and, of course, ourselves, of the validity of the models. To this end we adopt a strategy analogous to testing; animation of models using scenarios. We envisage a growing reliance on scenarios as we seek to integrate formal systems level modelling with industrial development processes. Scenarios are a reformulation of the specification and, no matter what format they are expressed in, errors may be introduced. However, errors are equally likely to exist in the original specification. We have found that scenarios aid detection of specification errors by allowing validation of the behaviour by domain experts. If errors are introduced into the scenarios these will be discovered when they are used to animate the model.

An important step is to make the scenarios more precise so that they are clear and unambiguous while remaining easily understood by all stakeholders. To achieve this, we have suggested deriving a scenario DSL from the particular specification in question, prior to commencing the formal modelling. Scenarios that illustrate the desired behaviour embodied by the specification, may then be expressed in a clear, precise and concise way. For early detection of problems, it is important that we can use the scenarios at stages when our abstract models do not contain all of the detail involved in the concrete scenario. We therefore propose a technique of synthesising abstract versions of the scenario that are suitable for use with the abstract refinement levels of the model. The abstraction technique uses the data refinement of the model (including superposition of new data as well as refinement of data representation) to make corresponding abstractions in scenarios. We propose to develop these techniques in the future as we continue to build our formal model based development process.

References

1. Abrial, J.-R.: Modeling in Event-B: System and Software Engineering. Cambridge University Press, Cambridge (2010)
2. Abrial, J.-R., Butler, M., Hallerstede, S., Hoang, T.S., Mehta, F., Voisin, L.: Rodin: an open toolset for modelling and reasoning in Event-B. STTT **12**(6), 447–466 (2010)
3. Cybulski, J.L.: The formal and the informal in requirements engineering. Technical report, Technical Report 96/7, Department of Information Systems, The University of Melbourne (1996)
4. Dghaym, D., Poppleton, M., Snook, C.: Diagram-led formal modelling using iUML-B for hybrid ERTMS level 3. In: Butler, M., Raschke, A., Hoang, T.S., Reichl, K. (eds.) ABZ 2018. LNCS, vol. 10817, pp. 338–352. Springer, Cham (2018). https://doi.org/10.1007/978-3-319-91271-4_23
5. Fischer, T.: Cucumber for Event-B and iUML-B (2018). https://github.com/tofische/cucumber-event-b
6. Fischer, T., Dghyam, D.: Formal model validation through acceptance tests. In: Collart-Dutilleul, S., Lecomte, T., Romanovsky, A. (eds.) RSSRail 2019. LNCS, vol. 11495, pp. 159–169. Springer, Cham (2019). https://doi.org/10.1007/978-3-030-18744-6_10
7. EEIG ERTMS Users Group. Hybrid ERTMS/ETCS Level 3: Principles, July 2017. Ref. 16E042 Version 1A
8. Hoang, T.S.: An introduction to the Event-B modelling method. In: Industrial Deployment of System Engineering Methods, pp. 211–236. Springer (2013)
9. Snook, C., et al.: Behaviour-driven formal model development. In: Sun, J., Sun, M. (eds.) ICFEM 2018. LNCS, vol. 11232, pp. 21–36. Springer, Cham (2018). https://doi.org/10.1007/978-3-030-02450-5_2
10. Wynne, M., Hellesøy, A.: The cucumber book: behaviour-driven development for testers and developers. Pragmatic Programmers, LLC (2012)

On Reconciling Schedulability Analysis and Model Checking in Robotics

Mohammed Foughali[(⊠)]

LAAS-CNRS, Université de Toulouse, CNRS, INSA, Toulouse, France
mfoughal@laas.fr

Abstract. The challenges of deploying robots and autonomous vehicles call for further efforts to bring the real-time systems and the formal methods communities together. In this paper, we discuss the practicality of paramount model checking formalisms in implementing dynamic-priority-based cooperative schedulers, where capturing the waiting time of tasks has a major impact on scalability. Subsequently, we propose a novel technique that alleviates such an impact, and thus enables schedulability analysis and verification of real-time/behavioral properties within the same model checking framework, while taking into account hardware and OS specificities. The technique is implemented in an automatic translation from a robotic framework to UPPAAL, and evaluated on a real robotic example.

1 Introduction

In robotics, schedulability analysis needs to be consolidated with the verification of other important properties such as *bounded response* and *safety*. This need is flagrant in *e.g.* mixed-criticality software, where some tasks are allowed to exceed their deadlines. Dually, important hardware-software settings (*e.g.* number of cores, scheduling policy) are classically abstracted away in formal verification. This renders verification results valid only if all tasks run in parallel at all times, which is seldom a realistic assumption.

Bridging the gap between these communities would be of a great benefit to practitioners and researchers: one could imagine a unified framework where schedulability, but also other properties can be verified, on a model that is faithful to both the underlying robotic specification and the characteristics of the OS and the robotic platform. This is however very difficult in practice. For instance, theoretical results on schedulers are difficult to exploit given *e.g.* the low-level fine-grain concurrency at the *functional layer* of robotic systems, where *components* directly interact with sensors and actuators (details in Sect. 3.1). Similarly, enriching formal models with *e.g.* dynamic-priority-based scheduling policies usually penalizes the scalability of their verification, even in non-preemptive settings. As an example, cooperative EDF [20] requires knowing the waiting time of tasks in order to compute their priorities. Model checking frameworks are hostile to this kind of behavior: UPPAAL [7], for instance, does not allow reading

© Springer Nature Switzerland AG 2019
C. Attiogbé et al. (Eds.): MEDI 2019 Workshops, CCIS 1085, pp. 32–48, 2019.
https://doi.org/10.1007/978-3-030-32213-7_3

the value of a clock (to capture waiting time), which requires using discrete-time-like methods that create further transitions in the model [19], leading to unscalable verification in the context of complex robotic systems.

In this paper, we propose a novel approach that allows schedulability analysis and formal verification of other properties within the same framework. We transform capturing waiting times from a counting problem to a search problem, which we solve using a binary-search-inspired technique. Integrated within a *template*, this technique allows us to automatically obtain, from functional robotic specifications, scalable formal models enriched with dynamic-priority cooperative schedulers. Our contribution is thus threefold: we (i) propose a novel approach for the general problem of capturing, at the model level, the value of time elapsed between some events, (ii) enable model checking robotic specifications while taking into account hardware- and OS-related specificities and (iii) automatize the process so the formal models are obtained promptly from any robotic specification with no further modeling efforts. We pay a particular attention to the readability of this paper by a broad audience in the different communities of robotics, formal methods and real-time systems. In that regard, we adopt a level of vulgarization with simple mathematical notions, together with sufficient references for further readings.

The rest of this paper is organized as follows. First, we propose a novel technique that ensures alleviating the effect of modeling schedulers on scalability (Sect. 2). Then, in Sect. 3, we present the *UPPAAL template* [15], which automatically generates formal models from robotic specifications, and show how we extend it with dynamic-priority schedulers using the solution shown in Sect. 2. In Sect. 4, we use the automatically generated models to verify properties over a real-world case study, before we explore the related work in Sect. 5 and conclude with a discussion and possible future work (Sect. 6).

2   Capturing Time

In this paper, we focus on dynamic-priority *cooperative* (*i.e. non preemptive*) schedulers, namely cooperative *Earliest Deadline First (EDF)* and *Highest Response Rate Next (HRRN)*. The computations of either of these schedulers rely on a key information: the *waiting time*. Let us consider n tasks $T_1 .. T_n$. Whenever a core is free, w_i, the time each task T_i has been waiting in the queue so far, is used to compute its priority. In EDF (resp. HRRN), the smaller (resp. higher) the value of $d_i - w_i$ (resp. $1 + \frac{w_i}{e_i}$), the higher the priority of T_i, where d_i is the (relative to task activation) *deadline* (resp. e_i is the *estimated execution time*) of T_i (more in Sect. 3.3). The task with the highest priority is then *released*: it is removed from the queue and a core is assigned to it.

Now, we need to integrate these schedulers into "model-checkable" formal models of robotic and autonomous systems. We explore thus two main formalisms: time Petri nets TPN and timed automata extended with urgencies UTA, both extended with data variables. This is because most of paramount model checkers are based either on the former (*e.g.* Fiacre/TINA [8] and

Romeo [22]) or the latter (*e.g.* UPPAAL [7] and IMITATOR [6]). Also, we already have templates that translate robotic specifications to both Fiacre/TINA [12] and UPPAAL [15]. Exploring both TPN and UTA will help us conclude on which of these templates we need to extend with schedulers.

2.1   Preliminaries

We (very briefly) present TPN and UTA as to show the difference between these formalisms in the context of this paper. In the original "model checkable" version of each formalism, timing constraints (bounds of time intervals in TPN and clock constraints in UTA) are allowed in $\mathbb{Q}_{\geq 0} \cup \infty$. Since we can always multiply all timing constraints by a natural that brings them to $\mathbb{N} \cup \infty$ (that is the *lowest common multiple LCM* of their denominators), we use natural constraints in our presentation.

Time Petri Nets TPN: Time Petri nets TPN [24] are Petri nets extended with time intervals (we only focus on closed intervals in this succinct presentation). Each transition t is associated with an interval $I(t) = [a_t, b_t]$ over $\mathbb{R}_{\geq 0}$ where $a_t \in \mathbb{N}$ (resp. $b_t \in \mathbb{N} \cup \infty$) is the *earliest* (resp. *latest*) *firing deadline* of t. The semantics of $I(t)$ is as follows: if t was last enabled since date d, t may not fire before $d + a_t$ and *must* fire before or at $d + b_t$ unless it is disabled before then by firing another transition. Time intervals in TPN are thus *relative* to the *enabledness* of transitions: if t is disabled, then $I(t)$ has no semantic effect. We consider a version of TPN where guards and operations over data variables are possible on transitions.

Timed Automata with Urgencies UTA: Timed automata TA [4] extend *finite-state Büchi automata* with real-valued clocks. The behavior of TA is thus restricted by defining (natural) constraints on the clock variables and a set of accepting states. A simpler version allowing local invariant conditions is introduced in [18], on which this paper (and tools like UPPAAL) relies. The syntax and semantics of TA in this paper follow those in [2] except that we refer to *switches* as *edges*. UTA [9] extend TA with a notion of urgency on edges, mainly (i) the *strong* urgency *eager, denoted* ⚡, meaning the edge is to be taken as soon as enabled and (ii) the *weak* (by default) urgency *lazy*, meaning the edge *may* be taken when enabled. *Transitions* resulting from synchronizing some clock-constraint-free edges inherit the strongest urgency (if there is at least one ⚡ edge in the synchronization, the resulting transition is also ⚡). We consider a version of UTA where guards and operations over data variables are possible on edges.

TPN vs UTA: What we need to retain for the sake of understanding this paper relates uniquely to the way time is handled in both formalisms. The main difference is that TPN feature no clocks (time intervals depend on transitions enabledness) whereas clocks in UTA evolve monotonically and independently from edges/transitions enabledness.

2.2   A High Level Presentation: Problem and Solution

We analyze the problem of capturing an arbitrary time, in both TPN and UTA models, at a framework-independent high level. We consider in each case a "process" that needs to store the value of time τ separating two events e and e', captured through the Booleans b and b', respectively. The value of τ is needed to perform further computations in the model. Since we are reasoning at a high level, we use standard algorithmic notations: $\leftarrow$ for assignment, $=$ for equality and $\neg$ for negation. In UTA, $reset(x)$ denotes resetting the valuation of clock x to zero. In graphical representations, guards are in green, operations in blue, and discontinued arcs/edges refer to missing parts of the model.

Before we go any further, it is very important to distinguish between the modeling and the verification levels. Here, it is essential to capture and store τ in order to construct the model (the model depends on the value of τ, as explained for EDF and HRRN above, and further detailed in Sect. 3.3). We cannot just use verification techniques to *e.g.* look for the bounds τ lies within, because the model itself relies on the *exact* value of τ for each $e->e'$ sequence, the tracking of which is far from obvious. Indeed, TPN feature no clocks to capture τ directly in the model. Surprisingly, this is also the case for UTA: UTA-based model-checkers allow comparing a clock value to some constraints, but none of them permits *reading* such a value as to *e.g.* store it in a variable, since that would prevent *symbolic* representations like regions [3]. It follows that we can only approximate τ to its truncated natural value (or the natural that upper-bounds it).

The Classical Method: Figure 1 shows the "classical" way to capture τ in TPN. The original net is in black stroke: as soon as (denoted by the interval $[0,0]$) b (resp. b') is true, transition t (resp. t') is fired, which unmarks place p (resp. the "waiting" place w) and marks place w (resp. p'). When p' is marked, we need the value of τ to perform further computations. The part in light blue is thus added to the net. Transition t_count, whose input and output place is w, is fired at each time unit as long as event e' is not received, which increments the value of τ. Consequently, as soon as p' is marked, τ holds the truncated natural value of the real duration d separating e and e' ($d-1$ if d is natural).

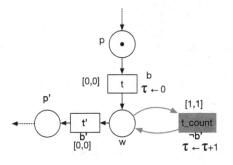

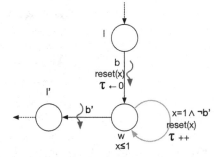

Fig. 1. Capturing waiting time in TPN (Color figure online)

Fig. 2. Capturing waiting time in UTA (Color figure online)

An equivalent solution is implemented in UTA (Fig. 2). Location l is to wait for event e. Eager ($\lightning$) edges are taken as soon as their guard is true. The invariant on clock x at location w enforces taking the added edge (in light blue) at each time unit, which increments the value of τ. This method, referred to as *integer clocks*, is proposed to solve a similar problem in [19].

Now, in either formalism, this solution is very costly: adding transitions triggered at each time unit creates further interleavings and complexity that leads to combinatory explosion in real-world robotic case studies (Sect. 4.1).

An Optimized Method: A key idea of this paper relies on transforming the *counting* problem into a *search* problem: instead of counting the time elapsed between e and e', we *search* for the value of τ once e' is received. This technique requires however an upper bound of τ (that is a value UP we know τ will never exceed). In our solution, this value may change for each sequence $e \rightarrow e'$ (UP may take a different value each time location l (or place p) is (re-)reached).

The solution in UTA is shown in Fig. 3. At location s (for *search*), at which time cannot elapse (all outgoing edges are $\lightning$), we undertake a binary search (*aka half-interval search*) that swings the value of τ within the bounds u (upper bound, initially UP) and d (lower bound, initially 0) till x lies within $[\tau - 1, \tau + 1]$, after which we simply assign τ the natural that lower-bounds the real value of x (by taking one of the edges from s to l'). This method is not implementable in TPN due to the absence of clocks.

Now, we already know that, generally, binary search algorithms (logarithmic complexity) are faster than linear ones. We extrapolate that the number of times edges from location s (in the optimized solution, Fig. 3) are taken is generally (and noticeably) smaller than the one of taking the self-loop at location w (in the classical solution, Fig. 2). Thus, there is a considerable gain in terms of state space size (and therefore scalability) when using the optimized technique, as we will confirm in Sect. 4.1.

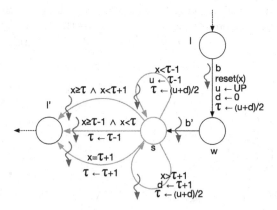

Fig. 3. Capturing waiting time in UTA (optimized solution) (Color figure online)

Note that we can think of more optimized solutions, like simply testing the value of x between each pair of integers i and $i + 1$ within the range $0 .. UP$ on separate edges from s to l'. This would not, however, work if the value of UP varies from an $e -> e'$ sequence to another, which renders the solution less generic (*e.g.* in the context of schedulability, it would not work for tasks with variable deadlines [29]).

3   Application to Robotic Systems

In previous work, we bridged the robotic framework G^{en}₀M3 (Sect. 3.1) with Fiacre/TINA [12,13] and UPPAAL [15] through *templates*. Now, we only extend the UPPAAL template (since the optimized method, Sect. 2, is only implementable in UTA) with EDF and HRRN schedulers. The UPPAAL template output is proven faithful to the semantics of G^{en}₀M3 [14,15]. Therefore, we present briefly G^{en}₀M3 in this section, then explain some of the former's important behavioral and real-time aspects using an example of an automatically generated UPPAAL model of a G^{en}₀M3 *component*.

3.1   G^{en}₀M3

G^{en}₀M3 [14,23] is a component-based framework for specifying and implementing functional layer specifications. Figure 4 shows the organization of a G^{en}₀M3 component. *Activities*, executed following *requests* from external *clients*, implement the core algorithms of the functionality the component is in charge of (*e.g.* reading laser sensor, navigation). Two types of tasks are therefore provided: (i) a *control Task* to *process* requests, *validate* the requested activity (if the processing returns no errors), and *report* to the clients and (ii) *execution task(s)* to execute activities. Tasks (resp. components) share data through the *Internal Data Structure IDS* (resp. *ports*).

An execution task is in charge of a number of activities. With each period, it will run sequentially, among such activities, those that have been already validated by the control task. Activities are *finite-state machines* FSM, each state called a *codel*, at which a piece of C or C++ code is executed. Each codel specifies a WCET (worst case execution time) on a given platform, and the possible *transitions* following its execution. Taking a *pause* transition or a transition to the special codel **ether** ends the execution of the activity. In the former (resp. latter) case, the activity is resumed at the next period (resp. *terminated*).

IDS, Ports & Concurrency: At ths OS level, tasks are parallel threads, with fine-grain concurrent access to the IDS and the ports: a codel (in its activity, run by a task) locks only the IDS field(s) and/or port(s) required for its execution (simultaneous readings are allowed). A codel *in conflict* (cannot execute at the same time) with another codel because of this locking mechanism is called *thread unsafe* (*thread safe* otherwise). Because of the concurrency over ports, codels in conflict may belong to different components. This aspect renders generalizing results on optimal schedulers very difficult in the context of robotics, as referred to in Sect. 1.

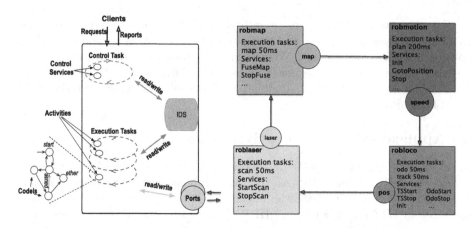

Fig. 4. A generic G^{en}₀M3 component   **Fig. 5.** The RobNav application

Case Study: In this paper, we consider a variation of the RobNav application developed by fellow researchers at LAAS-CNRS (Fig. 5, technical details in [13]). The G^{en}₀M3 specification includes four components interacting to achieve autonomous terrestrial navigation. There are five execution tasks. Additionally, each component has a control task. The total number of tasks is therefore nine. The presentation in this paper focuses mainly on execution tasks and is greatly simplified. For more details on control tasks (*e.g.* how they are activated) and more complex aspects (*e.g.* interruption of activities), we refer the interested reader to [14].

3.2 UPPAAL Template

We show in Fig. 6 a very simplified version of the automatically generated UPPAAL model of the periodic execution tasks odo and track (ROBLOCO component, one time unit in the model is equal to 1 ms). This model follows the implementation model shown in [15], proven faithful to the semantics of G^{en}₀M3 [14,15]. The *urgency* process is to enforce ⚡ transitions through the urgent channel *exe* (UPPAAL supports ⚡ transitions only, not ⚡ edges). Note that not all activities are shown.

Each task t is composed of a *manager* (to execute, at its location *manage*, activities sequentially), a *timer* (to send, through the Boolean $tick\_t$, period signals to the *manager*), and a number of activities the task executes. The $next()$ function browses the array tab_t, whose cells are records with two fields: n (activity name) and s (activity status), and returns the index of the first activity that is previously validated by the control task and still not executed in this cycle (an information retrieved through the s fields). The *manager* and the activities use this function, together with the variables $lock\_t$ and $turn\_t$, to communicate: the *manager* computes the identity of the next activity to execute and gives it the control (through $turn\_t$ and $lock\_t$). The activity will then execute until it pauses (*e.g.* reaching *track_pause* in *TrackSpeedStart*) or terminates (*e.g.* reaching *ether* in *InitPosPort*), in which case it computes the identity of the next activity to execute (in i) and gives the control back to the *manager*. When there are no more activities to execute (i is equal to the size of *tab_t* and the *manager* has the control through *lock_t*), the *manager* transits back to its initial location *start*.

Now, at the activity level, a signal is transmitted when the activity pauses or terminates (through the Boolean *finished_t*) to the control task (not shown here), so the latter informs the client that requested such activity and updates the status of the activity in *tab_t*. A thread-unsafe codel c is represented using two locations, c and *c_exec* (*e.g.* *compute* and *compute_exec* in *TrackOdoStart*). The guards and operations over the array of Booleans *mut* ensure no codels in conflict (*e.g.* codel *track* in *TrackSpeedStart* and codel *compute* in *TrackOdoStart*) execute simultaneously, and the urgency on $c \rightarrow$ *c_exec* edges ensures the codel executes (or loses some resources) *as soon as* it has the required resources. The invariants on locations *c_exec* and the guards on the clock on the edges of the form *c_exec* $\rightarrow$ reflect the fact that a codel is executed in a non-zero time that cannot exceed its WCET. For thread-safe codels, *c_exec* locations are not needed, and the invariant is thus associated with c locations.

As we can see, this model is highly concurrent: tasks may run on different cores and locking shared resources is fine grain (at the codels level) with simultaneous readings allowed. These features allow to maximally parallelize the tasks, but render manual verification and analytical techniques for schedulability analysis impractical.

3.3   Extending with Schedulers

We show how to extend the UPPAAL template with cooperative EDF and HRRN schedulers. First, we use the case study to exemplify on how to adapt the solution shown in Sect. 2 to efficiently and correctly integrate such schedulers. Then, we automatize such integration within the template.

Example: Let us get back to the ROBLOCO example. The *manager* processes are the only ones that will be affected. Also, we will need a *scheduler* process. Let us first introduce the constants, shared variables and channels that the scheduler and managers need to communicate and synchronize.

Constants: The number of tasks in the application is denoted by the constant *size_sched*. An array of constant naturals *periods* is introduced in which, with each task denoted by index i, a period *periods*[i] is associated.

Shared Variables: We need a queue (array) T of size *size_sched* in which we insert tasks dynamic priorities. Then, since priorities change their position when T is dequeued, we need an array p such that $p[i]$ tracks the index of T that points to the cell holding the dynamic priority of task i (that is $T[p[i]]$). Also, we need a natural *len* to store the number of waiting tasks, an array w to store the waiting time for each task i, and a natural *s_count* to store the number of

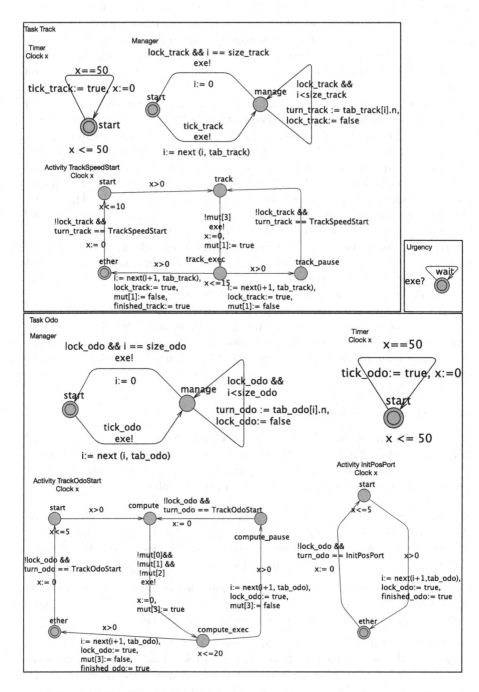

Fig. 6. UPPAAL model of tasks odo and track (automatically generated)

tasks for which the *search* for the waiting time has already finished. Finally, the natural *nc* stores the number of available cores.

Channels: A handshake channel *insert* is introduced to increment *len*. A broadcast channel *up* synchronizes with as many tasks as *len* to start the search operation. Besides, a broadcast channel *en* synchronizes the scheduler with all waiting tasks in order to diffuse the decision for each task on whether it is released (given a core to execute) or not (needs to wait further). Finally, a broadcast channel *srch* eliminates interleaving between managers during the search operation (more explanation below).

We show now the scheduler, then how the *manager* of odo is modified accordingly:

Scheduler: The scheduler (Fig. 7) has three locations: *start* (initial), *update* and *give*. The last two are *committed*, which (i) prevents interleaving with other interactions in the system and (ii) enforces urgency on all their outgoing edges (time cannot elapse).

The self-loop edge at location *start*, synchronized on *insert*, increments the number of waiting tasks each time a task wants to execute (we do not need a guard on this edge because the size of T is already equal to the number of tasks in the application). From location *start*, it is possible to reach location *update* providing there is at least one task to release.

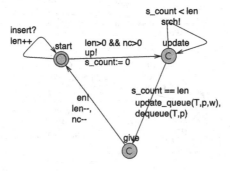

Fig. 7. UPPAAL model of the scheduler

At location *update*, an edge synchronized over the channel *srch* allows looping as long as the search has not finished for all waiting tasks (with one search operation for all tasks at once thanks to the broadcast channel *srch*). Another edge permits reaching the location *give* as soon as the search has finished for all waiting tasks (captured through the value of *s_count*). On this very edge, the core of the scheduling algorithm is implemented: function *update_queue*() updates the dynamic priorities in each $T[p[i]]$ before the function *dequeue*() finds the task with the highest priority and removes its priority by updating both p and T. The core of *update_queue*() is given later in this section.

Now, from location *give*, the initial location is immediately reached through an edge synchronized on the channel *en*. The number of cores as well as the number of waiting tasks is decremented as the task having the highest priority is released.

Manager: In the new manager model (Fig. 8), we have a clock x and four intermediate locations: *ask*, *search*, *decide*, and *error*. To meet the upper-bound condition (Sect. 2), we reason as follows. In such a real-time system, we do not tolerate that a task is still waiting (for a core) since a duration equal to its period. Thus, we enforce an urgency (through an invariant) from location *ask* (at which the clock x tracks the waiting time) to location *error* as soon as the waiting time is equal to the task period. Then, at the analysis step, we start by checking whether *error* is reachable in any manager in the model, in which case we drop the analysis and increase the number of cores.

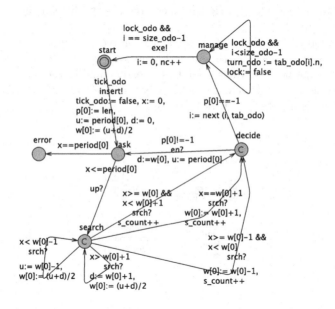

Fig. 8. UPPAAL model of the *odo* manager (enriched)

The remaining aspects are rather trivial considering the scheduler model and the search technique in Sect. 2 (we reuse the variable names for search bounds, u and d, from Fig. 3): $p[i]$ is updated from *start* to *ask*, the edge from *ask* to *search* is synchronized on *up* to drag all waiting tasks managers to the committed location *search* at which they loop, synchronized on *srch*, until the search ends. When all managers reach their respective *decide* locations, s_count is equal to *len* (the number of waiting tasks) and, in each manager, either the edge to *manage* or *ask* is taken, depending on whether the task i is released (recognized through $p[i]$ equalling -1), or not (otherwise). In the latter case, d (resp. u), the lower (resp. upper) bound for the next search is updated to the current value of $w[i]$ (resp. *period*$[i]$). Finally, the task frees the core at the end of execution (operation $nc + +$ on the edge from *manage* to *start*).

Automatic Synthesis: At this stage, we are ready to automatize the process. The user may pass the flag -sched to the UPPAAL template, followed by two numbers: the scheduling policy (HRRN (1) or EDF (2)) and the number of cores (a natural in $0 .. 9$). For instance, the following command line generates the UPPAAL model of the G^{en}_oM3 specification *spec.gen*, that integrates a cooperative EDF scheduler over four cores:

```
genom3 uppaal/model -sched=24 spec.gen
```

Now, the core of the UPPAAL template is enriched to automatically integrate such specificities in the generated model. As an example, the listing below shows the piece of the template that generates the *update_queue*() function. The interpreter evaluates what is enclosed in $<'$ $'>$ in Tcl and outputs the rest as is. Line 1 conditions generating the function with the validity of the option passed by the programmer and lines 8–9 generates the right dynamic-priority formula according to the specified scheduler in the option. In the case of EDF, we simply subtract the waiting time $w[i]$ from the (relative) deadline, fixed to the period *period*$[i]$. For HRRN, we proceed as follows. The estimated execution time is usually an average computed dynamically. Here, we fix it statically to the period of the task (the same reasoning was followed in [12] for the SJF scheduling policy). Then, since we can only perform integer divisions in UPPAAL, we look for the LCM *lcm_p* of all periods and multiply the priority formula by it. Since *lcm_p* is strictly positive, the inequality sign is not affected.

```
1   <'if {$argv >= 10} {'>
2   /* scheduling */
3   /* update dynamic priorities */
4   void update_queue (int &T[size_sched], int &p[size_sched], int
        &w[size_sched]) {
5   int i;
6   for (i:= 0; i<size_sched; i++) {
7       if (p[i] >= 0) {T[p[i]]:=
8   <'if {$argv < 20} {'>lcm_p + w[i] * (lcm_p/period[i])
9   <'} else {'>period[i] - w[i]<'}'>;}}
10  }
11  <'}'>
```

4   Results

We aim to analyze the deployability of the case study (Sect. 3.1) on the *Robotnik Summit-XL platform* [1], featuring an embedded four-core PC running Linux. There are two requirements, which we are unable to guarantee using classical FCFS and SJF schedulers from [12]. The track task is *hard real-time* (R1): it must always finish executing its activities within its period (new computed speeds must be sent to the controller at a fixed rate of 20 Hz). The remaining tasks are *soft real-time*, with the condition that the time by which a task exceeds its period must be always smaller than the period itself (R2). R1 is a typical *schedulability* property, whereas R2 is a *bounded response* property. UPPAAL models extended with EDF and HRRN are automatically generated from the case study. The results presented below are identical for both schedulers.

Schedulability: To check the schedulability of a task t, we first make sure such a task never waits for a duration equal to its period before starting to execute its activities, that is location *error* of its *manager* is unreachable:

`A[] not manager_t.error`

This *safety* property does not guarantee schedulability, but its falsification allows to quickly invalidate R1 (and is generally unacceptable for any task). Thus, we start by one core ($nc = 1$) and increase as soon as the safety property is violated for any task. We stop when nc is equal to four, the number of cores on the platform. The results show that as soon as nc reaches three, the property is satisfied for all tasks.

At this point, we fix nc to three and verify R1 (task track). The reasoning is as follows. A task is busy (waiting or executing activities) as long as its *manager* is not at location *start* (we verify beforehand that locations *ask* and *manage* are reachable in all managers). Thus, we check whether no new signal from the *timer* is sent while the *manager* is not at location *start*:

`A[] (not manager_track.start imply not tick_track)`

This safety property is violated for $nc = 3$, which means R1 is dissatisfied, which is no longer the case as soon as we increase nc to four. We fix thus nc to four and pursue the verification for the remaining tasks in order to assess R2.

Bounded Response: Now, for each task t that is not schedulable, we ask for the maximum value of clock x at location *manage*, at which activities are executed:
$sup\{manager\_t.manage\} : manager\_t.x$

Then, we simply subtract the period of t from the result to get exc_t, the maximum amount of time by which t exceeds its period.

The results for both schedulability and bounded response are given in Table 1. All tasks are feasible, besides scan (component roblaser) that may exceed its period by up to 20 ms (which is inferior to its period). R1 and R2 are thus both met on the four-core platform, and we can provide the precise maximum amount of time by which the only non schedulable task may overrun its period.

Table 1. Verification results (four cores).

t	odo	track	plan	fuse	scan
schedulabe	Yes	Yes	Yes	Yes	No
exc_t	/	/	/	/	20

4.1 Discussion

The results are encouraging: (i) schedulability is verified for all tasks and (ii) if schedulability is violated, the precise upper bound of the time the period is exceeded is retrieved. All this is done automatically at both the modeling (template) and verification (model checker) levels, while taking into account the real hardware and OS specificities. As expected, the search technique used to capture waiting times scales much better than the classical counting one: with the former, verification results are obtained within around 80 s for each property with less than 1 Gb of RAM usage, while with the latter no answer is given after several minutes and 4 Gb. However, we do not know whether we can obtain better results (*e.g.* schedulability of all tasks or shorter exceeding time) with preemptive schedulers. Indeed, we may not rely on generic theoretical results to know whether preemptive schedulers may perform better than cooperative ones in this case, and, unfortunately, preemption do generally not scale with model checking (Sect. 5). Possible directions to deal with this issue are given in Sect. 6.

5 Related Work

Real-Time Analysis and Model Checking in Robotics: Bridging the gap between analytical techniques (*e.g.* in schedulability analysis) and model checking is generally not explored at the functional layer of robotic and autonomous systems. On one hand, works focusing on model checking [21, 25, 30] ignore hardware and OS constraints (number of cores and scheduling policy) which restricts the validity of results to only when the number of cores in the platform is at least equal to that of the robotic tasks, which is usually an unrealistic assumption. On the other hand, real-time analysis of functional robotic components [16, 17, 28], mainly focusing on schedulability, is non automatic, gives no guarantees on other important properties and is hard to extend to verify specific temporal constraints (such as bounded response). Moreover, theoretical results on optimized schedulers are hard to generalize to the case of robotics due to the complexity of multitasking models. For instance, the experiments in [26] show how, contrary to generic theoretical results, some non preemptive schedulers perform better than preemptive ones in the case of a mobile robot application.

Model-Checking for Schedulability: Using model-checking-based techniques to verify schedulability has been studied in the past, producing tools such as TIMES [5]. Unfortunately, such tools are too high-level to implement complex robotic applications, which prevents their use as a uniform environment to verify various real-time and behavioral properties, including schedulability. Furthermore, they target mainly preemptive schedulers, and consequently suffer from scalability issues in large applications.

Capturing Time in Formal Models: To the best of our knowledge, enriching formal models of robotic applications with dynamic-priority cooperative schedulers is a non-explored research direction. Still, the problem that arises, *i.e.* storing arbitrary time values in variables to construct the model, has been already encountered in other domains. It is the case of [19], where the authors use *integer clocks* to perform arithmetics on clock values stored in natural variables. Such integer clocks, relying on a classical counting algorithm, lead to unscalable models in the case of large robotic applications.

Comparison to Our Previous Work: In [12], we extended the Fiacre template with FCFS and SJF cooperative schedulers. We concluded that we would need to integrate more "intelligent" schedulers with dynamic priorities, which we efficiently achieve in this paper using a novel binary-search-based technique. Practitioners can thus automatically generate, from any robotic specification, a formal model enriched with EDF or HRRN, on which various properties can be verified within the same framework, UPPAAL. The results enable deploying the case study on a four-core platform.

6   Conclusion

In this paper, we elaborate an effort to bring the robotics, the real-time systems and the formal methods communities together. We aim at providing, automatically, formal models of robotic specifications that take into account the actual hardware and OS specificities. In order to consider optimized (dynamic-priority) schedulers, we propose a scalable *search* method that we automatize within the UPPAAL template developed in [15]. The obtained results are encouraging, and allow to deploy the case study on a four-core robotic platform while fulfilling real-time requirements. This work gives also insights on the use of formalisms in practice. For instance, we favor TA-based to TPN models for this particular problem, where it was the other way around in [11].

A possible direction of future work is considering preemptive schedulers. Indeed, those may further improve the deployability, but do unfortunately not scale with model checking. We are exploring the extension of the UPPAAL-SMC (*Statistical Model Checking*) template [15] with preemptive schedulers in order to verify the properties up to some high probability. In that regard, works like [10] may help us deal with the lack of probabilistic requirements in the robotics domain (what could be considered as a "sufficiently high probability" for a robotic application?). Another direction is to integrate more low-level specificities, such as cache interferences (modeled using UPPAAL in [27]), in our models as to gain a higher confidence in the verification results.

References

1. Robotnik Summit-XL data sheet. https://www.robotnik.eu/web/wp-content/uploads//2019/03/Robotnik_DATASHEET_SUMMIT-XL-HL_EN-web-1.pdf
2. Alur, R.: Timed automata. In: Halbwachs, N., Peled, D. (eds.) CAV 1999. LNCS, vol. 1633, pp. 8–22. Springer, Heidelberg (1999). https://doi.org/10.1007/3-540-48683-6_3

3. Alur, R., Courcoubetis, C., Dill, D.: Model-checking in dense real-time. Inf. Comput. **104**(1), 2–34 (1993)
4. Alur, R., Dill, D.: A theory of timed automata. Theor. Comput. Sci. **126**(2), 183–235 (1994)
5. Amnell, T., Fersman, E., Mokrushin, L., Pettersson, P., Yi, W.: TIMES: a tool for schedulability analysis and code generation of real-time systems. In: Larsen, K.G., Niebert, P. (eds.) FORMATS 2003. LNCS, vol. 2791, pp. 60–72. Springer, Heidelberg (2004). https://doi.org/10.1007/978-3-540-40903-8_6
6. André, É., Fribourg, L., Kühne, U., Soulat, R.: IMITATOR 2.5: a tool for analyzing robustness in scheduling problems. In: Giannakopoulou, D., Méry, D. (eds.) FM 2012. LNCS, vol. 7436, pp. 33–36. Springer, Heidelberg (2012). https://doi.org/10.1007/978-3-642-32759-9_6
7. Behrmann, G., David, A., Larsen, K.G.: A tutorial on UPPAAL. In: Bernardo, M., Corradini, F. (eds.) SFM-RT 2004. LNCS, vol. 3185, pp. 200–236. Springer, Heidelberg (2004). https://doi.org/10.1007/978-3-540-30080-9_7
8. Berthomieu, B., Ribet, P.-O., Vernadat, F.: The tool TINA-construction of abstract state spaces for Petri nets and time Petri nets. J. Prod. Res. **42**(14), 2741–2756 (2004)
9. Bornot, S., Sifakis, J., Tripakis, S.: Modeling urgency in timed systems. In: de Roever, W.-P., Langmaack, H., Pnueli, A. (eds.) COMPOS 1997. LNCS, vol. 1536, pp. 103–129. Springer, Heidelberg (1998). https://doi.org/10.1007/3-540-49213-5_5
10. Díaz, J., et al.: Stochastic analysis of periodic real-time systems. In: RTSS, pp. 289–300. IEEE (2002)
11. Foughali, M.: Toward a correct-and-scalable verification of concurrent robotic systems: insights on formalisms and tools. In: ACSD, pp. 29–38 (2017)
12. Foughali, M., Berthomieu, B., Dal Zilio, S., Hladik, P.-E., Ingrand, F., Mallet, A.: Formal verification of complex robotic systems on resource-constrained platforms. In: FormaliSE, pp. 2–9 (2018)
13. Foughali, M., Berthomieu, B., Dal Zilio, S., Ingrand, F., Mallet, A.: Model checking real-time properties on the functional layer of autonomous robots. In: Ogata, K., Lawford, M., Liu, S. (eds.) ICFEM 2016. LNCS, vol. 10009, pp. 383–399. Springer, Cham (2016). https://doi.org/10.1007/978-3-319-47846-3_24
14. Foughali, M., Dal Zilio, S., Ingrand, F.: On the Semantics of the GenoM3 Framework. Technical report (2019)
15. Foughali, M., Ingrand, F., Seceleanu, C.: Statistical model checking of complex robotic systems. In: SPIN (2019)
16. Gobillot, N., Guet, F., Doose, D., Grand, C., Lesire, C., Santinelli, L.: Measurement-based real-time analysis of robotic software architectures. In: IROS, pp. 3306–3311. IEEE (2016)
17. Goddard, S., Huang, J., Farritor, S., et al.: A performance and schedulability analysis of an autonomous mobile robot. In: ECRTS, pp. 239–248. IEEE (2005)
18. Henzinger, T., Nicollin, X., Sifakis, J., Yovine, S.: Symbolic model checking for real-time systems. Inf. Comput. **111**(2), 193–244 (1994)
19. Huang, X., Singh, A., Smolka, S.: Using integer clocks to verify clock-synchronization protocols. Innov. Syst. Softw. Eng. **7**(2), 119–130 (2011)
20. Kargahi, M., Movaghar, A.: Non-preemptive earliest-deadline-first scheduling policy: a performance study. In: MASCOTS, pp. 201–208. IEEE (2005)
21. Kim, M., Kang, K.C.: Formal construction and verification of home service robots: a case study. In: Peled, D.A., Tsay, Y.-K. (eds.) ATVA 2005. LNCS, vol. 3707, pp. 429–443. Springer, Heidelberg (2005). https://doi.org/10.1007/11562948_32

22. Lime, D., Roux, O.H., Seidner, C., Traonouez, L.-M.: Romeo: a parametric model-checker for petri nets with stopwatches. In: Kowalewski, S., Philippou, A. (eds.) TACAS 2009. LNCS, vol. 5505, pp. 54–57. Springer, Heidelberg (2009). https://doi.org/10.1007/978-3-642-00768-2_6

23. Mallet, A., Pasteur, C., Herrb, M., Lemaignan, S., Ingrand, F.: GenoM3: building middleware-independent robotic components. In: ICRA, pp. 4627–4632. IEEE (2010)

24. Merlin, P., Farber, D.: Recoverability of Communication Protocols: Implications of a Theoretical Study. IEEE Transactions on Communications **24**(9), 1036–1043 (1976)

25. Miyazawa, A., Ribeiro, P., Li, W., Cavalcanti, A., Timmis, J.: Automatic property checking of robotic applications. In: IROS, pp. 3869–3876. IEEE (2017)

26. Piaggio, M., Sgorbissa, A., Zaccaria, R.: Pre-emptive versus non-pre-emptive real time scheduling in intelligent mobile robotics. J. Exp. Theor. Artif. Intell. **12**(2), 235–245 (2000)

27. Sensfelder, N., Brunel, J., Pagetti, C.: Modeling cache coherence to expose interference. In: ECRTS (2019)

28. Shi, J., Goddard, S., Lal, A., Farritor, S.: A real-time model for the robotic highway safety marker system. In: RTAS, pp. 331–340. IEEE (2004)

29. Shih, C., Sha, L., Liu, J.: Scheduling tasks with variable deadlines. In: RTAS, pp. 120–122. IEEE (2001)

30. Sowmya, A., Tsz-Wang So, D., Hung Tang, W.: Design of a mobile robot controller using Esterel tools. Electron. Not. Theor. Comput. Sci. **65**(5), 3–10 (2002)

Formalizing and Verifying UML Activity Diagrams

Messaoud Abbas[(✉)], Mounir Beggas, and Ammar Boucherit

Department of Computer Science, El Oued University, LABTHOP,
39000 El Oued, Algeria
{messaoud-abbas,beggas-mounir,ammar-boucherit}@univ-eloued.dz

Abstract. UML (Unified Modelling Language) is the de facto standard for the development of software models. Static aspects of systems are mainly described with UML class diagrams. However, the behavioral aspects are often designed by UML state machine and activity diagrams. Due to the ambiguous semantics of UML diagrams, formal methods can be used to generate the corresponding formal specifications and then check their properties. In this paper, we opt for functional semantics of UML activity diagrams by means of FoCaLiZe, a proof based formal method. Thus, we generate formal specifications in order to detect eventual inconsistencies of UML activity diagrams using Zenon, the automatic theorem prover of FoCaLiZe. The proposed approach directly supports action constraints, activity partitions and the communication between structural (classes) and dynamic (activity diagrams) aspects.

Keywords: UML activity diagram · UML semantics · Software engineering · Model proprieties · Model verification

1 Introduction

UML activity diagrams (UAD) [1] are graphical notations describing the behavior of UML class instances during their lifetime, without considering triggering events. They use the Object Constraint Language (OCL) [2] to specify action constraints and transition guards. UAD are frequently used in the area of workflow application modeling [3], such as software application modeling [4], web services composition modeling [5] and also in business process modeling [6]. The wide use of UAD is enhanced with MDE (Model Driven Engineering) tools for verification and code generation.

Because of the semantics of UAD, it is relevant to combine UML models (especially within the scope of critical systems) with formal methods in order to express and check software properties using the verification techniques provided by formal methods.

Many studies have focused on the transformation of UAD into formal methods, such as B language [7] based tools, Alloy formal tool [8], Petri Nets [9], Maude system [10] and model checkers [11]. However, the large gap between

© Springer Nature Switzerland AG 2019
C. Attiogbé et al. (Eds.): MEDI 2019 Workshops, CCIS 1085, pp. 49–63, 2019.
https://doi.org/10.1007/978-3-030-32213-7_4

UML (object oriented modeling) and formal methods (mathematical and logical specifications) leads in general to a manufactured transformation of models and loses essential semantics of the original UML/OCL models.

We have already formalized most UML class diagram features [12,13], OCL constraints [14] and UML state machines [15] with FoCaLiZe [16]. The latter is a formal programming environment with a purely functional language that shares with UML and OCL most of their architecture, design and specification features [13,17].

In this article, we opt for a functional semantics of UAD with FoCaLiZe. Firstly, we propose a functional semantics for UAD. Then, we implement the proposed semantics with FoCaLiZe. At the ultimate steps, we use FoCaLiZe proof techniques to check UAD properties. The proposed transformation considers OCL pre/post-conditions of class's operations and action constraints. It also supports activity partitions (activities that invoke several actors) and the communication between UML activity diagrams and their corresponding classes. Furthermore, the transformation of UAD into FoCaLiZe is realized in such a way that it could be naturally integrated with the proposals of the aforementioned UML class diagram transformation [13,17].

The remainder of this document is organized as follows: Sects. 2 and 3 present basic concepts of FoCaLiZe and define the subset of UML activity diagram and OCL constraints supported by our transformation. In Sect. 4, the semantics of UML activity diagrams is studied, followed by the specification of the transformation rules. The next section presents an approach that integrates UML classes, activity diagrams and the FoCaLiZe environment for error detection. Before concluding, Sect. 6 discusses some related works.

2   The FoCaLiZe Environment

FoCaLiZe [16] is an integrated development environment with formal features including a programming language, a constraint (property) specification language and theorem provers. A FoCaLiZe project is organized as a hierarchy of species that may have several roots. The upper levels are built along the specification stages, while the lower ones correspond to the implementation. Each node of the hierarchy corresponds to a refinement step toward a complete implementation using object oriented features such as multiple inheritance and parameterization.

The main brick in a FoCaLiZe project is the **species**. It is a structure that groups together several methods: the carrier type of the species, functions to manipulate this carrier type and logical properties. The properties of a species express requirements that must be verified. Using EBNF (Extended Backus-Naur Form) notation, the general syntax of a species is (Table 1):

Table 1. The syntax of a species

spec	::=	**species** *species_name* [(*param* [{ , *param*}*])] =
		[**inherit** *spec_def* [{ , *spec_def*}*] ;] {*methods*;}* **end**;;
param	::=	*ident* **in** *type* | *ident* **is** *spec_def*
spec_def	::=	*species_name* | *species_name* (*param* [{ , *param*}*])
methods	::=	*rep* | *signature* | *let* | *property* | *theorem*
rep	::=	**representation** = *type*;
signature	::=	**signature** *function_name* : *function_type*;
let	::=	**let** [**rec**] *function_name* = *function_body*;
property	::=	**property** *property_name* : *property_specification* ;
theorem	::=	**theorem** *property_name* : *property_specification* **proof**= *theorem_proof*;

It regroups together the following methods:

- The **representation** describes the data structure of the species entities.
- A **signature** specifies a function without giving its computational body, only the functional type is provided at this stage. A signature is intended to be defined (will get its computational body) later in the subspecies (through inheritances).
- A **let** defines a function together with its computational body.
- A **property** is a statement expressed by a first-order formula specifying requirements to be satisfied in the context of the species. A property is intended to be defined (will get its proof) later in the subspecies (through inheritances).
- A **theorem** is a property provided together with its formal proof.

FoCaLiZe provides several means to write proofs. We can directly write Coq [18] proofs, but the usual way to write proofs consists to use the FoCaLiZe proof language (FPL). Using FPL, the developer organizes the proof in steps. Each step provides proof hints that will be exploited by Zenon (the automatic theorem prover of FoCaLiZe) [19] to generate, automatically, a Coq proof script. So, at the ultimate step, the compilation of FoCaLiZe sources produces an OCaml executable and proof.

3   UML Activity Diagrams

An activity diagram (of a UML class) describes the behavior of the class objects. It specifies the sequence of actions (workflow) of an object during its lifetime. For simplicity and clarity, we only focus on simple actions (class operation calls) in this paper.

In order to provide a formal framework for the transformation of UAD to FoCaLiZe specifications, we propose an abstract syntax for the subset of UAD constructs that we consider, using mostly **UML metamodel syntax** [1]. Also here, the proposed syntax is written in EBNF notation (see Table 2) in order to improve the readability of our transformation rules.

An activity diagram consists of a set of nodes and a set of transitions (5). Each transition (flow) is a directed edge interconnecting two nodes. It specifies

Table 2. Abstract syntax of UML activity diagrams

ActivityDiagram	::= *ActivityDiagramIdent declaration**
declaration	::= *node*	*transition*
node	::= *sourceNode*	*targetNode*
sourceNode	::= **InitialNode** |*actionNode* |*controlNode*
targetNode	::= **FinalNode** |*actionNode* |*controlNode*
actionNode	::= *nodeIdent* [**«localprecondition»** *Pre-Condition*] *operation_call* [**«localpostcondition»** *Post-Condition*]
controlNode	::= *nodeIdent* {**DecisionNode** |**ForkNode** |**JoinNode** |**MergeNode**}[1]
operation_call	::= *self.operationIdent* ([*actualParameter* {, *actualParameter*}*])
guard	::= *OclExpression*
Pre-Condition	::= *OclExpression*
Post-Condition	::= *OclExpression*
transition	::= **transition** *transitionIdent* (*sourceNodeIdent* [[*guard*]] *targetNodeIdent*)

that the system moves from one action to another. We distinguish between two types of nodes: control nodes and action nodes.

Control nodes are used to specify choice (**DecisionNode** and **MergeNode**), parallelism (**ForkNode** and **JoinNode**), initial nodes (**InitialNode**) or final nodes (**FinalNode**).

The decision nodes choose one of the outgoing transitions and the merge nodes merge several incoming transitions, so the first incoming transition will be the first outgoing one. The Join nodes synchronize different parallel transitions, while the fork nodes split a transition into different parallel flows.

Action nodes are calls to classes operations (*operation_ call*). The initial node starts the global flow.

Action constraints are presented as notes attached to action nodes, specified with the stereotypes «localprecondition» and «localpostcondition». The local pre-condition describes a constraint which is assumed to be true before the action is executed. The local post-condition describes a constraint which has to be satisfied after the action is executed. We use OCL syntax to specify local pre and post-conditions on actions.

A transition guard ([*guard*]) is an optional constraint that controls the firing of the transition. If the guard is true, the transition may be enabled, otherwise it is disabled.

In this work, we consider the two main OCL constraints: class invariant and pre and post-conditions on classes operations. An invariant is an OCL expression attached to one class and must be true for all instances of that class at any time. The pre-condition of a class operation describes a constraint which is assumed to be true before the operation is executed. The post-condition describes a constraint which has to be satisfied after the operation is executed.

Activity Diagram Example: Orders Processing

We present here the activity diagram of the class Order (see Figs. 1 and 2).

First, an order (a new instance o of the class Order is created) is received by the action receive_order (the operation initOrder() of the class Order is invoked).Then, if the condition guard (Self.rejectOrder()) of the decision node is not true (the order is not rejected), the flow goes to the next

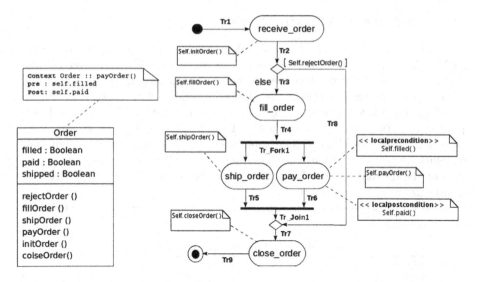

Fig. 1. The class Order   **Fig. 2.** UML activity diagram: orders processing

step: the action fill_order (Self.fillOrder()). After that, the fork node splits the path of the control flow into two parallel tasks. On the left path, the action ship_order (call of the operation shipOrder()) is executed. On the right path, to bill the order and process its payment, the action pay_order (Self.payOrder()) is handled. When the two paths are accomplished, the join node may take place and the action close_order (Self.closeOrder()) is achieved. Returning back to the above decision node, if the order is rejected, the flow is directly passed on the action close_order.

4   From UAD to FoCaLiZe

A UML activity diagram describes the behavior of a UML class and uses OCL expressions. Therefore, we will start with an overview on the transformation of UML classes and OCL expressions, then we describe the semantics and transformation rules for activity diagrams.

During the transformation from UML/OCL to FoCaLiZe, we will use the following notations:

- The term "class c_n" refers to the UML class named c_n and the term "species c_n" refers to the FoCaLiZe species named c_n.
- For a UML/OCL element E, $[\![E]\!]$ denotes its transformation into FoCaLiZe. We will also preserve the same UML/OCL elements identifiers in the transformations, taking into account upper and lower cases to respect FoCaLiZe syntax if necessary.

4.1   Transformation of UML Classes

The similarities between species and UML class [20], have led us to transform a UML class into a FoCaLiZe species. Class attributes will be converted into a representation of the derived species. For each attribute of the original class we generate a getter-function in the derived species. Class operations will be converted into species functions (signatures). OCL constraints are mapped into species properties. In the transformation from UML to FoCaLiZe we only generate an abstract FoCaLiZe specification, each attribute gives rise to a signature modeling its getter function and class operations will be converted into signatures of the derived species. Formal transformations for classes attributes and operations are given in [12,13].

Code 1.1 illustrates the transformation of the class Order (see Fig. 1) and its OCL constraints.

Code 1.1. The species Order

```
species Order =
 (* Transformation of attributes *)
 signature get_filled : Self -> bool;
 signature get_shipped : Self -> bool;
 signature get_paid : Self -> bool;

 (* Transformation of operations *)
 signature newOrder :   bool -> bool -> bool -> Self; (*Transformation of the class constructor*)
 signature rejectOrder : Self -> bool ;
 signature fillOrder   : Self -> Self;
 signature shipOrder   : Self -> Self;
 signature payOrder    : Self -> Self;
 signature initOrder   : Self -> Self ;
 signature closeOrder  : Self -> Self ;

 (* Transformation of payOrder pre/post-constraints *)
 property payOrder_pre_post: all e:Self, (get_filled(e)) -> (get_paid(payOrder(e)));
end;;
```

4.2   Transformation of Activity Diagrams

Let us start by the description of a functional semantics for a simple control flow (without emphasis on the sequence and conditions of the flow). Then, we present the implementation of this semantics with FoCaLiZe. After that, we describe the transformation of control nodes (decision, merge, fork and join nodes) using FoCaLiZe functional statements.

Functional Semantics for Activity Diagrams: An activity diagram $\mathbb{AD}$ of a class c_n consists of a set of nodes ($\mathbb{ND}$) and a set of transitions ($\mathbb{TR}$):

$$\mathbb{ND} = \{\texttt{InitialNode}, nd_1, \ldots, nd_k, \texttt{FinalNode}\}$$
$$\mathbb{TR} = \{ tr_1, \ldots, tr_m\}.$$

Each action node nd has form:

$$nd = nodeIdent \; [\text{«localprecondition»} \; Pre\text{-}Condition]$$
$$self.action \; (\text{param}_1 \ldots \text{param}_n)$$
$$[\text{«localpostcondition»} \; Post\text{-}Condition]$$

where $self.action \; (\text{param}_1 \ldots \text{param}_n)$ is an operation call of the class c_n. Thus, the set of nodes identifiers is:

$$\mathbb{NI} = \{\texttt{InitialNode}, \texttt{FinalNode}, nodeIdent_1, \ldots, nodeIdent_k\}.$$

Each transition tr has form:

$$tr = \textbf{transition} \; trIdent \; (sourceNode \; [[guard]] \; targetNode)$$

where the pair $(sourceNode, \; targetNode) \in \mathbb{NI}^2$ represents the source and target node identifiers (in addition to $\texttt{InitialNode}$ and $\texttt{FinalNode}$, we only have action nodes at this step) of the transition tr.

The optional transition guard ($[guard]$) conditions the transition, it is a logical formula specified by an OCL expression.

The set of transition identifiers is $\mathbb{TI} = \{ trIdent_1, \ldots, trIdent_m\}$.

Let $\mathbb{I}$ be the list of instances (snapshots) of the class c_n, for an instance o, $state(o)$ denotes its current action node in the activity diagram of the class c_n.

$$state : \mathbb{I} \to \mathbb{NI} \tag{1}$$
$$(o) \longmapsto state(o)$$

An activity diagram of the class c_n can be thought of as a **function** that takes a transition tr and an instance $o \in \mathbb{I}$ such that $state(o) = sourceNode$ (the source node identifier of the transition tr) as parameters and returns the instance $o\prime$ such that $state(o\prime) = targetNode$ (the target node identifier of the transition tr). The instance $o\prime = o.action(\text{param}_1 \ldots \text{param}_n)$ is the result of the execution of the action (operation call) in the source action node ($sourceNode$):

$$AD : \mathbb{I} \times \mathbb{TI} \to \mathbb{I} \tag{2}$$
$$(o, tr_i) \longmapsto o\prime$$

In the context of object oriented programming languages o and $o\prime$ are the same object (instance), but with different memory states. In functional languages (without memory states) such as FoCaLiZe, o and $o\prime$ are two different entities, which makes the transformation of that latter interpretation of the activity diagram perfectly suitable for FoCaLiZe.

Using the functional semantics presented in (2), the activity diagram of one class directly communicates with the structural aspect of the same class and with the other classes of the model. In such a way, all behavior actions are directly expressed using class operation calls.

The mapping of the UML activity diagram of the class c_n into FoCaLiZe translates the function AD (modeling the activity diagram, see formula (2)).

Table 3. General transformation of UAD into FoCaLiZe

UML:

  public class c_n = A ; $\mathbb{O}$ **end**

$$\left(\begin{array}{l} nd_1[\text{«localprecondition»}\ PreCondition_1]\ self.action_1(prm_{11}\ldots prm_{1n}) \\ \quad [\text{«localpostcondition»}\ PostCondition_1] \\ \ldots \\ nd_k[\text{«localprecondition»}\ PreCondition_k]\ self.action_k(prm_{k1}\ldots prm_{kn}) \\ \quad [\text{«localpostcondition»}\ PostCondition_k] \end{array} \right)$$

$$\left(\begin{array}{l} \textbf{transition}\ tr_1(sourceNode_1\ [[guard_1]]targetNode_1) \\ \ldots \\ \textbf{transition}\ tr_m(sourceNode_m\ [[guard_m]]targetNode_m) \end{array} \right)$$

FoCaLiZe

```
type nodes = | [[nd₁]] ... | [[ndₖ]]  ;;

type transitions = | [[tr₁]] ... | [[trₘ]]  ;;

species c_n =
...
signature state: Self -> nodes ;
signature [[action₁]]: Self -> [[prmType₁₁]]...  -> [[prmType₁ₙ]] -> Self ;
...
signature [[actionₖ]]: Self -> [[prmTypeₖ₁]]...  -> [[prmTypeₖₙ]] -> Self ;
let aD(t:transitions, e:Self): Self = match t with
(* Transformation of the first transition: No action is executed *)
| [[tr₁]] ->  if ([[guard₁]] ∧ (state(e) = [[sourceNode₁]]))
          then e
          else focalize_error ("ERROR");
...
| [[trᵢ]] ->    if ([[guardᵢ]] ∧ (state(e) = [[sourceNodeᵢ]]))
          then [[actionₛₙᵢ(e, prmₛₙᵢ1,...,prmₛₙᵢn)]]
          else focalize_error ("ERROR");
...
| [[trₘ]] ->    if ([[guardₘ]] ∧ (state(e) = [[sourceNodeₘ]]))
          then [[actionₛₙₘ(e, prmₛₙₘ1,...,prmₛₙₘn)]]
          else focalize_error ("ERROR");
| _   ->  focalize_error("ERROR") ;
end;;
```

It is transformed into a function aD (function names must start with a lowercase letter, in FoCaLiZe syntax) of the species c_n derived from the class c_n.

In order to group the transformation of all transitions of one activity diagram within a single function (see Table 3), we use the **pattern matching** in FoCaLiZe. So, each time we call the function aD only one pattern will be invoked. This is, of course, according to the state of the entity passed as parameter. if no pattern matches the state of the entity, the function will return an error message that expresses a system deadlock.

Using the transformation presented in Table 3, the decision nodes and merge nodes have straightforward counterparts as FoCaLiZe expressions. However, for the transformation of fork nodes we need to define a particular function (ADFN) that should generate as many copies of the resulted object as the outgoing transitions (paths) from the fork node. For this purpose, we use the FoCaLiZe type list(t) that groups several elements of the same type t. Note that a fork node is always followed by the parallel execution of its issued tasks using elements of the list list(t). Therefore, we use the following parallel execution statement in FoCaLiZe:

let $def_1 = exp_1$ and $def_2 = exp_2$ and... $def_n = exp_n$ in EXP;

This statement shows that all the definitions $(def_1, def_2, ... def_n)$ are separately evaluated (parallel execution).

Also for the transformation of join nodes, we need to define a particular function (ADJN) that associates a collection of objects of the class c_n and a transition as parameters and returns one object of the class.

Action constraints (local pre and post-conditions) are transformed in a similar way as OCL pre/post-conditions. We convert local pre and post-conditions together into a FoCaLiZe implication ($\mathbb{L}_{pre} \Rightarrow \mathbb{L}_{post}$) of the corresponding species.

We can now complete our species Order (see Code 1.2) by the transformation of the class Order activity diagram (see Figs. 1 and 2, page 5) and its action constraints.

The property action_pay_order_property represents the transformation of the action pay_order localprecondition and localpostcondition.

Code 1.2. Transformation of the class Order activity diagram

```
open "basics" ;;
type transitions =  | Tr1 | Tr2 | Tr3 | Tr4 | Tr5 | Tr6 | Tr7  | Tr8 | Tr9 | Tr_Fork1
                   | Tr_Join1 | Tr_final;;
type nodes =  | InitialNode| Receive_order  | Decision1   | Fill_order | Fork1 | Ship_order
              | Pay_order  | Join1 | Merge1 | Close_order | FinalNode;;
(* The species Order, derived from the class Order *)
species Order =
signature get_filled : Self -> bool;    signature get_shipped : Self -> bool;
signature get_paid : Self -> bool;
signature newOrder :  bool -> bool -> bool -> Self;
signature rejectOrder : Self -> bool ;    signature fillOrder : Self -> Self;
signature billOrder : Self -> Self;    signature shipOrder : Self -> Self;
signature payOrder : Self -> Self;    signature joinOrder : list(Self)-> Self ;
signature closeOrder : Self -> Self ;    signature initOrder : Self -> Self ;
signature state: Self -> nodes;

(* Transformation of the class order activity diagram *)
let aD (t:transitions, e:Self): Self = match t  with
| Tr1 -> if (state(e) = InitialNode) then e  else focalize_error('ERROR')
| Tr2 -> if state(e)= Receive_order then initOrder(e) else focalize_error('ERROR')

(* Handling of the node Decision1 - Decision not satisfied *)
| Tr3 -> if ((state(e)= Decision1) && (~~ rejectOrder(e) )) then e  else focalize_error('ERROR')
| Tr4 -> if (state(e) = Fill_order) then fillOrder(e) else focalize_error('ERROR')
| Tr5 -> if (state(e) = Ship_order) then shipOrder(e) else focalize_error('ERROR')
| Tr6 -> if (state(e) = Pay_order) then payOrder(e)   else focalize_error('ERROR')
```

```
(* Handling of the node Merge1 *)
| Tr7 -> if (state(e) = Merge1) then e else focalize_error('ERROR')

(* Handling of the node Decision1 - Decision satisfied *)
| Tr8 -> if ((state(e) = Decision1) && (rejectOrder(e))) then e else focalize_error('ERROR')
| Tr9 -> if (state(e) = Close_order) then closeOrder(e) else focalize_error('ERROR')
| _    -> focalize_error('ERROR');
(* Handling of Fork Nodes *)
let rec aDFN (t:transitions, e:Self):list(Self)= match t with
| Tr_Fork1 -> if state(e)= Fork1 then [e; e] else focalize_error('ERROR') ;
| _    -> focalize_error('ERROR') ;
(* Handling of Join Nodes *)
let rec aDJN (t:transitions,
le:list(Self)):Self = match t with
| Tr_Join1 ->
    if (let rec states (l:list(Self)):bool = match l with
    | [] -> true
    | x::r -> (state(x) = Join1) && (states(r)) in states(le) ) then joinOrder(le)
                                                    else focalize_error('ERROR')
| _    -> focalize_error('ERROR') ;
(* Transformation of payOrder pre/post-constraints *)
property payOrder_pre_post: all e:Self, get_filled(e) -> get_paid(payOrder(e)) ;
(* Transformation of the action pay_order constraints *)
property action_pay_order_property: all e:Self, get_filled(e) -> get_paid(aD(Tr6, e)) ;
end;;
```

An activity partition is an activity group for actions that invoke more than one class and have some common characteristics. To transform activity partitions, we use the same semantics and techniques as for activity diagrams (see Table 3). In addition, we use FoCaLiZe parameterized species to group the transformation of several classes within a single species. The full description of activity partition transformation is beyond the scope of this conference paper.

5   A Framework for Errors Detection

Our goal is to provide a framework that generates automatically FoCaLiZe abstract specifications from UAD and OCL constraints. Then, we use these specifications to check the consistency of the original model.

Using the proposed transformation, we obtain two kinds of properties from the original UML/OCL model:

- The properties derived from the OCL pre and post-conditions.
- The properties derived from action (action local pre/post-conditions) specifications.

When a particular action of an activity diagram invokes one operation of the class and this operation is attached to an OCL pre and post-conditions, we obtain (in the FoCaLiZe specification) two properties referring the same operation: the OCL pre/post-conditions and the action local pre/post-conditions. To detect eventual errors, we assume that the property derived from the OCL pre/post-conditions (*pre-post_property*) is satisfied, then we try to provide a proof (using FPL) of the property derived from the action specification (*action_property*) as follows:

proof of *action_property* = by property *pre-post_property* ;

If there is no contradiction between the two properties, Zenon will get the proof. Otherwise, the proof will be impossible.

To clarify this proof process, we complete the species `Order` with the following proof statements (Code 1.3):

Code 1.3. Successful proof of action_pay_order_property

```
species Order =
...
(* Transformation of payOrder
pre/post-constraints *)
property payOrder_pre_post: all e:Self, get_filled(e) -> get_paid(payOrder(e)) ;

(* Transformation of the action pay_order constraints *)
property action_pay_order_property: all e:Self, get_filled(e) -> get_paid(aD(Tr6, e)) ;

proof of action_pay_order_property = by  property payOrder_pre_post;
end;;
```

This example provides the proof of the property `action_pay_order_property`. It specifies the action `pay_order` of the class `Order` activity diagram.

The compilation of the above FoCaLiZe source ensures the correctness of the specification. No error has occurred, this means that the compilation, code generation and Coq verification were successful.

Imagine now that the UML user swaps (by mistake) the specification of the OCL pre/post-conditions of the operation `payOrder`. In this case, we will get the following FoCaLiZe source (Code 1.4):

Code 1.4. Unsuccessful proof of action_pay_order_property

```
species Order =
...
property payOrder_pre_post: all e:Self,
get_paid(e) -> get_filled(payOrder(e)) ;

property action_pay_order_property: all e:Self, get_filled(e) -> get_paid(aD(Tr6, e)) ;

proof of action_pay_order_property = by  property payOrder_pre_post;
end;;
```

The compilation of this FoCaLiZe source returns the following message:

```
File "order.fcl", line 85, characters 27-57:
Zenon error: exhausted search space
without finding a proof
### proof failed
```

When Zenon cannot find a proof automatically, the FoCaLiZe compiler indicates the line of code that is responsible for the error, if any.

To implement the proposed transformation, we considered using transformation tools such as QVT, ATL, ETL, etc. But, unfortunately, there is no sound meta-model for FoCaLiZe and there are not many modeling tools that combine UML/OCL, FoCaLiZe and the transformation tools. Therefore, we preferred to use the XSLT[1] [21]. Its processor is available in most programming environ-

---

[1] A usable language for the transformation of XML documents, recommended by the World Wide Web Consortium (W3C).

ments and allows us to transform an XML document into various formats (XML, HTML, PDF, Text, etc.). So, we have developed an XSLT stylesheet specifying the transformation rules from a UML model expressed in the XMI interchange format (generated by the **Papyrus** graphical tool) into FoCaLiZe (see Fig. 3).

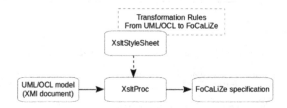

Fig. 3. Systematic transformation of UML models into FoCaLiZe

Additional information about the transformation tool (**UML2FOC**) are now available on-site[2], where instructions for installation and use are detailed.

6   Related Work

Some works deal with the transformation from UAD to the B method based tools. For instance, authors of [22] have proposed the translation of activity diagrams into Event B, in order to verify workflow properties of distributed and parallel applications with the B prover. In a second work [23], a meta-model transformation from UAD to Event-B models in order to verify functional properties of workflow models. However, OCL constraints transformation are not exploited to check the consistency of activity diagram transitions.

The Alloy tool is another formal method which has been used in the framework Alloy4SPV [24] for the verification of software process. The proposed framework uses a subset of UML2 Activity Diagrams as a process modeling language. However, class structures are isolated from activity diagrams.

Another approach consists to translate a UML activity diagram to CPN (Colored Petri Nets) specifications [4] to attribute a formal semantics for UML activity diagrams and verify their properties. Recent contributions focus on the verification of SysML activity diagrams through their translation into Recursive RECATNets [25] and into Modular Petri Nets [26]. Yet here, neither OCL and action constraints nor activity partitions are considered. Another proposal using Colored Petri Nets [27] consists in the modeling of dynamic process aspects with CPN transformed from UAD.

A formal transformation of UAD based on rewriting logic and Graph Transformation [28] is also proposed using the Maude system and its Real Time Checker.

---

[2] http://www.univ-eloued.dz/uml2foc/.

Some other contributions are summarized as follows: all the basic building blocks of UML 2.5 Activity Diagrams and their structural semantics have been formalized using Z Schemas [29]. In [30], there is a comparison of the different translations for four model checkers in particular: UPPAAL, PES, SPIN and NuSMV. The performance of these model checkers is then compared using a suite of UAD. Using the aforementioned model checkers (UPPAAL, PES, SPIN and NuSMV), a translation tool of UAD is also presented in [31]. It supports formal verification of UAD. Moreover, an extension of the UAD is presented in [32], in order to enable the stochastic modeling of user inputs and action executions, which strongly affect the overall timing behaviors of systems.

7   Conclusion and Perspectives

In this paper, we have proposed a functional semantics for UAD, with OCL constraints, and its transformation into FoCaLiZe. The proposal supports the communication between a class structure and its activity diagram, action constraints and activity partitions. In fact, the high level design and architectural features of FoCaLiZe reduces significantly the gaps between UML/OCL and formal methods. The generated formal specification reflects perfectly both structural and behavioral aspects of the original UML/OCL model. These results are very promotional for both structural and behavioral aspects. Moreover, by using the automatic theorem prover Zenon, it is possible to automatically detect eventual contradictions between the specification of OCL constraints and the specification of activity diagrams.

As a first future work, we will use the proposed transformation to deal with the verification of additional properties such as the absence of deadlock and the availability of system services. As a second future work, we intend to study the combination of our proposal and the reverse transformation from FoCaLiZe to UML [20]. We believe that the two formalisms could further cooperate, using the graphical expressiveness of UML/OCL and FoCaLiZe proof capabilities.

References

1. OMG: UML: Unified Modeling Language, version 2.5, March 2015. http://www.omg.org/spec/UML/2.5/PDF
2. OMG: OCL: Object Constraint Language 2.4, January 2014. http://www.omg.org/spec/OCL
3. Younes, A.B., Ayed, L.J.B.: An UMLAD-to-event_B refinement based approach for specifying and verifying workflow applications. In: Proceedings of the 13th International Conference on Information Integration and Web-based Applications and Services, pp. 523–526. ACM (2011)
4. Czopik, J., Košinár, M.A., Štolfa, J., Štolfa, S.: Formalization of software process using intuitive mapping of UML activity diagram to CPN. In: Kömer, P., Abraham, A., Snášel, V. (eds.) Proceedings of the Fifth International Conference on Innovations in Bio-Inspired Computing and Applications IBICA 2014. AISC, vol. 303, pp. 365–374. Springer, Cham (2014). https://doi.org/10.1007/978-3-319-08156-4_36

5. Grønmo, R., Solheim, I.: Towards modeling web service composition in UML. In: Web Services: Modeling, Architecture and Infrastructure, WSMAI 2004 **4**, pp. 72–86 (2004)
6. de Aalst, W.M.P., et al.: Workflow verification: finding control-flow errors using Petri-Net-based techniques. In: van der Aalst, W., Desel, J., Oberweis, A. (eds.) Business Process Management. LNCS, vol. 1806, pp. 161–183. Springer, Heidelberg (2000). https://doi.org/10.1007/3-540-45594-9_11
7. Abrial, J.R.: The B-Book: Assigning Programs to Meanings. Cambridge University Press, Cambridge (2005)
8. Jackson, D.: Software Abstractions: Logic, Language and Anlysis. MIT Press, Cambridge (2012)
9. Murata, T.: Petri Nets: properties, analysis and applications. Proc. IEEE **77**(4), 541–580 (1989)
10. Clavel, M., et al.: All About Maude - A High-Performance Logical Framework, How to Specify, Program, and Verify Systems in Rewriting Logic. LNCS, vol. 4350. Springer, Heidelberg (2007). https://doi.org/10.1007/978-3-540-71999-1
11. Eker, S., Meseguer, J., Sridharanarayanan, A.: The Maude LTL model checker. Electron. Notes Theor. Comput. Sci. **71**, 162–187 (2004)
12. Messaoud, A., Choukri-Bey, B.Y., Renaud, R.: Generating FoCaLiZe specifications from UML models. In: Proceedings of the International Conference on Advanced Aspects of Software Engineering, ICAASE 2014, Constantine Algeria, pp. 157–164 (2014)
13. Abbas, M., Ben-Yelles, C.-B., Rioboo, R.: Modeling UML template classes with FoCaLiZe. In: Albert, E., Sekerinski, E. (eds.) IFM 2014. LNCS, vol. 8739, pp. 87–102. Springer, Cham (2014). https://doi.org/10.1007/978-3-319-10181-1_6
14. Messaoud, A.: Using FoCaLiZe to check OCL constraints on UML classes. In: Proceedings of the International Conference on Information Technology for Organization Development, IT4OD 2014, Tebessa Algeria, pp. 31–38 (2014)
15. Messaoud, A., Choukri-Bey, B.Y., Renaud, R.: Modelling UML state machines with focalize. IJICT **13**(1), 34–54 (2018)
16. Thérèse, H., Francois, P., Pierre, W., Damien, D.: FoCaLiZe: Tutorial and Reference Manual, version 0.9.2. CNAM-INRIA-LIP6 (2018). http://focalize.inria.fr
17. Ayrault, P., Thérèse, H., François, P.: Development life-cycle of critical software under focal. Electr. Notes Theor. Comput. Sci. **243**, 15–31 (2009)
18. Coq: The Coq Proof Assistant, Tutorial and Reference Manual, Version 8.5.INRIA - LIP - LRI - LIX - PPS (2016). Distribution: http://coq.inria.fr/
19. Bonichon, R., Delahaye, D., Doligez, D.: Zenon: an extensible automated theorem prover producing checkable proofs. In: Dershowitz, N., Voronkov, A. (eds.) LPAR 2007. LNCS (LNAI), vol. 4790, pp. 151–165. Springer, Heidelberg (2007). https://doi.org/10.1007/978-3-540-75560-9_13
20. Delahaye, D., Étienne, J., Donzeau-Gouge, V.: Producing UML models from focal specifications: an application to airport security regulations. In: 2nd IFIP/IEEE International Symposium on Theoretical Aspects of Software Engineering, pp. 121–124 (2008)
21. W3C: XSL Transformations (XSLT) Version 3.0, W3C Recommendation, October 2014 (2015). http://www.w3.org/TR/2014/WD-xslt-30-20141002/
22. Younes, A.B., Ayed, L.J.B.: Using UML activity diagrams and event B for distributed and parallel applications. In: 31st Annual International Computer Software and Applications Conference, COMPSAC 2007, vol. 1, pp. 163–170. IEEE (2007)

23. Younes, A.B., Hlaoui, Y.B., Ayed, L.J.B.: A meta-model Transformation from UML activity diagrams to Event-B models. In: Computer Software and Applications Conference Workshops (COMPSACW), pp. 740–745. IEEE (2014)
24. Laurent, Y., Bendraou, R., Baarir, S., Gervais, M.-P.: Alloy4SPV: a formal framework for software process verification. In: Cabot, J., Rubin, J. (eds.) ECMFA 2014. LNCS, vol. 8569, pp. 83–100. Springer, Cham (2014). https://doi.org/10.1007/978-3-319-09195-2_6
25. Rahim, M., Kheldoun, A., Boukala-Ioualalen, M., Hammad, A.: Recursive ECATNets-based approach for formally verifying System Modelling Language activity diagrams. IET Softw. **9**(5), 119–128 (2015)
26. Rahim, M., Hammad, A., Boukala-Ioualalen, M.: Towards the formal verification of SysML specifications: translation of activity diagrams into modular Petri Nets. In: 2015 3rd International Conference on Applied Computing and Information Technology/2nd International Conference on Computational Science and Intelligence (ACIT-CSI), pp. 509–516. IEEE (2015)
27. Czopik, J., Košinár, M.A., Štolfa, J., Štolfa, S.: Addition of static aspects to the intuitive mapping of UML activity diagram to CPN. In: Abraham, A., Krömer, P., Snasel, V. (eds.) Afro-European Conference for Industrial Advancement. AISC, vol. 334, pp. 77–86. Springer, Cham (2015). https://doi.org/10.1007/978-3-319-13572-4_6
28. Kerkouche, E., Khalfaoui, K., Chaoui, A., Aldahoud, A.: UML activity diagrams and maude integrated modeling and analysis approach using graph transformation. In: Proceedings of ICIT 2015 The 7th International Conference on Information Technology, Amman, Jordan, pp. 515–521 (2015)
29. Jamal, M., Zafar, N.A.: Formalizing structural semantics of UML 2.5 activity diagram in Z notation. In: 2016 International Conference on Open Source Systems & Technologies (ICOSST), Lahore, Pakistan, pp. 66–71. IEEE (2016)
30. Daw, Z., Cleaveland, R.: Comparing model checkers for timed UML activity diagrams. Sci. Comput. Program. **111**, 277–299 (2015)
31. Daw, Z., Mangino, J., Cleaveland, R.: UML-VT: A formal verification environment for UML activity diagrams. In: Proceedings of the MoDELS 2015 Demo and Poster Session co-located with ACM/IEEE 18th International Conference on Model Driven Engineering Languages and Systems (MoDELS 2015), Ottawa, Canada, 27 September 2015, pp. 48–51 (2015)
32. Gu, F., Zhang, X., Chen, M., Große, D., Drechsler, R.: Quantitative timing analysis of UML activity diagrams using statistical model checking. In: Proceedings of the 2016 Conference on Design, Automation & Test in Europe, EDA Consortium, pp. 780–785 (2016)

Formal Modeling and Verification
of Cloud Elasticity with Maude and LTL

Khaled Khebbeb[1,2]($\boxtimes$), Nabil Hameurlain[1], and Faiza Belala[2]

[1] LIUPPA, University of Pau, Pau, France
{khaled.khebbeb,nabil.hameurlain}@univ-pau.fr
[2] LIRE, University of Constantine 2, Constantine, Algeria
{khaled.khebbeb,faiza.belala}@univ-constantine2.dz

Abstract. Elasticity allows Cloud systems to adapt to the demand by (de)provisioning resources as the input workload rises and drops. Given the numerous overlapping factors that impact their elastic behavior, the specification and verification of Cloud elasticity is a particularly challenging task. In this paper, we propose a Maude-based approach to formalize Cloud systems' elastic behaviors, as a first step towards the verification of their correctness through a LTL (Linear Temporal Logic) state-based model-checking technique.

Keywords: Formal modeling and verification · Maude · Linear Temporal Logic · Self-adaptive systems · Cloud computing

1   Introduction

Cloud elasticity [10] endows Cloud systems with the ability to adapt computing resource provisioning, in order to cope with the demand as closely as possible. Elasticity allows to control resources provisioning according to workload fluctuation in a way to maintain a good quality of service (QoS) while reducing infrastructure costs. Cloud elasticity is ensured by an elasticity controller: an entity usually based on a closed control loop that decides which of the elasticity methods (horizontal scale, vertical scale, etc.), to be triggered, to adapt to the demand [9]. In terms of specification, Cloud elasticity is particularly challenging to manage. Elasticity relies on numerous overlapping factors such as current demand, available resources, etc., and has to consider the unpredictable nature of input workload. These complex dependencies significantly increase the difficulty of specifying and verifying Cloud elasticity controller's behaviors.

In this paper, we provide a formal modeling approach which reduces the complexity of designing Cloud elasticity control. We rely on Maude, which is an implementation of rewrite logic [6], as a semantic framework to specify Cloud systems elasticity. Maude is a formal environment which can be used as a declarative and executable formal specification language, and as a formal verification system. It provides good representation and verification capabilities for a wide

© Springer Nature Switzerland AG 2019
C. Attiogbé et al. (Eds.): MEDI 2019 Workshops, CCIS 1085, pp. 64–77, 2019.
https://doi.org/10.1007/978-3-030-32213-7_5

range of systems including models for concurrency. Precisely, we propose a state-based model-checking technique, supported by the Linear Temporal Logic (LTL), to conduct formal analysis of the introduced behaviors, in order to verify their correctness.

The remainder of the paper is structured as follows. In Sect. 2, we introduce the elasticity controller's principles and behaviors. In Sect. 3, we introduce Maude system and explain our formal modeling approach of Cloud elasticity. In Sect. 4, we present our Maude-based solution for formal verification of Cloud elasticity correctness. In Sect. 5, we review some works about formal specification and verification of Cloud elasticity. Finally, Sect. 6 summarizes and concludes the paper.

2   The Elasticity Controller

Cloud elasticity is generally of an autonomic nature, i.e., it is self-managed and categorized with minimal human intervention [11]. Elasticity is generally ensured by an *elasticity controller*. This entity decides on the elasticity actions to be applied over a controlled Cloud system in order to adapt resource provisioning to the demand. The elasticity controller is generally referred to as an *autonomic manager* and usually works as follows. It periodically monitors the managed Cloud system, i.e., it considers numerous factors such as the amount of available resource and input workload. It diagnoses (by analyzing the monitored data) the controlled Cloud system's state in terms of resource provisioning: *Overprovisioning* (i.e., over-billing) and *Underprovisioning* (i.e., poor quality of service). The controller then provides action plans to ensure the managed Cloud elasticity, i.e., it calculates a way to reach a *Stable* state where the amount of available resource matches as closely as possible the actual demand. Finally, the proper adaptation actions are triggered at the proper Cloud layer (infrastructure and/or application) to fulfill the controller's plan.

In previous work [12,13], we defined different elasticity strategies to describe a logic which governs the elasticity controller's decision-making behavior for elasticity management. The introduced strategies are of reactive nature and take the form: **IF** *Condition* **THEN** *Action*. Conditions are given with monitoring predicates φi (in first-order logic) and actions Ai are elasticity adaptations to be triggered. We defined horizontal scale (*scale-out* and *scale-in*), migration and load balancing strategies which operate at infrastructure and application Cloud layers in a complementary way. Table 1 gives informal descriptions of the strategies. Note that we defined a high (V1, S1) and limited (V2, S2) resource provisioning models for scaling-out at both infrastructure and application layers.

The elastic behavior of a Cloud system, i.e., dynamically scaling up and scaling down resource allocation, is determined by numerous overlapping factors, such as the input workload (which can be unpredictable), the amount of available resource, their usage rate, the logic that describes the elasticity controller's reasoning (i.e., the strategies), etc. These complex dependencies and their hard to determine outcomes on the behavior of the system, make understanding, modeling and analyzing Cloud elasticity very challenging. In terms of specification

Table 1. Elasticity strategies description

Layer	Strategy	Condition	Action
Infrastructure	(V1) Scale-out	(φ1) A VM is overloaded	(A1) Deploy a new VM
	(V2) Scale-out	(φ2) All VMs are overloaded	
	(Vin) Scale-in	(φ3) A VM is unused	(A2) Remove the VM
	(MIG) Migration	(φ4) A VM is overloaded and a VM is unused	(A3) Migrate a service instance to the less loaded VM
Application	(S1) Scale-out	(φ5) A Service is overloaded	(A4) Deploy a new service
	(S2) Scale-out	(φ6) All services are overloaded	
	(Sin) Scale-in	(φ7) A service is unused	(A5) Remove a service
	(LBS) Load balacing	(φ8) A service is overloaded and a service is unused	(A6) Move a request to the less loaded service

and verification, the main research challenges are: (1) how to specify the desired elastic behavior of Cloud systems? (2) how to check whether they fulfill, or not, such a behavior? (3) how to identify when and how they deviate from their intended elastic behavior?

In this paper, we intend to answer these questions, and propose a formal approach for the specification and verification of Cloud elasticity. We specify an elasticity controller to manage elasticity at both infrastructure and application Cloud layers in a complementary way, relying on elasticity strategies. Precisely, we provide a rewrite-logic-based formal modeling of Cloud elasticity, through the Maude language [7], to manage the elasticity controller's behavior complexity. In addition, we propose a state-based model-checking technique [3], supported by Linear Temporal Logic (LTL), to formally verify its correctness.

3   Maude-Based Specification of Elasticity

Maude is a high-level formal specification language based on rewrite and equational logic. A Maude program defines a logical theory and a Maude computation implements a logical deduction using axioms specified in the theory. A Maude specification is structured in two parts [5]:

– A *functional module* which specifies a theory in *membership equational logic*: a pair (Σ, $E \cup A$), where signature Σ specifies the type structure (sorts, subsorts, operators etc.). E is the collection of possibly conditional equations, and A is a collection of equational attributes for the operators (i.e., associative, commutative, etc.).

- A *system module* which specifies a rewrite theory as a triple $(\Sigma, E \cup A, R)$, where $(\Sigma, E \cup A)$ is the module's equational theory part, and R is a collection of possibly conditional rewrite rules.

To specify Cloud elasticity, a Maude functional module can define Cloud systems' structures (i.e., configurations) together with monitoring predicates and other actions to be applied over them, to diagnose their state. A Maude system module can specify conditional rewrite rules to express elasticity strategies to be applied.

3.1   Cloud Stuctures and Monitoring Predicates

In the functional module (i.e., Listing 1.1), the Cloud physical server, virtual machines and service instances are defined as CS, VM and S sorts. A sort is built according to its associated constructor (see lines $6-8$). For instance, a Cloud server is built by the term CS<x,y,z/VML:state>, where x, y and z are naturals which encode upper hosting thresholds at server, VM and service levels. VML, respectively, SL is a list of VMs and services. This relationship is expressed by the declaration of sort VM, respectively S as a subsort of sort VML and SL (lines $11-14$).

Listing 1.1. Functional module: Elastic_Cloud_System decalarations

```
1  fmod Elastic_Cloud_System is
2  protecting NAT BOOL .
3  sorts HSCALE CS VM S VML SL state.
4  subsort VM < VML . subsort S < SL .
5  ——Cloud systems construction axioms
6  op CS<_,_,_/_:_> : Nat Nat Nat VML state -> CS [ctor] .
7  op VM{_,_:_} : Nat SL state -> VM [ctor] .
8  op S[_,_:_] : Nat Nat state -> S [ctor] .
9  ops stable overloaded unused ... : -> state [ctor]
10 ——VM and services lists
11 op nilv : -> VML [ctor] .
12 op _|_ : VML VML -> VML [ctor assoc comm id: nilv] .
13 op nils : -> SL [ctor] .1
14 op _+_ : SL SL -> SL [ctor assoc comm id: nils] .
15 ——Monitoring predicates
16 ops isStable(_) isUnstable(_) isOverprovisioned(_)
17       isUnderprovisioned(_): CS -> Bool .
18 ops AoverV(_) EoverV(_) EunV(_) AoverS(_) EoverS(_)
19       EunS(_) MIGpred LBSpred: CS -> Bool .
20 ops overV(_) unV(_) : VM -> Bool .
21 ops overS(_) unS(_) : S -> Bool .
22 ...
23 ——Operations
```

```
24 op loadCS (_) : CS -> Nat . op loadV (_) : VM -> Nat .
25 op loadS (_) : S -> Nat .
26 ...
27 endfm
```

Sort **state** gives a state out of the constructors overloaded, unused, stable, etc. (line 9). An instance (server, VM and service) is overloaded if its load (lines 24−25) reaches its upper hosting threshold (i.e., x, y and z). It is unused if it reaches zero. To calculate states, we define a set of monitoring predicates which give information about the managed Cloud system configuration. For instance, *AoverV()* is a predicate for "all VMs are overloaded" and *EunS()* is a predicate for "there exists an unused service instance" (lines 18−21). Predicates *isStable()*, *isUnstable()*, *isUnderprovisioned()* and *isOverprovisioned()* define the global system state of provisioning (lines 16−17). Table 2 gives the correspondence between strategies' triggering predicates ($\varphi1$−8) identified in Sect. 2 and their encoding into the *Elastic_Cloud_System* functional module.

Table 2. Strategies predicates encoded into Maude

Triggering predicate	Maude encoding
$\varphi1$	*EoverV(cs)*
$\varphi2$	*AoverV(cs)*
$\varphi3$	*EunV(cs)*
$\varphi4$	*MIGpred(cs)*
$\varphi5$	*EoverS(cs)*
$\varphi6$	*AoverS(cs)*
$\varphi7$	*EunS(cs)*
$\varphi8$	*LBSpred(cs)*

cs: managed Cloud system of sort *CS*

3.2 Elastic Behaviors and Strategies

In the system module (i.e., Listing 1.2), we define a sort HSCALE to compose horizontal scale strategies at infrastructure and application levels. It is given with a term HSCALE(V i, S j) :: cs (lines 2−4), where parameters $i, j \in [1, 2]$ indicate which strategies are applied at infrastructure (V1 or V2) and service (S1 or S2) levels of the Cloud system cs. The equational theory, defined in the previously introduced functional module, is imported as a basis through the **including** primitive (line 2). Elasticity actions are defined as rewrite operations which operate over the Cloud system sort terms (lines 7−8). For instance, *newV()/Vin()* are used to deploy or remove a VM and *MIG()/LBS()* are for migration and load balancing.

Listing 1.2. System module: Elastic_Cloud_Behavior decalarations

```
1  mod Elastic_Cloud_Behavior is
2  including Elasti_Cloud_System .
3  sort HSCALE .
4  ---Horizontal scale specification
5  op HSCALE (V_ , S_) :: _ : Nat Nat CS -> HSCALE [ctor] .
6  ---Elasticity actions
7  ops newV(_) newS(_) MIG(_) LBS(_)
8        Vin(_) Sin(_) : CS -> CS .
9  ---Rewrite rules (strategies)
10 vars stratV stratS : NAT . var cs : CS .
11 crl [V1]: HSCALE (V 1, S stratS)::  cs
12        => HSCALE (V 1, S stratS)::  newV( cs ) if EoverV(cs)
13 crl [V2]: HSCALE (V 2, S stratS)::  cs
14        => HSCALE (V 2, S stratS)::  newV( cs ) if AoverV(cs)
15 crl [Vin]: HSCALE (V stratV, S stratS)::  cs
16        => HSCALE (V stratV, S stratS)::  Vin(cs) if (EunV(cs)))
17
18 crl [S1]: HSCALE (V stratV, S 1)::  cs
19        => HSCALE (V stratV, S 1)::  newS( cs ) if EoverS(cs) .
20 crl [S2]: HSCALE (V stratV, S 2)::  cs
21        => HSCALE (V stratV, S 2)::  newS( cs ) if AoverS(cs) .
22 crl [Sin]: HSCALE (V stratV, S stratS)::  cs
23        => HSCALE (V stratV, S stratS)::  Sin(cs) if (EunS(cs))
24
25 crl [Mig] : cs
26        => MIG(cs) if MIGpred(cs) .
27 crl [LBS] : cs
28        => LBS(cs) if LBSpred(cs) .
29 endm
```

From monitoring predicates and elasticity actions, we define a set of conditional rewrite rules, of the form `crl [name] term => term' if condition` to specify elasticity strategies (lines 11−28). Rewrite rules consist of rewriting the left-hand side of the rule as its right-hand side if the specified condition is satisfied. These rules describe generic behaviors as they support variables (line 10). Rule conditions are expressed in terms of the identified monitoring predicates and their right-hand side consists of applying an elasticity action in such a way to apply a desired operation. For instance, migration strategy at VM level (Mig) is specified as: `crl[Mig]:cs => MIG(cs) if MIGpred(cs)`. Where `cs` is a given Cloud system, `MIG(cs)` is an equation which reduces the term `cs` in such a way to apply migration at VM level and `MIGpred(cs)` is a predicate which triggers this strategy (as specified in Sect. 2). Table 3 gives the correspondence between the specified strategies actions and their encoding into Maude.

Note that the defined rewrite system (functional and system modules) ensure an autonomic executability of the defined behaviors. We designed the rewrite rules (i.e., elasticity strategies) to be complementary (i.e., every triggering condition is specific to a single elasticity anomaly to resolve). The rules' concurrent triggering nature define the desired autonomic behavior which is non-deterministic. Precise behavior patterns (which take the form of regular

Table 3. Strategies actions encoded into Maude

Triggered actions	Maude encoding
A1	newV(cs)
A2	Vin(cs)
A3	MIG(cs)
A4	newS(cs)
A5	Sin(cs)
A6	LBS(cs)

cs: managed Cloud system of sort CS

expressions) can be defined using inter-Maude strategies, as used in [15] in order to apply precedence and priorities between rules. However, inter-Maude strategies are out of scope of this paper.

In the next Section, we present our formal verification of our introduced Cloud elasticity strategies correctness.

4   Formal Verification of Elasticity

Formal verification consists of ensuring the defined behaviors correctness. In other terms, it consists of verifying the introduced strategies ability to manage a Cloud system's adaption in order to avoid over and underprovisioning in terms of deployed resources.

To proceed, we propose a LTL state-based model-checking technique. The first difficulty here is controlling the set of possible Cloud states (i.e., configurations). The proposed Maude specification allows modeling any Cloud configuration, which results in a potentially infinite set of structural states. Thus, we use a Kripke structure to identify symbolic states to manage the set of states complexity. Then we define a set of LTL propositional formulas to describe the desired transitions between those states. The verification process is explained in the following subsections.

4.1   Kripke Structure and LTL Formulas

A *Kripke* structure is a calculus model of temporal logic [3] which allows to identify symbolic states and define desired transitions between them. It is given formally with the following definition:

Definition (Kripke structure): Given a set AP of atomic propositions, a Kripke structure $\mathbf{A} = (A, \rightarrow_{\mathbf{A}}, L)$, where A is a set of symbolic states, $\rightarrow_{\mathbf{A}}$ is a transition relation, and $L : A \rightarrow AP$ is a labeling function associating to each state $a \in A$, a set $L(a)$ of atomic propositions in AP that hold in a. $LTL(AP)$ denotes the formulas of the propositional linear temporal logic. The semantics of $LTL(AP)$ is defined by a satisfaction relation: $\mathbf{A}, a \models \Phi$, where $\Phi \in LTL(AP)$.

In terms of elasticity management, we tend to have the following considerations:

– *Is there enough provisioned resource to satisfy the demand?*
   If the answer is *"no"*, the system is said to be *Underprovisioned* and more resources need to be provisioned (using scale-out strategies). But if the answer is *"yes"*, another consideration rises:
– *Are there too many deployed resource considering the demand?*
   If the answer is *"yes"*, the system is said to be *Overprovisioned* and unnecessarily provisioned resource need to be removed (using scale-in strategies). Otherwise, if the answer to the first question is still positive. The system is likely to be at a *Stable* state (i.e., desired state) in terms of elasticity, where no adaptation is required. However, one can consider another case:
– *Can the resource (VMs, services) usage be optimized?*
   It might be possible that some parts of the system are *Overloaded* while others are *Unused*. The system is then said to be *Unbalanced*, meaning that migration and/or load balancing strategies are required to balance the system's load.

Remember that answering these questions consists of monitoring the managed Cloud system, i.e., applying the specified monitoring predicates $\varphi 1-8$. In other words, these predicates constitute the set AP of atomic propositions:

$$AP = \{\varphi 1, \varphi 2, \varphi 3, \varphi 4, \varphi 5, \varphi 6, \varphi 7, \varphi 8\}$$

The set of symbolic states A express classes of equivalence with respect to the global system state in terms of elasticity. It is determined by answering the questions listed above (i.e., different Cloud configurations can have the same state of elasticity). Our considered symbolic states are given with:

$$A = \{S, P, O, B\}$$

A Cloud configuration is flagged with a symbolic state if the right atomic propositions subset in AP hold in it as follows, for each state $a \in A$:

– The system is *Stable*: $a = S \Leftrightarrow L(a) = \emptyset$
– The system is *Underprovisioned*: $a = P \Leftrightarrow L(a) \subseteq \{\varphi 1, \varphi 2, \varphi 5, \varphi 6\}$
– The system is *Overprovisioned*: $a = O \Leftrightarrow L(a) \subseteq \{\varphi 3, \varphi 7\}$
– The system is *Unbalanced*: $a = B \Leftrightarrow L(a) \subseteq \{\varphi 4, \varphi 8\}$

Now that symbolic states are identified, we define a set of LTL propositional formulas to describe the desired transitions (i.e., behavior) of the system. The set of LTL formulas is given with:

$$LTL(AP) = \{ScaleOut, ScaleIn, Balance, Elasticity\}$$

– $ScaleOut \equiv \mathbf{G}\ (P \rightarrow \mathbf{F}\ S)$
– $ScaleIn \equiv \mathbf{G}\ (O \rightarrow \mathbf{F}\ S)$
– $Balance \equiv \mathbf{G}\ (B \rightarrow \mathbf{F}\ S)$
– $Elasticity \equiv \mathbf{G}\ (\sim S \rightarrow \mathbf{F}\ S)$

Formulas *ScaleOut, ScaleIn* and *Balance* specify that the managed Cloud system which is *Underprovisioned* (P), *Overprovisioned* (O) or *Unbalanced* (B) will eventually end up by reaching the desired *Stable* (S) state, respectively. Formula *Elasticity* describes a general behavior where a system which is not stable will eventually reach the *Stable* state. Symbols **G** and **F** are LTL operators that stand for "always" and "eventually". Symbol $\sim$ is used to express negation.

A Kripke structure specification of a system's states and transitions can also be seen through a Labeled Transition System (LTS) [16]. The LTS shown in Fig. 1 gives a graphical view of these specification.

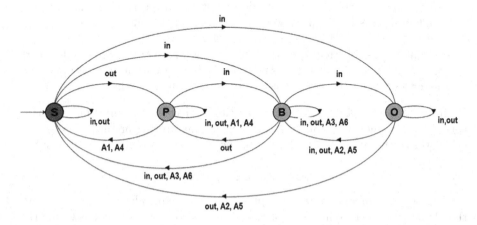

Fig. 1. LTS for Cloud elasticity

The shown transitions are the elasticity actions *Ai* (defined in Sect. 2) to be triggered by strategies, together with *in* and *out* events which stand for receiving and releasing a request. The transition system shows that the fundamental properties of *Safety* and *Liveness* are verified. Precisely, we can see that there is always a path which leads from undesirable states (*P, B, O*) to the desired one (*S*) and that no state is blocking. This globally shows the *Correctness* of the designed behaviors. In the shown representation, the stable state is initial, but any state can be the initial one as it is determined by monitoring. However, this shows the elasticity-linked property of *non-plasticity* which was defined in [4]. Meaning that an elastic system can always reach its initial state after adapting.

4.2 Maude Encoding of Properties

Maude allows associating a *Kripke* structure to a rewrite theory to define a module for property specification. Precisely, the introduced *Kripke* structure together with the identified LTL propositional formulas can be directly encoded into Maude in a system module, as shown in Listing 1.3. Such a specification configures the integrated Maude model-checker to conduct LTL state-based verification modulo a designer's property specification (lines 2−3). Cloud system sort (CS) is declared as a subsort of sort state in order to symbolically reason over it. Symbolic states and LTL formulas are declared as properties (lines 5−7), as a requirement of the satisfaction semantics [6], and are defined as (conditional) equations (lines 11−24).

For instance, determining that a Cloud configuration is in the *Stable* state is specified with

$$\text{ceq cs |= Stable = true if isStable(cs) == true}$$

Where cs is a given Cloud configuration, stable is a symbolic state for *Stable* ∈ A and iStable(cs) is a predicate for "the Cloud system is stable".

Propositional formulas ∈ $LTL(AP)$ are directly encoded into the Maude syntax. For instance, *Balance* formula is specified with

$$\text{eq Balance = [] (Unbalanced -> <> Stable) .}$$

Where Unbalanced and Stable are symbolic states ∈ A. The LTL operators **G**, **F** and ~ are directly encoded into Maude with [], <> and ~ respectively.

Listing 1.3. System module: Elastic_Cloud_Properties decalarations

```
1  mod Elastic_Cloud_Properties is
2  including MODEL-CHECKER LTL-SIMPLIFIER SATISFACTION .
3  protecting Elastic_Cloud_System Elastic_Cloud_Behavior .
4  subsort CS < State .
5  ops Stable Underprovisioned Overprovisioned
6          Unbalanced : -> Prop [ctor] .
7  ops ScaleOut ScaleIn Balance Elasticity : -> Prop [ctor] .
8
9  var cs : CS .
10 var P : Prop .
11 ——Symbolic states
12 ceq cs |= Stable = true if isStable( cs ) == true .
13 ceq cs |= Underprovisioned = true
14         if isUnderprovisioned( cs ) == true .
15 ceq cs |= Overprovisioned = true
16         if isOverprovisioned( cs ) == true .
17 ceq cs |= Unbalanced = true
18         if isUnbalanced( cs ) == true .
19 eq cs |= P = false [owise] .
20 ——LTL formulas
21 eq ScaleOut = [] ( Underprovisioned -> <> Stable ) .
22 eq ScaleIn = [] ( Overprovisioned -> <> Stable ) .
23 eq Balance = [] ( Unbalanced -> <> Stable ) .
24 eq Elasticity = [] ( ~ Stable -> <> Stable ) .
25 endm
```

4.3   LTL State-Based Model-Checking

Once system structures, behaviors and properties are defined, conducting model-checking to verify their correctness is now possible. The Maude-integrated LTL model-checker can be configured to conduct a designer's custom verification modulo their specified theory. Figure 2 gives a top view of the proposed solution for Cloud elasticity specification and verification using Maude and LTL.

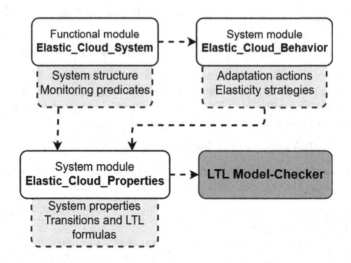

Fig. 2. Summary view of formal specification and verification approach

Cloud systems structures are encoded in a functional module *Elastic_Cloud_System*, where the declared operations and equations define the constructors that build the system's elements and the predicates that determine their states. Elasticity actions and strategies, which define the elasticity controller's behavior, are encoded in a system module *Elatic_Cloud_Behavior*, where the elasticity strategies are described as conditional rewrite rules. Their triggering conditions expressed as equations from the functional or system module encode the strategies' predicates. To verify the correctness of the defined Cloud systems' elastic behavior as encoded in the system module, we define a Maude property specification based on Linear Temporal Logic. It consists of an additional system module *Elastic_Cloud_Properties* which encodes the specified *Kripke* structure and LTL formulas, and provides a support for the verification of their satisfaction, through a LTL state-based model-checking technique. This technique consists of the verification of LTL formulas satisfaction, i.e., the reachability of the desired *Stable* state.

The model-checker is executed with, as parameters, a Cloud configuration as an initial state and a property expressed as a formula in $LTL(AP)$ to verify. The model-checker shows "True" if the property is satisfied. Otherwise, it gives counter examples showing a succession of rewrite rules, applied on the initial state, which lead to the violation of the property.

5   Related Work

In the last few years, Cloud elasticity has increasingly gained interest from both academic and industrial worlds. Some works such as [1,8,14] proposed environments for the autonomic management of Cloud elasticity. In these works, authors provide accurate executable and functional elasticity behaviors. However, the proposed approaches globally lack genericity and are highly dependent on precise technologies and/or programming languages. In addition, these works rely on simulation for the validation of their correctness and no qualitative study was provided.

Other research works provided formal models to specify and analyze Cloud elasticity. In [4], the time constraint linear temporal logic CLTLt(D) was used to specify some elasticity-related properties, such as *resource management* and *quality of service*. Authors provided horizontal scale (scale-out/in) elastic behavior. Specified behaviors and properties were analyzed using an offline SAT and SMT-solvers-based verification tool, to validate simulation results. Authors in [2] proposed a Petri Nets based formalization to describe Cloud elasticity. They introduced multiple horizontal elasticity strategies at application level. Their approach's correctness was analyzed using a Petri-nets-based reachability graph. Globally, these approaches rely on verification techniques which were adapted to their specification support. The authors respectively consider infrastructure or application Cloud layers only, and define simple elasticity behaviors at a high level of abstraction. Besides, the proposed verification processes lack simplicity and reusability.

In this paper, we propose a generic and original solution for self-adaptive behaviors formal specification and verification, illustrated on Cloud elasticity. We propose a generic way to model system structures with equational theories and system behaviors with rewrite theories, both using Maude, a rewrite-logic-based environment. Furthermore, we showed that custom designer theories could be used as a basis for a state-based model-checking technique, supported by LTL, in order to conduct formal verification of any desired behaviors, in a generic way. We showed that the Maude integrated model-checker can be configured, to conduct properties verification modulo any designer custom specifications.

6   Conclusion

Cloud elasticity is an important property. It allows Cloud systems to control their resource provisioning in order to avoid *Overprovisioning* (i.e., over-billing) and *Underprovisioning* (i.e., poor quality of service). Elastic behaviors are of a significant complexity as they rely on numerous overlapping factors, and considering the unpredictable nature of input workload.

In this paper, we provide a solution to formally specify and verify Cloud elasticity. We propose a Maude-based specification of Cloud systems structure, to master the complexity of their configuration. We propose a Maude-based specification of Cloud elastic behaviors, through elasticity strategies, describing a logic which governs the elasticity controller decision-making at infrastructure and application layers.

To formally verify the correctness of the introduced behaviors, we define elasticity desirable states and transitions, respectively using a Kripke structure and LTL propositional formulas. Such specification is encoded directly into Maude to enable a formal verification (in terms of *safety, liveness, non-plasticity*) to show the correctness of the defined behaviors. The conducted verification relies on a LTL state-based model-checking technique, which is supported by the Maude language.

In the presented approach, and for the sake of simplicity, we adopted a single controller to manage elasticity at both infrastructure and application layers, according to corss-layer elasticity strategies from previous work. This representation implies designing different elasticity actions of a concurrent triggering nature. To improve elasticity control efficiency and accuracy, and to enlarge adaptation capabilities while mastering the underlying complexity, we aim, as future work, at enlarging elasticity control specifications in order to consider elasticity controllers' coordination for infrastructure and application Cloud layers, together with the coordination between different elasticity methods (horizontal scaling, vertical scaling, etc.).

References

1. Al-Dhuraibi, Y., Paraiso, F., Djarallah, N., Merle, P.: Autonomic vertical elasticity of Docker containers with ElasticDocker. In: 2017 IEEE 10th International Conference on Cloud Computing (CLOUD), pp. 472–479. IEEE (2017)
2. Amziani, M.: Modeling, evaluation and provisioning of elastic service-based business processes in the cloud. Theses, Institut National des Télécommunications, June 2015
3. Baier, C., Katoen, J.P.: Principles of Model Checking. MIT Press, Cambridge (2008)
4. Bersani, M.M., Bianculli, D., Dustdar, S., Gambi, A., Ghezzi, C., Krstić, S.: Towards the formalization of properties of cloud-based elastic systems. In: Proceedings of the 6th International Workshop on Principles of Engineering Service-Oriented and Cloud Systems, pp. 38–47. ACM (2014)
5. Clavel, M., et al.: Maude Manual (Version 2.7. 1) (2016)
6. Clavel, M., et al.: All About Maude - A High-Performance Logical Framework: How to Specify, Program and Verify Systems in Rewriting Logic. LNCS, vol. 4350. Springer, Heidelberg (2007). https://doi.org/10.1007/978-3-540-71999-1
7. Clavel, M., et al.: Maude: specification and programming in rewriting logic. Theor. Comput. Sci. **285**(2), 187–243 (2002)
8. Dupont, S., Lejeune, J., Alvares, F., Ledoux, T.: Experimental analysis on autonomic strategies for cloud elasticity. In: 2015 International Conference on Cloud and Autonomic Computing, pp. 81–92. IEEE (2015)
9. IBM Group, et al.: An architectural blueprint for autonomic computing. IBM White paper (2005)
10. Herbst, N.R., Kounev, S., Reussner, R.H.: Elasticity in cloud computing: what it is, and what it is not. In: ICAC, vol. 13, pp. 23–27 (2013)

11. Huebscher, M.C., McCann, J.A.: A survey of autonomic computing–degrees, models, and applications. ACM Comput. Surv. (CSUR) **40**(3), 7 (2008)

12. Khebbeb, K., Hameurlain, N., Belala, F.: Modeling and evaluating cross-layer elasticity strategies in cloud systems. In: Abdelwahed, E.H., Bellatreche, L., Golfarelli, M., Méry, D., Ordonez, C. (eds.) MEDI 2018. LNCS, vol. 11163, pp. 168–183. Springer, Cham (2018). https://doi.org/10.1007/978-3-030-00856-7_11

13. Khebbeb, K., Hameurlain, N., Belala, F., Sahli, H.: Formal modelling and verifying elasticity strategies in cloud systems. IET Softw. Inst. Eng. Technol. **13**(1), 25–35 (2018)

14. Letondeur, L., Etchevers, X., Coupaye, T., Boyer, F., De Palma, N.: Architectural model and planification algorithm for the self-management of elastic cloud applications. In: 2014 International Conference on Cloud and Autonomic Computing, pp. 172–179. IEEE (2014)

15. Sahli, H.: A formal framework for modelling and verifying cloud-based elastic systems. Theses, Université Constantine 2 - Abdelhamid Mehri, February 2017. https://hal.archives-ouvertes.fr/tel-01484662

16. Schoren, R.: Correspondence between Kripke structures and labeled transition systems for model minimization. In: Seminar Project, Department of Computer Science, Technische Universiteit Eindhoven (2011)

Optimizing the Performance of Timed-Constrained Business Processes in Cloud-Fog Environment

Fairouz Fakhfakh[✉], Ahemd Neji, Saoussen Cheikhrouhou, and Slim Kallel

ReDCAD Laboratory, University of Sfax, Sfax, Tunisia
{fairouz.fakhfakh,saoussen.Cheikhrouhou,slim.kallel}@redcad.org,
Ahmed.neji@fsegs.tn

Abstract. Fog computing has emerged as a promising paradigm which aims to solve several problems of Cloud based systems. It aims to reduce the financial cost as well as the transmission latency compared to Cloud resources. One of the key issues in a Cloud-Fog environment is how to find the assignment of business process tasks to the most suitable resources while seeking the trade-off between cost and execution time. Business processes are often constrained by hard timing constraints which are specified by the designer. To address such a problem, we propose in this paper two resource allocation algorithms. The first one is based on an exact solution that aims to provide an optimal assignment. However, the second represents a meta-heuristic solution which uses the particle swarm optimization (PSO) technique. Our algorithms aim to optimize the financial cost of Cloud-Fog resources while satisfying the time constraint of the business process. A set of simulation experiments are presented to illustrate the performance of the approach.

Keywords: Business process · Resource allocation · Cloud computing · Fog computing · Time constraints

1 Introduction

Recently, Fog computing has become a popular paradigm, which provides computing resources for end-user applications [1]. It can solve several shortages of Cloud Computing based systems such as the poor support of user mobility, unexpected delays and heavy communication [2].

The architecture of Fog computing consists of three layers. The bottom layer contains IoT devices such as smart wearable devices, smartphone, etc. The middle layer is composed of Fog devices which can be used by near devices to quickly achieve some time-constrained tasks. These Fog devices need to connect to the upper layer (Cloud layer) which hosts different resources that process the request dispatched from the middle layer.

Due to the different types of Cloud and Fog computing resources, the optimization problem of these resources has become a major challenge. In fact, it

C. Attiogbé et al. (Eds.): MEDI 2019 Workshops, CCIS 1085, pp. 78–90, 2019.
https://doi.org/10.1007/978-3-030-32213-7_6

is difficult to make an appropriate decision when mapping tasks to resources considering multiple objectives that are often contradictory. This problem has become so complex for business processes which impose dependencies and order constraints between tasks. While there exist works on resource allocation for business processes, only few authors have paid attention to the collaboration between Cloud and Fog computing. Also, to the best of our knowledge, existing works have not yet handled the optimization cost of business processes enriched with temporal constraints in a Cloud-Fog environment.

For that, we propose in this paper, an approach that offers two methods for enterprises to minimize the cost of their processes without violating their time constraints. Concretely, given: (i) a business process with its set of tasks' requirements and (ii) a set of resource types delivered from Cloud and Fog providers, our approach provides the assignment of tasks to resources while reducing the allocation cost and satisfying the time constraint of the process. Two algorithms for resource allocation are proposed. They are based on different optimization methods: exact method and meta-heuristic method.

The remainder of this paper is organized as follows: In Sect. 2, we show a motivating scenario based on the collaboration between Cloud and Fog computing. Section 3 describes the assumptions considered on application and resource levels. In Sect. 4, we detail our proposed algorithms for resource allocation. In Sect. 5, we describe the experimental settings of our evaluation and we discuss the experimental results. A review of the related literature is presented in Sect. 6. Finally, the last section concludes the paper and outlines some future works.

2 Motivation Scenario

Time-based competition is one of the most important modes to gain competitive advantage in today's economy. This competition focuses on time management, especially delivery lead time, to quickly respond to customer requirements.

If organisations assign a short promised delivery lead time (i.e., process deadline) to attract more customer demand, respecting all the orders on time (i.e., respecting process deadlines) is harder given the increased number of customer orders, uncertainties in available resources and delivery processes, or other unpredictable events.

The firm will thus, assume the poor on-time delivery and will be charged with higher tardiness cost, and thereby threaten the firm's long-term competitive advantage.

In this work, we assume that controlling the execution of process tasks in cloud and/or Fog will have significant effects on avoiding the late deliveries of processes (i.e, avoiding deadline violations).

For example, Amazon, the online retailer depends not only on the selling price but also on the promised delivery lead time. Indeed, it launched the Amazon's Prime Air project[1], in which the firm revealed its somewhat audacious plan to

---

[1] https://www.engadget.com/2016/12/14/amazon-completes-its-first-drone-powered-delivery/.

make deliveries by drone. On December 7th 2016, the firm announced that it completed the first Amazon Prime Air delivery, with a shipment lasting 13 min from order to delivery.

To illustrate the features of the proposed approach, we introduce a toy process to exemplify the Prime Air drone delivery of Amazon.

When ordering goods that weigh less than 2.6 kg, and being close to an Amazon depot, Amazon can offer the Prime Air drone delivery service. In this case, the process needs to migrate some tasks from Cloud to Fog to respond to the drone real-time needs, reaching thus the specified *lead time.*

To illustrate the features of the proposed approach, we introduce a toy process to exemplify the drone delivery process of Amazon.

Figure 1 represents a simple scenario of drone shipping process, in which, Amazon collects delivery instructions (T_1) and starts pick process (T_2). In parallel with sensing drone position (T_3), it receives current position sent by drone (T_4), maintains a logbook of drone flying/delivery activities (T_5), processes received information (T_6), sends instructions to avoid accidents or violations (T_7), and updates drone position (T_8). And finally, it notifies the customer about product arrival (T_9). Each task of this business process has a temporal duration constraint defined by the designer.

The combination of a huge network of warehouses, excellent transportation, and most importantly the use of information technology such as Cloud and Fog computing, makes Amazon online retailer the most efficient compared to major companies in the world. In the case of Amazon's local distribution system, distribution tasks may benefit from both cloud and Fog computing capabilities to ensure rapid fulfillment to consumers.

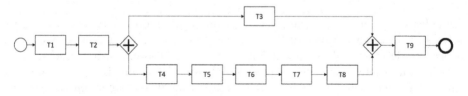

Fig. 1. Drone shipping scenario

3   Preliminaries

In this section, we introduce the main concepts and assumptions related to our application and resources model.

3.1   Application Model

A business process model is represented by a directed acyclic graph (DAG), denoted $G = (T, E)$, where $T = \{T_1, T_2, ..., T_N\}$ is the task set and E is the edge set defining the precedence constraints between tasks. An edge $e_{i,j} = (T_i, T_j) \in E$ means that T_j cannot be executed until T_i is completed. The task T_i without any predecessors is denoted T_{start} and the task T_j without any successors is denoted T_{end}. Each edge $e_{i,j}$ has its weight value $w_{i,j}$ which designates the amount of data that must be transferred from T_i to T_j.

In our work, each process has a deadline constraint (D) within which all tasks must complete their execution. Also, we use temporal constraints associated with tasks to limit their execution duration. For example, DC_i designates the duration constraint of task T_i.

3.2   Resources Model

The resource model can be expressed as a collection $R = R_c \cup R_f$ which represents the Cloud nodes and the Fog nodes. We consider M resources types which have different capacities $R = \{R_1, R_2, ..., R_M\}$. We assume that each resource can only process one task at the same time. In addition, we adopt the hourly pricing model. Then, resources are purchased according to the number of usage hours.

- The total execution time of a business process consists of two parts: the execution time of tasks and the communication time.
  (i) The execution time of the task T_i running on the resource R_t is denoted as d_i^t.
  (ii) The communication time required to transfer data from the task T_i to T_j is defined as follows:

$$CT_{ij} = \frac{w_{i,j}}{B}$$

  where B represents the bandwidth between the resources assigned respectively to T_i and T_j and $w_{i,j}$ is the amount of communication data transferred between these two tasks.
- The start execution time SET_i and the finish execution time FET_i of a task T_i running on a resource R_t are defined by the following equations:

$$SET_i = \max \{FET_j + CT_{ji}\}, (T_j, T_i) \in E$$
$$FET_i = SET_i + d_i^t$$

- The financial cost of the task T_i running on the resource R_t is denoted as C_i^t.

4   Proposed Algorithms

The big challenge of an enterprise is to reduce its expenditure as well as the execution time of its processes. Thus, it should use the adequate resources to run the different tasks at an optimal cost while satisfying the time constraints of the business process. In the rest of this section, we present two solutions. In the first one, we adopt an exact optimization method which, optimally schedules the process tasks. The second solution is based on the meta-heuristic particle swarm optimization (PSO) that generates a good solution with no guarantee of optimality, but with the benefit of a shorter computation time.

4.1   Exact Solution

We formulate the assignment problem of business process tasks to resources as a Mixed Integer Linear Programming (MILP) model. In fact, mathematical programming, particularly MILP, has become one of the most widely used methods for resource allocation problems [3].

We designate by X_i^t the decision variable of our mathematical problem:

$$X_i^t = \begin{cases} 1 & \text{if the resource } R_t \text{ is assigned to the task } T_i; 1 \leq i \leq N \\ 0 & \text{Otherwise.} \end{cases}$$

The goal of our algorithm is to reduce the financial cost of resources. Hence, the objective function of the model is defined as follows:

$$\min \sum_{i=1}^{N} \sum_{t=1}^{M} C_i^t \tag{1}$$

Subject to the following constraints:

$$\sum_{t=1}^{M} X_i^t = 1; 1 \leq i \leq N \tag{2}$$

$$f_i + \sum_{t=2}^{M} X_j^t * d_j^t + CT_{ij} \leq f_j, \forall (i,j) \in E \tag{3}$$

$$f_1 \geq \sum_{t=1}^{M} d_1^t X_1^t \tag{4}$$

$$X_i^t \in \{0,1\}, 1 \leq t \leq M \tag{5}$$

$$d_i^t \leq DC_i, 1 \leq i \leq N, 1 \leq t \leq M \tag{6}$$

$$f_N \leq D \tag{7}$$

Constraint (2) ensures that every task is assigned to only one resource type. According to the constraints (3) and (4), the precedence constraints of tasks are guaranteed. We denote by f_i the finish execution time of the task T_i. Constraint (5) is used to define the binary decision variable X_i. Constraint (6) denotes that each task has to meet its duration constraint. The final constraint (7) defines the deadline constraint (D) of the business process.

4.2   Meta-Heuristic Solution

PSO is a swarm-based intelligence algorithm [4] derived from the behavior of animals such as a flock of birds looking for a source of food. The main idea of PSO consists in searching an optimization solution by sharing information between the members of a group which is commonly called "population". PSO begins with a set of potential solutions which are initialized randomly. Each solution, called particle, has two parameters that are the position and the velocity. The position of a particle Pi is affected by its optimal position denoted as *pbest* and the best position of the whole population denoted as *gbest*. The performance of a particle is evaluated based on the value of its fitness function which is specific to the studied problem. At an iteration k of the algorithm, the position and the velocity of a particle are updated according to the following equations:

$$x_i^{k+1} = x_i^k + v_i^{k+1} \tag{8}$$
$$v_i^{k+1} = wv_i^k + c_1 r_1 (pbest_i - x_i^k) + c_2 r_2 (gbest - x_i^k) \tag{9}$$

$c1$ and $c2$ designate the acceleration factors, $r1$ and $r2$ are two random numbers within $[0, 1]$ and w represents the inertia weight. x_i^k and x_i^{k+1} indicate respectively the current position of a particle i at the iteration k and k+1. Also, $pbest_i$ is the best position of the particle i and $gbest$ represents the position of the best particle in a population.

In order to provide a mapping solution of all process tasks to the appropriate resource types, we represent a particle as a process and its resources. The dimension of a particle is defined as the number of the process tasks. The range in which a particle can be positioned is determined by the indices of the available resource types. Figure 2 shows a particle for a process formed by 6 tasks.

T_1	T_2	T_3	T_4	T_5	T_6
3	1	2	1	4	2

Fig. 2. A particle for a process formed by 6 tasks

In this work, our purpose is to reduce the financial cost of resources, while executing the process before the user's defined deadline (D) and the duration constraints associated with tasks. So, the value of the fitness function represents the cost of resources used to complete the process execution. To take into account the deadline constraint, we adopt the strategy proposed in [5] to handle constraints in PSO algorithm. This strategy consists in verifying whether a mapping solution is feasible. A solution is called feasible if it satisfies the deadline of the business process. When comparing two solutions, we distinguish three situations: (1) If both solutions are feasible, the solution with better fitness is chosen. (2) If one solution is feasible and the other is not, then the feasible one is choosed. (3) If both solutions are infeasible, the solution with smaller overall constraint violation is choosed. In our work, we define the constraint violation value as the difference between the total execution time of the process and the deadline.

Algorithm 1 shows the different steps of our assignment algorithm based on PSO.

Algorithm 1. Resource allocation algorithm based on PSO

1: **Input:** A business process (BP), number of iteration, a set of Cloud and fog resources
2: **Output:** The mapping of tasks to resources
3: Set particle dimension as equal to the size of process tasks
4: Initialize particles population randomly while satisfying the temporal constraints of tasks
5: **while** maximum iteration is not reached **do**
6:     **for** each particle i with position x_i **do**
7:         calculate fitness value $f(x_i)$
8:         **if** $f(x_i)$ is better than $f(pbest_i)$ **then**
9:             $pbest_i \longleftarrow x_i$
10:        **end if**
11:    **end for**
12:    $gbest_i \longleftarrow$ The position of the best particle
13:    **for** each particle i **do**
14:        calculate the position and velocity of the particle according to equation (4) and (5)
15:    **end for**
16: **end while**

Firstly, it begins by setting the particle dimension as equal to the number of process tasks (line 3). Secondly, the initialization of the particles population is performed randomly, but, each task must be assigned to the resource that satisfies its duration constraint (line 4). After that, for each position x_i of a particle i, the value of the objective function (f) is computed (line 7). If this position x_i is better than its best position $pbest_i$, then $pbest_i$ takes the value x_i (line 8–9). This is repeated for all particles. Then, the best position of the swarm $gbest$ takes the best position $pbest$ among all the particles (line 12). The values of the velocity and position of each particle will be updated based on the Eqs. ((8) and (9)) cited previously to process the next iteration (line 14). The algorithm stops when the maximum number of iterations is reached.

5 Evaluation

In this section, we describe the experimental settings of our business processes, resources and algorithms. After that, we present the simulation experiments that we have conducted to evaluate the efficiency of the proposed algorithms in terms of resources cost and computation time.

5.1 Experimental Setup

The different experiments were performed on a laptop that has 64-bit Intel Core, 2.6 GHz CPU, 8 GB of RAM and Windows 7 as OS. For tasks of business processes, we generated randomly a set of data. The computation workload of each task has a size from 400 to 16000 MI and the size of data transferred from a task to another is ranging from 100 to 600 MB. Also, each task of the business process has a duration constraint which represents the time limit within which a task must finish its execution.

We show in Table 1 the configurations and prices of Cloud and Fog resources.

Table 1. Configurations and prices of Cloud and Fog resources

Type of resources	Number of CPUs	Memory (GiB)	Cost ($)
Cloud resources			
large	6	8	1.2
medium	4	4	1.0
small	2	2	0.7
Fog resources			
large	4	3	0.6
medium	2	2	0.45
small	0.5	1	0.3

- In order to implement the algorithm based on the exact method, we have used IBM-ILOG Cplex[2] Optimization Studio V12.6.3 to solve the MILP formulation.
- For the algorithm based on the meta-heuristic method, the population size is set as 30 and the dimension of each particle is equal to the number of process tasks. We define the learning factors $c1 = c2 = 2$ and the inertia value $w = 0.5$. In order to determine the number of iterations required for our experiments, we present in Fig. 3 the convergence of the financial cost of PSO while increasing the number of iterations. We realize four scenarios using different number of tasks (10, 20, 40 and 80). We have executed each scenario 50 times while using different size of data and the average value of these executions is reported. At the beginning, the particles are randomly initialized. So, the resource cost is quite high. This cost corresponds to the 0th iteration of the algorithm. We can determine the number of iterations needed for the convergence when the cost becomes stable. For example, we notice that 16 iterations are needed for a business process with 20 tasks.

5.2 Experimental Results

- **Evaluation of the financial cost**
  In this experiment, we analyze the results of the two proposed algorithms focusing on their performances in term of the financial cost.

---

[2] https://www.ibm.com/products/ilog-cplex-optimization-studio.

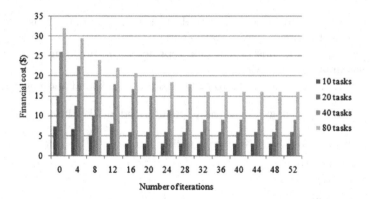

Fig. 3. Convergence of PSO

Figure 4 shows the cost of resources needed for the process execution while varying the number of tasks. Each experiment runs for 50 times and the average value of these executions is reported. The results provided in Fig. 4 show a considerable gain in financial cost when applying the exact method. In fact, this method provides the optimal assignment of tasks to resources. However, the meta-heuristic algorithm generates a good solution after a certain number of iterations.

- **Evaluation of the computation time**
  In this experiment, we report the execution time required to compute the mapping solutions using the two algorithms. We present our evaluation in the case of two scenarios: increasing the number of tasks and increasing the number of resource types. The results are depicted respectively in Figs. 5 and 6.

We notice that the algorithm solved by the CPLEX solver takes more time to find the assignment solutions. The additional computing time of this algorithm exceeds 27% compared to the meta-heuristic algorithm based on PSO.

The solver cannot find the optimal solution for large-sized business processes such as scientific workflows [6] due to lack of memory. So, the exact method is not suitable for problems, which need the reassignment of tasks to resources at runtime. Among these problems, we cite: the violation of duration constraints related to tasks and the dynamic adaptation of business processes (such as adding and deleting tasks during execution) which aims to cope with unexpected events. In these cases, it may be profitable to recompute the allocation solutions of unexecuted tasks to resources according to the fluctuation of the process or the requirements. This method is widely used in the literature to deal with similar problems [7].

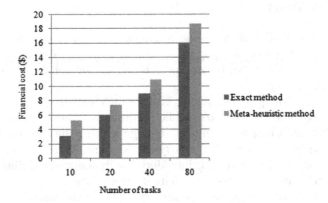

Fig. 4. Comparison of the financial cost

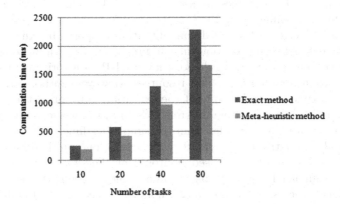

Fig. 5. Comparison of the computation time while increasing the number of tasks

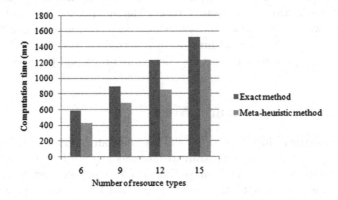

Fig. 6. Comparison of the computation time while increasing the number of resource types

6   Related Work

Many research studies dealt with the problem of resource allocation for business processes as it is a challenging up-to-date issue [8–11]. Whereas, few works addressed this problem in an environment based on the collaboration between Cloud and Fog computing.

In [12], the authors proposed an algorithm which aims to optimize the financial cost of Cloud and Fog resources while taking into account the network condition. In addition, a task reassignment strategy which refines the output of the proposed algorithm is presented to satisfy the deadline of the business process.

The approach proposed in [13] introduced a dynamic scheduling heuristic for multiple real-time IoT processes. This heuristic attempts to schedule the tasks which need height computation and low communication requirements in the Cloud. However, the communication intensive tasks which need low computational demands are scheduled in the Fog. During the scheduling, the possible gaps of Cloud and Fog resources are used to reduce the financial cost and satisfy the user-defined deadline.

The main objective of the scheduling algorithm proposed by Xu et al. [14] is to seek a tradeoff between execution time and resource cost of a business process in a Cloud-Fog environment. To do so, they used PSO algorithm to solve the mapping solution between tasks and resources. However, authors do not take into account a time constraint to limit the execution duration of the process.

Deal with CRs allocated from different PSs to run processes where the temporal constraint are more complex than the simple deadline.

Ding et al. [15] introduced a strategy for scheduling multiple business processes utilizing Fog and Cloud based environment. The goal of this strategy is to reduce the financial cost of resources taking into account the deadline constraint of each process. To do so, the authors are based on PSO and Min-Min algorithms.

Though there has been some research on resource allocation for business processes in a Cloud-Fog environment, to the best of our knowledge, no previous work considers duration constraints of tasks. The main contribution of our work is to propose two resource allocation algorithms based on the exact and the metaheuristic methods. These algorithms achieve a tradeoff between the execution time and resource cost under tasks duration constraints and the overall process deadline.

7   Conclusion and Future Work

In this paper, we introduced an approach that helps an enterprise optimizing the deployment cost of its timed-constrained business process based on the collaboration between Cloud and Fog computing. For this purpose, we proposed two algorithms which determine the resources required to execute a process while respecting the user-defined constraints. Through the conducted experiments, we have compared the efficiency of these algorithms in terms of resource cost and computation time.

In this work, we have assumed that a process model has only ANDsplit branching. We intend in the future to take into account other branching types such as XORsplit and ORsplit. In addition, we have considered only a deadline constraint of the overall process. We plan to extend our approach to deal with other temporal constraints such as duration constraints of tasks, temporal dependencies between tasks and absolute temporal constraints which specify the start and end times of process tasks. Furthermore, in this work, we have considered on demand instances offered by Amazon Cloud. However, it is interesting to extend our approach to take into account other pricing strategies such as reserved and spot instances.

References

1. Bonomi, F., Milito, R., Zhu, J., Addepalli, S.: Fog computing and its role in the internet of things. In: Proceedings of the First Edition of the MCC Workshop on Mobile Cloud Computing, pp. 13–16. ACM (2012)
2. Lin, Y., Shen, H.: Leveraging fog to extend cloud gaming for thin-client MMOG with high quality of experience. In: Proceedings of the 35th International Conference on Distributed Computing Systems, pp. 734–735. IEEE (2015)
3. Floudas, C.A., Lin, X.: Mixed integer linear programming in process scheduling: modeling, algorithms, and applications. Ann. Oper. Res. **139**(1), 131–162 (2005)
4. Kennedy, J., Eberhart, R.: Particle swarm optimization. In: IEEE International Conference on Neural Networks, vol. 4, pp. 1942–1948 (1995)
5. Deb, K., Pratap, A., Agarwal, S., Meyarivan, T.: A fast and elitist multiobjective genetic algorithm: Nsga-ii. IEEE Trans. Evol. Comput. **6**(2), 182–197 (2002)
6. Atkinson, M.P., Gesing, S., Montagnat, J., Taylor, I.J.: Scientific workflows: past, present and future. Future Gener. Comput. Syst. **75**, 216–227 (2017)
7. Lee, Y.C., Zomaya, A.Y.: Rescheduling for reliable job completion with the support of clouds. Future Gener. Comput. Syst. **26**(8), 1192–1199 (2010)
8. Xie, Y., Chen, S., Ni, Q., Wu, H.: Integration of resource allocation and task assignment for optimizing the cost and maximum throughput of business processes. J. Intell. Manuf. **30**(3), 1351–1369 (2019)
9. Halima, R.B., Kallel, S., Gaaloul, W., Jmaiel, M.: Optimal cost for time-aware cloud resource allocation in business process. In: IEEE International Conference on Services Computing (SCC), Honolulu, HI, USA, pp. 314–321. IEEE Computer Society, 25–30 June 2017
10. Ihde, S., Pufahl, L., Goel, A., Weske, M.: Towards dynamic resource management in business processes. In: Proceedings of the 11th Central European Workshop on Services and their Composition, Bayreuth, Germany, pp. 17–23, February 14–15 2019
11. Xu, X., Dou, W., Zhang, X., Chen, J.: Enreal: an energy-aware resource allocation method for scientific workflow executions in cloud environment. IEEE Trans. Cloud Comput. **4**(2), 166–179 (2015)
12. Pham, X., Nguyen, M.D., Tri, N.D.T., Ngo, Q.T., Huh, E.: A cost- and performance-effective approach for task scheduling based on collaboration between cloud and fog computing. In: International Journal of Distributed Sensor Networks (IJDSN), vol. 13(11) (2017)

13. Stavrinides, G.L., Karatza, H.D.: A hybrid approach to scheduling real-time IoT workflows in fog and cloud environments. Int. J. Multimedia Tools Appl. **78**(17), 24639–24655 (2018)

14. Xu, R., et al.: Improved particle swarm optimization based workflow scheduling in cloud-fog environment. In: Daniel, F., Sheng, Q.Z., Motahari, H. (eds.) BPM 2018. LNBIP, vol. 342, pp. 337–347. Springer, Cham (2019). https://doi.org/10.1007/978-3-030-11641-5_27

15. Ding, R., Li, X., Liu, X., Xu, J.: A cost-effective time-constrained multi-workflow scheduling strategy in fog computing. In: Liu, X., et al. (eds.) ICSOC 2018. LNCS, vol. 11434, pp. 194–207. Springer, Cham (2019). https://doi.org/10.1007/978-3-030-17642-6_17

A Temporal Approach for Testing Distributed Systems-A MapReduce Case Study

Sara Hsaini[✉], Salma Azzouzi, and My El Hassan Charaf

Laboratory of Informatics Systems and Optimization (ISO),
IbnTofail University, Kenitra, Morocco
hsaini.sara@gmail.com, salma.azzouzi@gmail.com, charaf@gmail.com

Abstract. To observe the behavior of a distributed implementation under test (IUT), we commonly coordinate parallel testers in order to check not only if the output events have been observed, but also the dates when these events have been occurred. However, the use of multiple testers can produce several coordination problems amongst remote testers known as Controllability and Observability issues. To cope with such problems, we suggest-in previous works- the inclusion of some timing constraints in the test architecture. In this paper, we choose as a case study the use of a MapReduce architecture with several worker components running essentially two functionalities: Map and Reduce tasks. These systems often face failures caused by various conditions, e.g., network connection delays, power outages or hardware problems. Moreover, we define the temporal properties in the specification of such systems. Then, we explain how to apply these properties in the case of MapReduce testing to identify faulty workers, in order to reschedule their tasks to a healthy worker.

Keywords: Distributed testing · Controllability · Observability ·
Timing constraints · MapReduce

1 Introduction

There has been growing interest in distributed testing where the implementation under test (IUT) has physically distributed ports. In such context, we place a tester at each port (interface) of the IUT and each tester observes only the events at its ports which brings out the possibility of controllability and observability problems. These problems occur if a tester cannot determine either when to apply a particular input to the IUT, or whether a particular output from the IUT has been generated in response to a specific input, respectively which often require the use of external coordination message exchanges among testers.

The basic challenge in such situations is to synchronize the correct execution sequence of test case steps. Moreover, it is still a difficult task to guarantee the test sequence execution to be correct at large-scale context in the way that a great

© Springer Nature Switzerland AG 2019
C. Attiogbé et al. (Eds.): MEDI 2019 Workshops, CCIS 1085, pp. 91–103, 2019.
https://doi.org/10.1007/978-3-030-32213-7_7

number of messages exchanged should be managed by some synchronization component. To illustrate our approach, we investigate in this paper a MapReduce case study.

A Mapreduce system is a distributed framework for processing large-scale data over clusters of computers using two high-order functions: Map and Reduce. These systems often face failures caused by various conditions, e.g. power outages, hardware problems or network connection delays particularly when the synchronization time is greater than the execution time of the IUT.

In this context, this paper extends previous work in order to check not only if the output events have been observed, but also the dates when these events have been occurred. We apply the temporal properties presented in [2] to the specification of Mapreduce implementation under test (MR-IUT), in order to identify faulty workers and to reschedule their tasks to healthy workers.

The paper is structured as follows: Sect. 2 describes some modeling concepts related to the distributed testing architecture, it presents the coordination issues arisen during the test execution, and how to cope with these problems by introducing some timing constraints. In Sect. 3, we give some related works. Then, we explain in Sects. 4 how to apply the temporal properties proposed previously in the case of Mapreduce systems- where several workers are running simultaneously- to identify faulty workers. Finally, the Sect. 5 gives some conclusions and identifies future works.

2   Distributed Testing

This section is devoted to deal with the test of open distributed systems. The principle is to apply input events to the IUT and compare the observed outputs with expected results. A set of input events and planned outputs is commonly called a test case and it is generated from the specification of the IUT.

2.1   Architecture

The basic idea of distributed testing architecture is to coordinate parallel testers called PTCs (Parallel Test Components) using a communication service in conjunction with the IUT (Implementation Under Test). Each tester interacts with the IUT through a port PCO (Point of Control and Observation), and communicates with other testers through a multicast channel.

Figure 1 gives an abstract view of classic architecture for testing distributed systems. An IUT is the implementation under test. It can be considered as a "black-box"; its behavior is known only by interactions through its interfaces with the environment or other systems. Each tester sends some stimulus to the IUT via their attached interfaces called PCOs (Points of Control and Observations) and from which it observes the output IUT reactions.

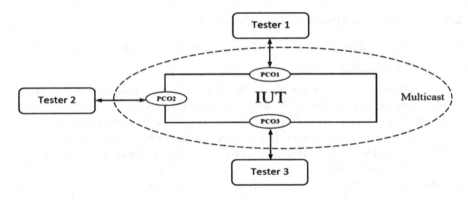

Fig. 1. IUT test architecture.

2.2 Test Process

To approach the testing process in a formal way, the specification and the IUT must be modeled using the same concepts. The specification of the behavior of a distributed application is described by an automaton with n-port (FSM Finite State Machine) [1] defining inputs and the results expected for each PCO. We denote by Σk the input alphabet of the port k (PCO number k), Γk the output alphabet of the port k and Q the finite set of states. Figure 2 gives an example of 3p-FSM with $Q = q_0, q_1, q_2, q_3, q_0$ initial state, $\Sigma_1 = x_1$, $\Sigma_2 = x_2$, $\Sigma_3 = x_3$ and $\Gamma_1 = a_1, a_2, a_3$, $\Gamma_2 = b_1, b_2, b_3$, $\Gamma_3 = c_1, c_2, c_3$. A test sequence of an np-FSM automaton is a sequence in the form: $!x_1?y_1!x_2?y_2!x_t?y_t$ that for $i = 1, \ldots, t : x_i \cup \Sigma = \Sigma_1 \cup \ldots \cup \Sigma_n$ with $\Sigma_i \cap \Sigma_j = \emptyset$ for $i \neq j$, $y_i \cup \Gamma_k$ and for each port k $-y_i \cap \Gamma_k - \leq 1$. We denote '$!x_i$' sending the message xi to MR-IUT and '$?y_i$' the reception of messages belonging to the yi from the IUT.

An example of a global test sequence (GTS) deduced form the 3p-FSM given in Fig. 2 is:

$$!a_1?\{x_1, y_1, \epsilon\}!b_1?\{x_2, y_2, z_2\}!c_1?\{\epsilon, \epsilon, z_3\} \tag{1}$$

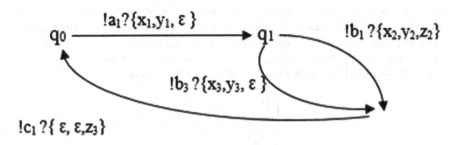

Fig. 2. An example of 3p-FSM.

2.3   Common Distributed Test Problems

Many kinds of problems can arise in the distributed test context; we define these notions by referring [1]

1. Controllability problem: It can be defined from Test System view as capability of a Test System to force the IUT (implementation under test) to receive inputs in the given order. It arises when Test cannot guarantee that IUT will receive event of transition (i) before event of transition $(i + 1)$. In other way, it's the capability of the test system to realize input events at corresponding PCOs in a given order.
2. Observability problem: It can be defined from Test System view as capability of a Test System to observe the outputs of the IUT and decide which input is the cause of each output, it arises when two consecutive transition (i) and transition $(i + 1)$ occur on the same port k but only one of the transitions has an output in port k and the other one is an empty transition with no output. In this case the Test System cannot decide whether transition (i) or transition $(i + 1)$ is the cause of output.

   To solve such problems, authors in [4] propose an algorithm to generate Local Test Sequences (LTS) from Global Test Sequence (GTS). The following LTS are the results given by applying the proposed algorithm to test sequence (1):

$$\begin{cases} W_1 = !a_1?x_1?x_2?O^3 \\ W_2 = ?y_1!b_1?y_2!C^3 \\ W_3 = ?C^2!O^1!c_1?z_1 \end{cases} \quad (2)$$

   where:
   - $!x$ denotes sending of message x to IUT
   - $?y$ denotes receiving of message y from the IUT
   - $!C^k$ denotes sending coordination message to tester k and $?C^k$ receiving coordination message from tester k.
   - $!O^k$ denotes sending observation message to tester k and $?O^k$ receiving observation message from tester k.
3. Synchronization Problem: As explained above, the algorithm in [3] allows the generation of local test sequences to be performed by each tester. Then, each tester is running its local test sequence. Thus, the testers are working together but independently, which leads us to manage the problem of synchronization of testers. Let the execution of the first fragment of each local test sequence W_{f1}, W_{f2} and W_{f3} select from W_1, W_2 and W_3 as follows:

$$\begin{cases} W_{f1} = !a_1?x_1?x_2 \\ W_{f2} = ?y_1!b_1 \\ W_{f3} = ?C^2!O^1 \end{cases} \quad (3)$$

The execution of local test sequences W_f1, W_f2 and W_f3 must give the result shown in Fig. 3(a) but the execution of our prototype provides an incorrect result given in Fig. 3(b).

Indeed, in the diagram Fig. 3(b) the second tester sends the message "b2" to the IUT before the first tester receives the message "x_1" from the IUT. So, the execution of local testing does not conform with the specification given in (1), where the message "b_2" must be sent only if all messages due to the sending of "a1" by the tester-1 are received by the IUT.

In this perspective, the distributed testing process must not only check if the output events have been observed, but also the dates when these events have been occurred especially if the system has to respect some timing constraints. For example, in the execution of the first fragment of the GTS given in (1): $!a_1?\{x_1, y_1\}!b_1?\{x_2, y_2\}$, the tester-1 begins by sending a message "!a1" to the IUT. However, the tester-2 can't send the message "$!b_1$" and must wait until receiving the message "$?y_1$" from the IUT and the message "?x1" to be received by the tester-1. Now, the principal question that can be studied and discussed is how much time the tester-2 and tester-1 can wait for receiving "$?y_1$" and "$?x_1$" respectively, so that the tester-2 can send "$!b_2$" to the IUT.

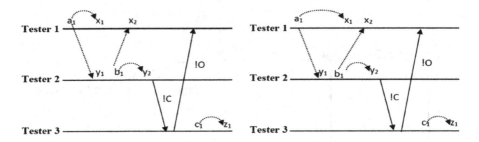

Fig. 3. Example of the synchronization problem.

2.4   Temporal Based Approach

The proposed architecture operates in an environment with some timing constraints needed to check not only if the IUT produces the correct outputs "$?y_i$" but to check also if the timings of outputs are corrects. To this end, we define the following constraints:

Intra-port Timing Constraints. The intra-port timing constraints occur when communication is established between a tester and the IUT, it could be the reaction time required for a tester receiving a message belonging to "y_i" in response to the reception of the input "x_i" by the IUT. Where the different computing times used in Fig. 4 are defined as follows:

- T_{TBIT}: Transfer time between the IUT and the Tester is the time separating: (i) the instant when a Message M is sent by the IUT (resp. the tester) and (ii) the instant when M is received by the Tester (resp. IUT).

- T_{iut}: the reaction time of the IUT is an upper bound of the time separating: (i) any instant when an event e is received by the IUT and (ii) the instant when the IUT has terminated to send all the outputs (if any) in response to the reception of e. We emphasize the word "all" because the definition includes possible unexpected outputs (in the case of a non-conformant IUT) [8,9].
- Time Out is the waiting time that a tester can wait for receiving a message. In case where this time is elapsed the test system should return Failed.
- Master Clock provides the reference time for all clocks in the testing system.

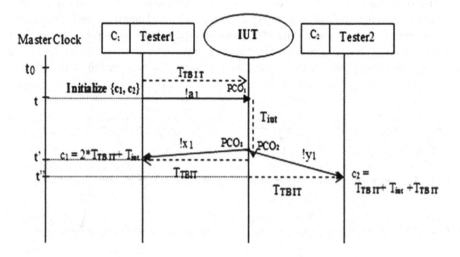

Fig. 4. Transfer time required to receive outputs.

The implementation under test must respect the inter-port constraints described by the following formula, where C is reception time measured by the clock port(a)

$$T_{TBIT(1)} + T_{IUT} + T_{TBIT(2)} <= c <= TimeOut \tag{4}$$

Inter-port Timing Constraints. The inter-port timing constraints may be the transfer time required when testers communicate on different ports. The implementation under test must respect the inter-port constraints described by the following formula. Where TTBTT is the transfer time between tester-i and Tester-j:

$$T_{TBTT} <= c <= TimeOut \tag{5}$$

Further works for covering previous issues comes from studies exploring different architectures of distributed testing. We review that literature in the next section.

3   Literature Review

Many works have been made to avoid the problems described in the previous section. Indeed, the authors in [3] explain how both controllability and observability problems can be overcame through the use of coordination messages among remote testers. The basic idea in [4,5] is to build a test sequence that causes no coordination problems during its application in a distributed test architecture. The work [6] proposes a new method to generate a test sequence utilizing multiple unique input/output (UIO) sequences. The method is essentially guided by the way of minimizing the use of external coordination messages and input/output operations.

The authors in [7] present DTRON, a framework for model-based testing that addresses the issues of distributed execution and real-time constraints imposed by the design of networked Cyber-Physical Systems.

The work in [8] presents a complete formal framework to perform passive testing of software systems with asynchronous communications where actions are timestamped with the time when they were observed at the monitor.

In [9], the authors introduce conformance relations where, for a given metric, a re-ordering is only considered if the distance between the two traces is at most a certain bound.

Moreover, the authors in [10] suggest a new approach whose main ingredient is to combine timing attacks with fuzzing techniques. This new approach, which is dedicated to work on Java Card, allows not only reducing the test space explosion, but also to simplify the fuzzing process configuration.

In other hand, the author in [11] presents a test harness for Mapreduce-based implementations, he proposes a framework, called HadoopTest, that deploys and manages the execution of test cases across distributed nodes. Another work [12] introduces an approach addresses the tests from the standpoint of identification of potential functional faults, in order to derive repeatable tests that may be designed at an early stage, before program implementation. In [13], the authors present a novel technique that systematically searches for such bugs in MapReduce applications and generates corresponding test cases. The technique works by encoding the high-level MapReduce correctness conditions as symbolic program constraints and checking them for the program under test.

This paper is a continuity of the work [2] where we check not only if the output events have been observed, but also the dates when these events have been occurred. The work explains how to apply this approach in the context of Mapreduce systems. In the next section we give a brief overview of our case study, as motivation for temporal testing approach, which we define formally in Sect. 2.

4   Case Study: Testing MapReduce System

4.1   Basics Concepts

Mapreduce systems process large datasets distributed over clusters composed of multiple computers using two mains functionalities: Map and Reduce tasks.

The model breaks jobs into mapping/reduce phases. As explained in Fig. 5, the core concept of MapReduce is that input may be split into logical chunks, and each chunk may be initially processed independently, by a map task. The results of these individual processing chunks can be physically partitioned into distinct sets, which are then sorted. Each sorted chunk is passed to a reduce task. MapReduce makes the guarantee that the input to every reducer is sorted by key [14].

Therefore, testing MR-based systems is a complex task. The main issue is the co-ordination of distributed components of the system. Moreover, in order to reproduce a real-world environment during testing, we should take into consideration timing constraints to be respected by the implementation under test. Thus, it is not sufficient to check if the IUT produces the correct outputs but it should also checks if the timings of outputs are respected. Hence, several types of failures must be considered, such as: output faults, transfer faults or combination of both of them [15].

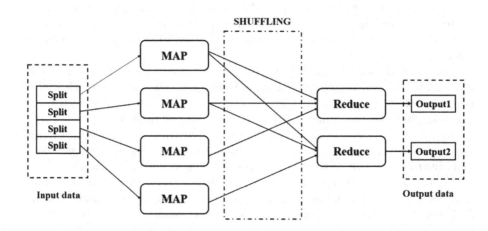

Fig. 5. The MapReduce model.

4.2   Architecture

The MapReduce framework was introduced to support distributed processing on large data sets distributed over clusters of computers and to solve large-data computational problems [14]. In other hand, testing is difficult and expensive, and testing distributed system, like a Mapreduce system, still more difficult due to issues such as coordination, synchronization. As shown in previous section, many works has been done to resolve such problems. We propose, in the following, our architecture for testing the MapReduce system behavior. In our approach, we focus firstly on conformance testing that is essentially a type of functional testing of a black box nature. The source code of the MR-IUT is unknown and his behavior is checked with respect to a specification (Fig. 6).

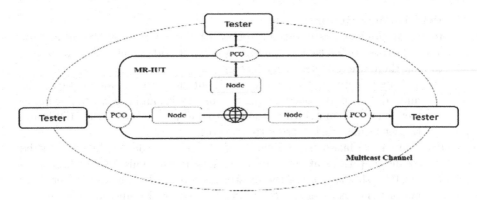

Fig. 6. MR-IUT test architecture.

In the context of mapreduce each input data is considered as an input element in the FSM model and each result generated by a reduce task correspond a an output element (Fig. 7).

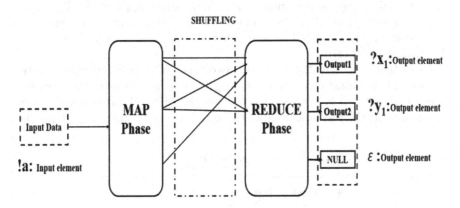

Fig. 7. MR-IUT input & outputs.

To cope with the coordination problems, i.e. Controllability and Observability issues, during the Mapreduce distributed testing process, we introduce the timings constraints.

4.3 Time Model

This section is dedicated to extend results from testing distributed system to deal with testing an implementation under test with some timing constraints. The new architecture for testing Mapreduce framework will take into account the delay of messages exchanged between testers and MR-IUT.

(a) **Performance Factors**

In the Mapreduce System, the response time is affected by several factors. These factors are focused on quantities of input and output data. According to [16], there are four necessary factors:

(1) The first factor is the volume of input data to the application. The input data is partitioned among the map tasks, and the key performance metric is the bandwidth of the end-to-end pipe between the HDFS and the set of map tasks across the network.

(2) The second factor is the volume of intermediate data, which is emitted by the map tasks at the end of the Map Phase. This intermediate data must be shuffled across the cluster and sorted by key value. Here, the performance is determined by both the bandwidth and the efficiency of the sort.

(3) Third is the volume of output data, which is emitted by the Reduce Tasks at the completion of the Reduce Phase. The performance metric during this process is the bandwidth available to send the output data to each Data Node, in addition to the write speed of each Data Node's storage devices.

(4) Beyond the data volumes, there are two other fundamental characteristics affecting the performance of a MapReduce application. The first is the number of Map Tasks among the available concurrently executing cores in the cluster. The second is the number of Reduce Tasks.

(b) **Timing constraints**

As presented in Sect. 2.4, there are two types of timing constraints: intra-port and inter-port constraints. Among the required times in the intra-port constraints there is the reaction time of the MR-IUT. This reaction time depends on the response time of the three necessary phases in Mapreduce

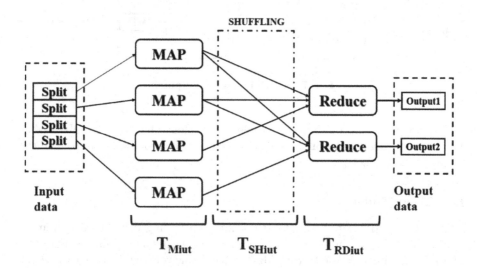

Fig. 8. Mapreduce reaction time.

processing: (1) Map phase is an initial ingestion and transformation step, in which individual input records can be processed in parallel, (2) Shuffle phase is the process of transferring data from the mappers to reducer, (3) Reduce phase is an aggregation or summarization step, in which all associated records, must be processed together by a single entity. And thus, the reaction time of MR-IUT is: $T_{Mriut} = T_{Mpiut} + T_{Shiut} + T_{RDiut}$., where:

- T_{Mpiut}: the reaction time of map phase.
- T_{Shiut}: the reaction time of shuffle phase.
- T_{RDiut} the reaction time of reduce phase (Fig. 8).

Map(resp. Reduce)Phase Reaction Time

The map phase execution depends on (1) the average response time of a map (resp. Reduce) task in mapreduce processing (T^{avg}), (2) the total number of map (resp. Reduce) tasks necessary to process the input data, (3) and depends on the total number of configured map (resp. Reduce) slots i.e. the maximum number of map (resp. reduce) tasks that will be run simultaneously by a task tracker. As presented in [17], the map phase execution time and reduce phase execution time can be computed using (1) and (2) respectively:

$$T_m^{total} = \frac{T_m^{avg} * N_m}{N_m^{slot}} \tag{6}$$

$$T_r^{total} = \frac{T_r^{avg} * N_r}{N_r^{slot}} \tag{7}$$

Shuffle Phase Reaction Time

The shuffle phase execution time depends on (1) The average execution duration of a shuffle task in mapreduce processing (T^{avg}), (2) the total number of Reduce tasks necessary to process the data, (3) and depends on the total number of configured Reduce slots i.e. the maximum number of reduce tasks that will be run simultaneously by a task tracker. As presented in [16], the shuffle phase execution time can be computed using (3):

$$T_{sh}^{total} = \frac{T_{sh}^{avg} * N_r}{N_r^{slot}} \tag{8}$$

Thereby, the inter-port constraints can be described by the following formula:

$$T_{TBIT(1)} + T_{Mriut} + T_{TBIT(2)} <= c <= TimeOut \tag{9}$$

with

$$T_{Mriut} = T_{Mpiut} + T_{Shiut} + T_{RDiut} \tag{10}$$

(c) **Testing process**

In this section, we describe the tester's behavior according to our distributed testing platform with temporal constraints. Actually, each tester executes its local test sequence as follows:

a. **For a communication with the IUT**
   - If the message is a reception (?y), the tester waits until that the reception of the message has been observed, and that the timing constraints have been verified.
   - If the message is a sending (!x), the tester sends this message and saves the sending time.

b. **For a communication with other testers**
   - If the message is a reception message (?O/?C), the tester waits of the receipt of the waiting message and that the timing constraints have been checked.
   - If the message is a sending message (!C/!O), the tester communicate with the tester that will receive this message. Then, it saves the sending time.

   Then during the test process of mapreduce framework:
   - If no message is received in a correct time, or if the received message is not expected, the tester returns a verdict Fail (fail).
   - If the tester reaches the end of its local test sequence, then it gives a verdict Accept (accepted).

   Thus, if all testers return a verdict Accept, then the test system ends the test with a global verdict Accept.

5   Conclusion

As conclusion, we can state that many important developments have been done over the last several decades to overcome problems of coordination in the distributed testing field.

We propose in this paper- as a main contribution- our prototype by introducing some timing properties to be respected by the distributed testing frameworks. On the other hand, we explain how to apply this timed approach on a system more complex like Mapreduce. More precisely, we define the inter/intra ports constraints according to response time of different phases (Map/Shuffle/Reduce). Furthermore, in order to validate our approach, the prototype realization of this case study is under experimentation in a Hadoop environment.

Finally, as prospects, we plan to improve the model performances and to implement such approach on a real system. Moreover, we work out to adapt and generalize our testing approach for more complex frameworks like distributed cloud.

References

1. Charaf, M.E.H., Azzouzi, S.: A colored Petri-net model for control execution of distributed systems. In: 2017 4th International Conference on Control, Decision and Information Technologies, CoDIT 2017, January 2017, vol. 2017, pp. 277–282 (2017)
2. Azzouzi, S., Benattou, M., Charaf, M.E.H.: A temporal agent based approach for testing open distributed systems. Comput. Stand. Interfaces **40**, 23–33 (2015)

3. Benattou, M., Cacciari, L., Pasini, R., Rafiq, O.: Principles and tools for testing open distributed systems. In: Csopaki, G., Dibuz, S., Tarnay, K. (eds.) Testing of Communicating Systems. IFIPAICT, vol. 21, pp. 77–92. Springer, Boston, MA (1999). https://doi.org/10.1007/978-0-387-35567-2_6
4. Hierons, R.M.: Testing a distributed system: generating minimal synchronised test sequences that detect output-shifting faults. Inf. Softw. Technol. **43**(9), 551–560 (2001)
5. Tai, K.-C., Young, Y.-C.: Synchronizable test sequences of finite state machines. Comput. Netw. ISDN Syst. **30**(12), 1111–1134 (1998)
6. Liu, W.Y., Zeng, H.W., Miao, H.K.: Multiple UIO-based test sequence generation for distributed systems. J. Shanghai Univ. **12**(5), 438–443 (2008)
7. Anier, A., Vain, J., Tsiopoulos, L.: DTRON: a tool for distributed model-based testing of time critical applications. Proc. Est. Acad. Sci. **66**(1), 75 (2017)
8. Merayo, M.G., Hierons, R.M., Núñez, M.: Passive testing with asynchronous communications and timestamps. Distrib. Comput. **31**(5), 327–342 (2018)
9. Hierons, R.M., Merayo, M.G., Núñez, M.: Bounded reordering in the distributed test architecture. IEEE Trans. Reliab. **67**(2), 522–537 (2018)
10. Lanet, J.L., Le Bouder, H., Benattou, M., Legay, A.: When time meets test. Int. J. Inf. Secur. **17**(4), 395–409 (2018)
11. Marynowski, J.E., Albonico, M., de Almeida, E.C., Sunyé, G.: Testing MapReduce-based systems. In: SBBD - XXVI Simpósio Bras, Banco Dados (2011)
12. Moran, J., La Riva, C.D., Tuya, J.: MRTree: functional testing based on MapReduce's execution behaviour. In: Proceedings of 2014 International Conference on Future Internet of Things and Clou, FiCloud 2014, pp. 379–384 (2014)
13. Csallner, C., Fegaras, L.: New ideas track: testing MapReduce style programs categories and subject descriptors. In: Engineering, pp. 504–507 (2011)
14. Lublinsky, B., Smith, K.T., Yakubovich, A.: Professional Hadoop Solutions (2013)
15. Petrenko, A., Bochmann, G.v., Yao, M.: On fault coverage of tests for finite state specifications. Comput. Netw. ISDN Syst. **29**(1), 81–106 (1996)
16. Wottrich, K., Bressoud, T.: The performance characteristics of mapreduce applications on scalable clusters. In: Proceedings of the Midstates Conference on Undergraduate Research in Computer Science and Mathematics, April 2011
17. Khan, M., Jin, Y., Li, M., Xiang, Y., Jiang, C.: Hadoop performance modeling for job estimation and resource provisioning. IEEE Trans. Parallel Distrib. Syst. **27**(2), 441–454 (2016)

Workshop on Data Science for Social Good in Africa

Workshop on Data Science for Social Good in Africa (DSSGA)

Workshop Description

Advances in Data Science and Artificial Intelligence are profoundly transforming economically advanced nations. Unfortunately, Africa is still lagging behind in these technological developments. If this technology gap is not closed, it could foster algorithmic bias, disparities in access to data and information, and lead to growing inequity between countries.

However, despite the barriers, Africa presents many opportunities. In fact, private and crowdsourced datasets from different sources are becoming available in many African countries. On other hand, Data Science and AI-related skills are being democratized and talents are emerging.

The aim of this workshop is to encourage researchers from data science and AI communities in Africa and worldwide, to think collectively and propose innovative solutions to bridge the digital divide, and use data science and AI to enhance quality of life in Africa and, therefore, contribute in achieving inclusive development.

Organization

DSSGA Chairs

El Adnani Mohammed   Cadi Ayyad University, Morocco
El Bachari Essaid   Cadi Ayyad University, Morocco
Zahir Jihad   Cadi Ayyad University, Morocco

International Program Committee

El Hassan Abdelwahed   Cadi Ayyad University, Morocco
Karine Ayoub   Haute-Alsace University, France
Nawal Alioua   Cadi Ayyad University, Morocco
Othmane Alaoui Fdili   Cadi Ayyad University, Morocco
Bubacarr Bah   African Institute for Mathematical Sciences, South Africa
Richard Chbeir   UPPA University, France
Patrick Corlay   Polytechnique Haut de France University, France
François-Xavier Coudoux Polytechnique Haut de France University, France
Rachida Dssouli   Concordia University, Canada
Noureddine Doghmane   Badji Mokhtar Annaba University, Algeria
Ahmed Ebamouh   IAV Hassan II, Morocco
Mohammed EL Adnani   Cadi Ayyad University, Morocco

Essaid El Bachari	Cadi Ayyad University, Morocco
Abdelhakim El Boustani	Cadi Ayyad University, Morocco
Mohammed El Hassouni	Mohammed V University, Morocco
Zahir Jihad	Cadi Ayyad University, Morocco
Mohammed Gharbi	Polytechnique Haut de France University, France
Abdelaziz Khadraoui	University of Geneva, Switzerland
Nasreddine Kouadria	Annaba University, Algeria
Eric Leclercq	University of Burgundy, France
Ciira Maina	Dedan Kimathi University of Technology, Kenya
Vukosi Marivate	University of Pretoria, South Africa
Abdelila Maach	Mohammed V University, Morocco
Vahid Meghdadi	Poitiers University, France
Chouaib Moujahdi	Mohammed V University, Morocco
Clency Perrine	Poitiers University, France
Yannis Pousset	Poitiers University, France
Esteban Vázquez Cano	National University of Distance Education, Spain
Amin Zribi	ENIT, Tunis Elmanar University, Tunisia

Semantic Graph-Based Recommender System. Application in Cultural Heritage

Sara Qassimi[1] and El Hassan Abdelwahed[1,2(✉)]

[1] Lisi Laboratory, Faculty of Science Semlalia,
Cadi Ayyad University, Marrakesh, Morocco
sara.qassimi@ced.uca.ma, abdelwahed@uca.ac.ma
[2] CSEHS, Mohammed VI Polytechnic University, Ben Guerir, Morocco

Abstract. Research on visitor support systems for museums and cultural sites has been particularly important in recent years. Many research projects have been created to assist the visitor before and during his visit. The cultural heritage area is affected by the problem of information overload. With the advent of the social web, a large number of available resources have emerged coming from the social information systems SocIS. Therefore, visitors are swamped with enormous choices in their visited cities. Even though, SocIS platforms use the features of collaborative tagging, named folksonomy, to commonly contribute to the management of the shared resources. Collaborative tagging lacks semantic which reduces the effectiveness of organizing resources. It decreases their findability and discoverability, thereby their recommendation. In this paper, we aim to personalize the cultural heritage visit, i.e., to suggest semantically related places that are most likely to interest a visitor. Our proposed approach represents a semantic graph-based recommender system of cultural heritage places by (1) constructing an emergent semantic description that semantically augments the place and (2) effectively modeling the emerging graphs representing the semantic relatedness of similar cultural heritage places and their related tags. The experimental evaluation shows relevant results attesting the efficiency of our proposal applied to recommend cultural heritage of Marrakesh city. Future perspectives will focus on creating a real-world application using augmented reality. It will include a semantic-based context-aware recommender system that rises in value the cultural heritage of the touristic city by suggesting historical places that suit the visitor's interests.

Keywords: Emergent semantic · Folksonomy · Graph-based recommender system · Context-awareness · Cultural heritage · Marrakesh

1 Introduction

Digital cultural heritage is now a mature field, in which novel information and communication technologies (ICT) are used in the service of preserving cultural

© Springer Nature Switzerland AG 2019
C. Attiogbé et al. (Eds.): MEDI 2019 Workshops, CCIS 1085, pp. 109–121, 2019.
https://doi.org/10.1007/978-3-030-32213-7_8

heritage and supporting its discovery by the public [1]. Research on visitor support systems for museums and cultural sites has been particularly important in recent years. Indeed, the museum is not only a place for the conservation of cultural sites and masterpieces of works showcased in an exhibit but also an institution for the education and entertainment of visitors. The cultural heritage area is particularly affected by the problem of information overload. For example, the Tripadvisor website lists more than 800 points of cultural visits for the city of Marrakesh, Morocco. Consequently, visitors are confronted with several challenges and issues. They are swamped with the enormous choices in their visited cities. Exploiting this long list of options is confusing and ambiguous for visitors. Therefore, they either spend time sifting through the options that best match their interests or to choose randomly. In addition, visitors do not necessarily know what they should visit or what they could appreciate. They are usually limited to visit the most popular places as in most guided tours. As a result, they may miss cultural heritage sites or places that might have interested them. One of the main research areas related to the problematic of information overload is the field of information retrieval. The general principle is to develop methods and algorithms to respond to the user's requests. However, it is not always easy for a user to know how to express his request especially within the large number of available resources coming from the social information systems SocIS.

The SocIS are information systems based on social technologies and open collaboration [2]. They have enabled social interaction giving rise to massive shared resources, any identifiable things (e.g. images, museums, videos, blogs, etc.). The SocIS platforms use the features of folksonomy to commonly contribute to the management of the shared resources. The collaborative tagging, named folksonomy, enables a collaborative classification of the shared resources. Folksonomy, unlike a taxonomy, includes terms without a hierarchy [16]. For example, Instagram provides collaborative tagging, sharing and categorizing photographs and short videos. Different aspects of folksonomy have been explored in information retrieval [3], social network analysis [4] , recommendation systems [5] and others. The collaborative tagging has led to an increasing amount of users providing information not only about the shared resources but also about their interest. The resulted growing and rich corpus of social knowledge can be exploited by recommendation technologies [6].

Regardless of its popularity and its widespread success, folksonomy lacks semantics. The tags come from an unsupervised and uncontrolled vocabulary which contains polysemous and synonymous words [7]. The unsupervised nature of folksonomy' tags semantically weakens the description of resources, consequently hindering their indexing, classification, and clustering. Indeed, a poor classification and clustering of resources decrease their retrieval and suggestion in recommender system RS. Therefore, the shared resources have to be pertinently described to ameliorate their recommendations.

In this regards, this article represents a semantic graph-based recommender system by (1) semantically enhancing the description of resources, in our case augmenting the cultural heritage place and (2) effectively modeling the emerging graphs representing the semantic relatedness of similar cultural heritage places and their related tags to perform graph-based recommendations. The recommender system is based on the emerging graphs representing the semantic relatedness of similar cultural heritage places and their related tags. In this paper, we present how the graph-oriented database leverages the building of flexible recommendation engines. This study is a part of a wider range of research project aiming to embrace digital culture in order to attract the attention of a wider audience. Many research projects have been created to assist the visitor before and during his visit. We aim to personalize the cultural visits, i.e., to suggest to the visitor cultural heritage places that are most likely to interest him.

The rest of the paper is organized as follows: A motivation scenario of graph-based recommendation of TripAdvisor museums is described in Sect. 2. Section 3 provides the literature review related to recommender system. Section 4 depicts the proposed approach of the semantic graph-based recommender system to suggest cultural heritage places. The experimental results and evaluation are described in Sect. 5. Finally, the conclusion and future directions are delineated in Sect. 6.

2   Motivating Scenario: Graph-Based Recommendation of TripAdvisor Museums Using Neo4j

A graph database is characterized by its distinct data model compared to traditional relational databases [12]. The flexible data model of a graph database enables stores data and represented it in a graph. Besides, the use of a graph database enables a great query performance regardless of number and depth of connections. Also, the graph database's processing at scale is inherently scalable for pattern-based queries.

Each graph database has its own specialized graph query language. For example, Neo4j uses Cypher language, and RDF (Resource Description Framework) databases use SPARQL (SPARQL Protocol and RDF Query Language). The integrity rules in a graph database are based on its graph constraints, rather than an imposed relational schema. The popularity of using graph databases has emerged with the increasing complexity of real-world data and growing needs for graph queries. For example, Neo4j is suited for online transaction processing (OLTP). Neo4j is a widely used open-source graph database, implemented in Java. Neo4j is characterized as an "embedded, disk-based, and fully transactional graph database engine" [13]. The Graph Model in the Neo4j database has the following components: Nodes (equivalent to vertices in graph theory) are the main data elements that are interconnected through relationships. A node can have one or more labels (that describe its role) and properties (i.e. attributes). Labels are used to group nodes, and each node can be assigned multiple labels. Labels are indexed to speed up finding nodes in a graph. Properties are attributes of both nodes and relationships. Neo4j allows for storing data as key-value pairs, which means properties can have any value (string, number, or boolean).

Recommendations can be computed thanks to graphs that create meaningful clusters of items reducing the dimensionality of the recommendation problem. To conduct cluster analysis using Neo4j , we perform the museums' recommendation using the collection and processed data of 1600 museums scraped from TripAdvisor [22].

The Cypher query bellow enables to recommend to the target user, having phone number "+1 412-622-3131", museums similar to the previously rated museum (see Fig. 1).

MATCH p=(user : User {phone: "+1412−622−3131"})−[:HAS_RATED]
−>()−[:HAS_TAG]−>()<−[:HAS_TAG]−(otherMusuem : Museum)
WHERE NOT (user)−[:HAS_RATED]−>(otherMusuem)
RETURN p

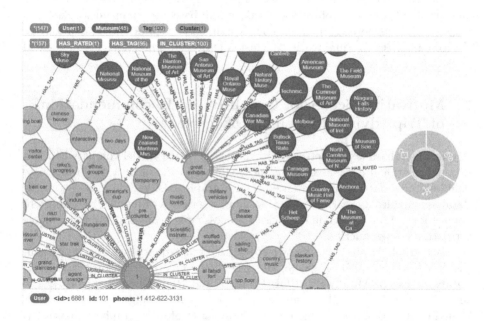

Fig. 1. Recommending never rated museums for the target user

3   Literature Review

A recommender system RS is a subclass of information filtering systems, that deals with information overload [8]. Recommender systems RSs are advantageous for both service providers and their users. They reduce the transaction cost of finding relevant items that interest users. Besides, RSs are proved to improve the decision-making process and quality [9]. The recommendations are based on the items' description, users' profile and their preferences. There are two approaches of recommendations either based on items' content or based on users' profile.

The two main recommendation paradigms are the collaborative filtering based recommendation and the content-based recommendation [10]. The content-based recommendations recommend similar items the user's previously preferred items (defined by aggregating the previous implicitly or explicitly rated items). The collaborative filtering recommendations suggested preferred items of the user's similar crowds [11]. Despite the success of the two filtering techniques, several problems were identified such as the limited content analysis for content-based and the cold start in collaborative filtering. In order to mitigate these problems, many hybrid filtering techniques were proposed by combining content-based, collaborative filtering and other filtering techniques [9].

The commonly used recommender system approaches rely on the exploitation of items-items similarities and users-items interactions. The integration of complex interactions between entities will be inflexibly integrated using these approaches. For instance, using the similarity matrix for recommending movies is unable to model and merge the explicit taste of a user about its favorite genres with its ratings and tagging for specific movies. A flexible approach would ease the exploitation of multiple kinds of possible interactions between different entities (users, items, genres, tags, and so on). Graphs are mathematical structures enabling to encode these interactions.

4   Proposed Approach: Semantic Graph-Based Recommender System of Cultural Heritage Places

The proposed approach (Fig. 2) presents the recommendation of cultural places based on graphs by harnessing the emergent semantic tags $T = \{t_i\}$ that aims to augment the places $P = \{p_i\}$ to be recommended.

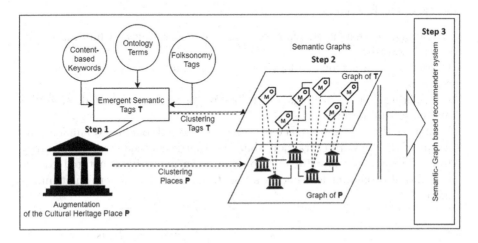

Fig. 2. Proposed approach of recommending Heritage places

4.1 Step 1: Emergent Semantic Using Collaborative Tagging

The first step mainly focuses on exploring collaborative tagging in order to pertinently extract descriptive metadata of resources, a.k.a. cultural heritage places.

Our previous works [7,14] present a deep explanation of the concept of the emergent semantic of resources through a combined semantic enrichment approach to augment the resource. The construction of the emergent semantic of resources is realized by extracting a different type of descriptive metadata, namely the relevant tags from the folksonomy, the matching terms from a domain ontology and the extracted content-based main keywords.

The augmentation of a resource (in the case study the resource is a cultural heritage place) is presented by the pertinently extract descriptive metadata by using collaborative tagging and ontology.

Folksonomy is known as collaborative tagging, social indexing or social classification. It refers to a set of keywords "tags" created by users to describe resources. Each user freely tags the resources using its own keywords, which aids him in categorizing information for his own personal management and also for sharing with others. For instance, the social annotation services Instagram is based on the exchange of tagged photos and videos. While ontology, the backbone of the semantic web, is a traditional taxonomy built with a controlled vocabulary and maintained by a limited number of experts. It is a representative knowledge structure of a field's descriptive. By representing the relationship between mental objects "concepts", ontology aims to "explicitly specify a conceptualization" [15].

The emergent semantic Tags T is a combined semantic enrichment of resources performed by extracting different type of descriptive metadata: Relevant tags extracted from the folksonomy; Extracted content-based main keywords; Matching terms from a domain ontology. The main steps of the emergent semantic are as follows:

- Extracting content-based main keywords by generating and filtering candidates keywords.
- Extracting of a set of ontology's terms matching the textual content of a resource.
- Considering folksonomy tags which are frequently used and understood by many users of a group.
- Exploring the relevant extracted tags from the folksonomy to enhance the model of the keyword extraction Maui [17] that learn the extraction strategy from the manually annotated corpus; i.e., the manually annotated corpus contains also relevant folksonomy's tags to additionally aliment the training data.

$$Emergent\ Semantic\ Tags\ T = \begin{cases} Folksonomy\ Tags \\ Main\ Keywords \\ Ontology\ Terms \end{cases}$$

4.2   Step 2: Semantic-Graph Based Recommender system

Graph of Cultural Heritage Places: Let $G_P = (V_P, E_P)$, with V_P vertices and E_P edges. G_P is a graph of cultural heritage places P, representing the vertices V_P or nodes as places connected with weighted edges $W(p_i, p_j)$ relating two places p_i and p_j. The two places are semantically similar when their weighted edge $W(p_i, p_j)$ is high.

$$W(p_i, p_j) = \sqrt{W_{semantic}(p_i, p_j)^2 + W_{context}(p_i, p_j)^2}$$

$$W_{semantic}(p_i, p_j) = \sqrt{\begin{aligned}&W_{folksonomy-tag}(p_i, p_j)^2 \\ &+ W_{main-keyword}(p_i, p_j)^2 \\ &+ W_{ontology-term}(p_i, p_j)^2\end{aligned}} \tag{1}$$

⚠ If the cultural heritage place is not described with textual descriptive $\Longrightarrow W_{main-keyword}(p_i, p_j) = 0$ and $W_{ontology-term}(p_i, p_j) = 0$

$$W_{folksonomy-tag}(p_i, p_j) = \frac{Number\ of\ folksonomy\ tags\ describing\ both\ p_i\ and\ p_j}{Total\ Number\ of\ folksonomy\ tags}$$

$$w_{main-keyword}(p_i, p_j) = \frac{Number\ of\ main\ keywords\ describing\ both\ p_i\ and\ p_j}{Total\ Number\ of\ main\ keywords}$$

$$w_{ontology-term}(p_i, p_j) = \frac{Number\ of\ ontology\ terms\ describing\ both\ p_i\ and\ p_j}{Total\ Number\ of\ ontology\ terms} \tag{2}$$

$$W_{context}(p_i, p_j) = \frac{\sum w_c(p_i, p_j)}{Total\ Number\ of\ contextual\ features}$$

$$w_c(r_i, r_j) = \begin{cases} 1\ if\ p_i\ and\ p_j\ are\ contextually\ related \\ 0\ else. \end{cases}$$

The places are clustered based on their same descriptive tags constructing an emergent graph of cultural heritage places. We use the folksonomy relevant tags to semantically relate places, in case, the textual content is absent to perform the extraction of main keywords and matching ontology's term. Besides, the weighted edges $W_{context}(p_i, p_j)$ consider the contextual features (contextual information: spatial, temporal and static) that conjointly describe the two places to enhance their relatedness. The static context characterizes a possessed attributes describing the places that are unchanged over time, like the category of a cultural place. The graph of places assembles semantically related places to formalize their similarity. Therefore, the recommender system will explore the place-place similarities among the graphs of cultural heritage places.

Graph of Emergent Semantic Tags : Let $G_T = (V_T, E_T)$ where vertices V_T are tags and E_T represents the edges relating the tags. G_T is a semantic graph of tags useful to further find semantic relationships among places annotated with connected tags. The graph is constructed with the weighted edge $W(t_i, t_j)$ relating two tags t_i and t_i.

$$W_{place}(t_i, t_j) = \frac{Number\ of\ places\ described\ by\ both\ tags\ t_i\ and\ t_j}{Total\ Number\ of\ tagged\ places} \qquad (3)$$

It enables graph-based reasoning about the relationships between tags attributed to describe different places.

4.3   Step 3: Recommendation Algorithm

The recommender system will explore the knowledge graphs to extract and recommend semantically related places.

Algorithm 1. Graph-based recommendations

$t \in T$; $t_{p_i} \in T_{p_i}$; $p_j, p_i \in P$; $Recom_t, Recom_p$, $RecomReturn_p \subset P$
$Recom_r$: a set of recommended resources based on the graph of places
$Recom_t$: a set of recommended places based on the graph of tags
k : a finite number of recommendations.
T_{p_i}: a finite number of tags describing the place p_i.
procedure RECOMMENDATIONGRAPHPLACES(p_i)
    for $p_j \in P$ **do**
      if $W(p_i, p_j) > 0$ **then**
         $Recom_p \leftarrow$ list of k-ranked p_j
      end if
    end for
    return $Recom_p$
end procedure
procedure RECOMMENDATIONGRAPHTAGS(p_i, t_{p_i})
    $RecomReturn_p \leftarrow$ RecommendationGraphResources(p_i)
    for $t \in T$ **do**
      if $W(t_{p_i}, t) > 0$ **then**
         $Recom_t \leftarrow$ list of k-ranked places annotated with t
      end if
    end for
    return $Recom_t$
end procedure

---

5   Evaluation and Results: Recommendation of Cultural Heritage Places in Marrakesh

We aim to personalize the cultural visits, i.e., to suggest to the visitors of Marrakesh city cultural heritage places that are most likely to interest them. The recommendations are implemented with queries using the Neo4j database and further processed in Python. We collected Wikipedia textual description of each of the list of World Heritage Sites in the Arab States [18] for training and 21 most cultural places of Marrakesh city for testing. We perform the augmentation of each place by constructing its Emergent Semantic Tags T using the three types of medatada considering: Relevant tags of the folksonomy TagsFinder [19] which are related hashtags used by Instagram and Twitters users; Ontology terms extracted from UNESCO Thesaurus [20]; Main keywords extracted from the Wikipedia descriptive content.

The model chosen for the graph (see Fig. 3) consists in:

- Three kinds of nodes: Places, Categories and Tags
- Two kind of edges: HAS_TAG expressing the relationship Place-Tag. HAS_CATEGORY relating Places to Categories. the category is defined as a static contextual information characterizing the cultural place.

The graph of emergent semantic tags are presented in Fig. 4. The 205 tags are clustered in 12 clusters with the edge In_CLUSTER relating the semantically related tags together.

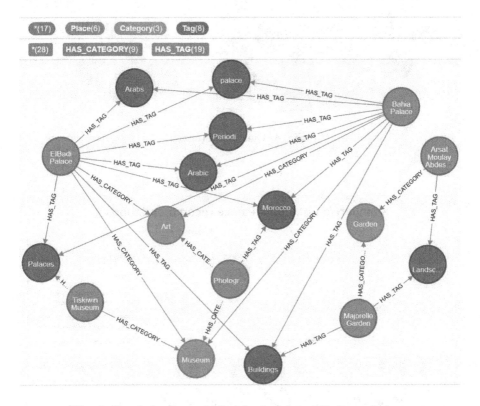

Fig. 3. Graph-database of Marrakesh Cultural Heritages Palaces

The semantic graph-based recommendations recommend the k-top places with similar tags and categories. We compare (see Fig. 5) the recommendations of places related to the ElBadi Palace suggested by our proposed approach and

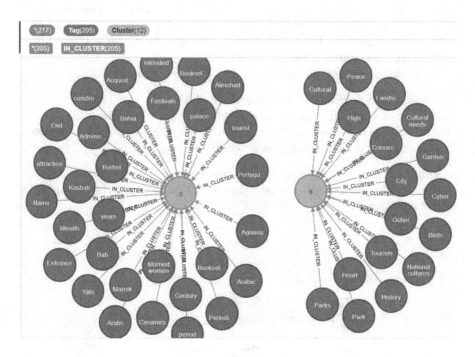

Fig. 4. Clusters of tags

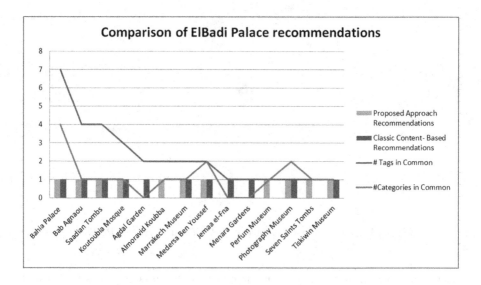

Fig. 5. Comparison of ElBadi Palace recommendations

the classic content-based recommender system CB-RS [21]. The CB-RS computes the similarity between all cultural places using SciKit Learn's linear_kernel (python library). Even though the CB recommendations of places are based on their textual descriptive and their emergent semantic Tags, they still provide irrelevant recommendations compared to our proposed RS. For example, CB-RS suggests Menara and Agdal Gardens which are not in the same category of ElBadi palace. Besides, It does not recommend three cultural places (Almoradive Koubba, Seven Saints Tombs and Perfume Museum) which have tags and categories in common with ElBadi Palace.

6   Conclusion and Perspectives

The need for embracing digital culture has increased in the cultural mediation in order to attract the attention of a wider audience. With the advent of social information systems SocIS, the digital cultural heritage area is affected by the problem of information overload. Consequently, visitors are confronted with several challenges and issues. They are swamped with the enormous choices in their visited cities. Choosing the options that best match their interests is time spending time and usually let the visitor choose randomly. Even though, SocIS platforms use the features of collaborative tagging, named folksonomy, to commonly organize the shared resources. Folksonomy lacks semantic which reduces its effectiveness of organizing resources. It decreases their findability and discoverability, thereby their recommendation. In this paper, our research study aims to enhance the visitor support system by recommending cultural sites that are most likely to interest visitors. Our proposed approach represents a semantic graph-based recommender system of cultural heritage places by (1) constructing an emergent semantic description that semantically augments the place and (2) effectively modeling the emerging graphs representing the semantic relatedness of similar cultural heritage places and their related tags. The experimental evaluation shows relevant results attesting the efficiency of our proposal applied to recommend cultural heritage of Marrakesh city. Future perspectives will focus on creating a real-world application enabling the recommendation of personalized content to visitors of cultural heritage sites in a context-aware manner. The challenge relies on creating a real-world mobile application using augmented reality (AR) that will allow the user to discover the cultural heritage of the visited city, like Marrakesh, without the help of a native citizen or a touristic guide offering excursions. The AR will help on directly deliver recommended information (e.i, cultural heritage sites, videos describing a place to visit, its most popular tags, and so on). This mobile application will include a semantic-based context-aware recommender system (CARS) that rises in value the cultural heritage of the touristic city by suggesting historical places that suit the visitor's interests. The CARS will filter similar users by analyzing their similar profiles (e.g., ethnicity, age, country of provenance, previous tags describing the visited historical places, etc.) to suggest fitting historical places with their descriptions.

References

1. López-Nores, M., Kuflik, T., Wallace, M., et al.: User Model User-Adap. Inter. **29**, 1 (2019). https://doi.org/10.1007/s11257-019-09230-x
2. Tilly, R., Posegga, O., Fischbach, K., et al.: Bus. Inf. Syst. Eng. **59**, 3 (2017). https://doi.org/10.1007/s12599-016-0459-8
3. Kumar, K.P., Srivastava, A., Geethakumari, G.: A psychometric analysis of information propagation in online social networks using latent trait theory. Computing **98**, 583–607 (2016). https://doi.org/10.1007/s00607-015-0472-7
4. Feicheng, M.A., Yating, L.: Utilising social network analysis to study the characteristics and functions of the co-occurrence network of online tags. Online Inf. Rev. **38**, 232–247 (2014). https://doi.org/10.1108/OIR-11-2012-0124
5. Sánchez-Bocanegra, C.L., et al.: HealthRecSys: a semantic content-based recommender system to complement health videos. BMC Med. Inf. Dec. Making **17**, 63 (2017)
6. Godoy, D., Corbellini, A.: Folksonomy-based recommender systems: a state-of-the-art review. Int. J. Intell. Syst. **31**, 314–346 (2016). https://doi.org/10.1002/int.21753
7. Qassimi, S., Abdelwahed, E.H., Hafidi, M., Lamrani, R.: Towards an emergent semantic of web resources using collaborative tagging. In: Ouhammou, Y., Ivanovic, M., Abelló, A., Bellatreche, L. (eds.) MEDI 2017. LNCS, vol. 10563, pp. 357–371. Springer, Cham (2017). https://doi.org/10.1007/978-3-319-66854-3_27
8. Konstan, J.A., Riedl, J.: Recommender systems: from algorithms to user experience. User Model. User-Adapt Inter. **22**, 101–23 (2012)
9. Isinkaye, F.O., Folajimi, Y.O., Ojokoh, B.: Recommendation systems: principles methods and evaluation. Egypt Inform. J. **16**, 261–273 (2015)
10. Yera, R., Martínez, L.: Fuzzy tools in recommender systems: a survey. Int. J. Comput. Intell. Syst. **10**(1), 776–803 (2017)
11. Villegas, N.M., Sánchez, C., Díaz-Cely, J., Tamura, G.: Characterizing context-aware recommender systems: a systematic literature review. Knowl. Based Syst. **140**, 173–200 (2018)
12. Angles, R., Gutierrez, C.: Survey of graph database models. ACM Comput. Surv. **40**, 1 (2008). https://doi.org/10.1145/1322432.1322433
13. Park, Y., Shankar, M., Park, B., Ghosh, J.: Graph databases for large-scale healthcare systems: a framework for efficient data management and data services. In: 2014 IEEE 30th International Conference on Data Engineering Workshops, Chicago, IL, pp. 12–19 (2014). https://doi.org/10.1109/ICDEW.2014.6818295
14. Qassimi, S., Abdelwahed, E.H.: The role of collaborative tagging and ontologies in emerging semantic of web resources, Computing 1–23 (2019)
15. Gruber, T.R.: A translation approach to portable ontology specifications. Knowl. Acquis. **5**, 199–220 (1993). https://doi.org/10.1006/knac.1993.1008
16. Qassimi, S., Abdelwahed, E.H., Hafidi, M., Lamrani, R.: Enrichment of ontology by exploiting collaborative tagging systems: a contextual semantic approach. In: Third International Conference on Systems of Collaboration (SysCo), IEEE Conference Publications, pp: 1–6 (2016)
17. Maui - Multi-purpose automatic topic indexing. http://www.medelyan.com/software. Accessed 30 June 2019
18. World Heritage Centre - World Heritage List. https://whc.unesco.org/pg.cfm?cid=31&l=en&&&mode=table&order=regi. Accessed 30 June 2019
19. Folksonomy TagsFinder. https://www.tagsfinder.com/. Accessed 30 June 2019

20. UNESCO Thesaurus SKOS. https://skos.um.es/unescothes/. Accessed 30 June 2019
21. simple content-based recommendation engine using python. https://www.kaggle.com/cclark/simple-content-based-recommendation-engine. Accessed 30 June 2019
22. Museum Reviews Collected from TripAdvisor. https://www.kaggle.com/annecool37/museum-data. Accessed 30 June 2019

MRI Brain Images Compression and Classification Using Different Classes of Neural Networks

Abdelhakim El Boustani$^{(\boxtimes)}$ and Essaid El Bachari

Cadi Ayyad University, Marrakesh, Morocco
a.elboustani@uca.ma, elbachari@uca.ac.ma

Abstract. The aim of this paper is to build an automatic system for compression and classification for magnetic resonance imaging brain images. The algorithm segments the images in order to separate regions of medical interest from its background. Only the regions of interest are compressed with a low-ratio scheme, while the rest of the image is compressed with a high-ratio scheme. Based on Convolutional Neural Network (CNN) method for classification and a Probabilistic Neural Network (PNN) for image segmentation, the system has been developed. Experiments were conducted to evaluate the performance of our approach using different optimizers with a huge dataset of MRI brain images. Results confirmed that the Root Mean Square Propagation (RMSprop) optimizer converges faster with a highest accuracy comparing to other optimizers and showed that the proposed preprocessing schema reduced the execution time.

Keywords: Machine learning · Classification · Convolutional Neural Networks · Deep learning · Resonance magnetic images · Big data

1 Introduction

Magnetic resonance imaging (MRI) is a technique of choice for studying brain structures, as it provides 3D high-resolution high-contrast images. However, since the memory space necessary to store the medical images and/or their transmission time increase with image quality, there is a strong need for their compression before processing them. Such image compression should not remove any medically relevant information in the process. This is why lossless compression techniques have been first applied to medical image compression [1]. The compression ratio can be increased by selecting the diagnostic regions which are medically interesting, and apply lossless techniques only to these regions [2]. This technique supposes that, prior to the compression; a classification process had to be applied on the image, with the classification criteria varying from one medical application to another.

Neural network-assisted segmentation and classification have been already applied successfully to MRI brain images [3]. Moreover, for image compression, neural networks (NNs) have been proven to be an approach of choice mainly because of their massively parallel computation, which provides fast algorithms [4]. This is a strong

© Springer Nature Switzerland AG 2019
C. Attiogbé et al. (Eds.): MEDI 2019 Workshops, CCIS 1085, pp. 122–134, 2019.
https://doi.org/10.1007/978-3-030-32213-7_9

advantage when the amount of data is important, as it is in the case of 3D high-resolution images.

Due to the huge amount of information coming from hospitals, especially medical images, it becomes so hard to classify every image manually and to store it into its appropriate folder to track the diseases of each subject. The new challenge now is how to build an automatic system that can classify and store images without human intervention. Otherwise, deep learning has demonstrated its superior performance on a wide variety of tasks including speech, natural language, and images. It has become the go-to technique for most Artificial Intelligence (AI) type problems, because its capacity to deal with big data, particularly to extract features and to classify medical images in order to store them in a distributed database.

Past work on image recognition has emerged strongly either using classical or modern methods often derived from machine learning algorithms. Authors in [7] proposed a method that combines digital image processing and a thresholding method for a segmentation algorithm. In [8, 9], a feature extractor based on the powerful machine learning model Support Vector Machine (SVM) was proposed and a state of the art survey on MRI brain tumor segmentation was presented. A new approach was proposed by Dimitrovski *et al.* in [10] where they used, among others, a standard classification of Medical Images using Convolutional Neural Networks. Another research in this field is the study of Erickson *et al.* in [11]. The objective of their work is to detect tumors using machine learning, such as SVM and K-Nearest Neighbors (K-NN), and they made a comparative study between traditional machine learning and deep learning. In [12], Affonso *et al.* used deep learning, especially CNN, with a combination of texture-based feature extraction techniques and traditional techniques. This work was relayed on Haralick's texture descriptors [13] to pre-process an image before training a model by different machine learning techniques. In the same context, Tanga *et al.*, in [14], used the multiscale Sparse Auto Encoders (SAEs) Networks from [15], which are the most popular representations of unsupervised learning methods to extract image features. Mohan and Subashini proposed a study of medical image classification using MRI format [16]. Descombes *et al.* presented a new approach for segmenting 3D tomographic vascular network images into pathological and normal regions from considering their micro-vessel 3D structure only [17, 18]. El-Boustani *et al.* used different neural networks architectures to compress MRI brain images [19]. More recently, Kheradpisheh *et al.* have shown that spike-timing-dependent plasticity (STDP) can be used in spiking neural networks (SNN) to extract visual features of low or intermediate complexity in an unsupervised manner [20].

While the basic image processing feature extraction and classification schemes are much easier to implement and are computationally less expensive, the modern techniques based on deep learning gives better performance, especially when dealing with huge amount of data. In our recent paper [25], we concluded that more importance must be given to the pre-processing step as this part can help us to build a stronger model and thus to obtain better results. This motivated our research for building an automatic system by combining preprocessing techniques from machine learning, a more sophisticated CNN, and a SVM decision model to improve the results. We propose in this paper to first compress the MRI images without losing the relevant information by using probabilistic and back-propagation neural networks; then, we design a deep CNN comprising several convolutional and pooling layers for tumor classification. We evaluate the proposed scheme using different optimizer functions.

The paper is structured as follows. In the next section, we present our proposed approach and the different tools used in our study. In Sect. 3, we present the used data and the design of our experiments. Section 4 sets out our key experimental results, including some statistical analysis and interpretations and a comparative study. And in Sect. 5, we state some concluding remarks and suggestions for future work.

2   The Proposed Approach

To build our system, two main steps are necessary. The first step revolves around the construction of a model using a training set where some medical images are chosen to extract the image features. The second step depends on medical images dataset to be classified. Images from this dataset will be processed by the system to extract its features and, based on the output data, the system determinates to which class an image will belong.

2.1   Image Pre-processing

As it's known, image in general contains two kinds of information: useful and un-useful information. So it's obvious that we need some methods that can remove useless information and keep just useful ones. Indeed, for neurological purposes, only the brain tissue region represents the relevant medical information in the entire head image, as usually acquired with the MRI technique. We then propose a preprocessing scheme consisting on first segmenting the brain image to separate brain tissue from the rest of the image (i.e., background and low part of the head), and then to apply compression algorithms with different compression ratios. Thus, only the brain tissue, i.e., the region of interest (ROI), should be considered for a low-ratio. In contrast, a strongly lossy compression technique can be applied on the rest of the image. The segmentation is performed using a probabilistic NN (PNN), and the compression is performed using two back-propagation NNs.

As shown on Fig. 1, the ROI is less than half the entire image. Thus, by applying a strong compression on the background, an interesting compression ratio can be achieved on the whole image.

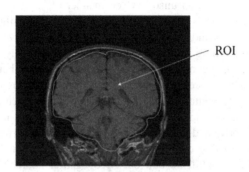

Fig. 1. Region of Interest (ROI) on MRI brain image

2.1.1 Probabilistic Neural Networks

The PNN is very well adapted to this segmentation purpose, as it allows classification by calculating the probability of a given input to belong to one of K predefined classes [5] as shown in Fig. 2.

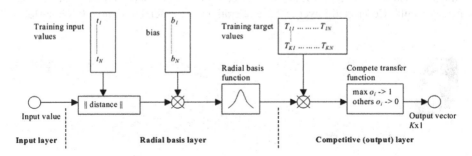

Fig. 2. Probabilistic Neural Network

The segmentation process consists of finding an estimator function $f_A(x, c)$ for each input x and each class c defined by

$$f_A(x,c) = \sum_{j=1}^{N_c} w_j b(\|x - t_j\|)$$ (1)

where the (t_j) are the N_c vectors in the training input set which are in the class c ($c = 1$, 2, 3), b is a decreasing radial basis function, and (w_j) is a set of weights. Then, a compete function classifies each pixel x in the class where $f_A(x, c)$ is maximum.

2.1.2 Back-Propagation Neural Networks

For compression purposes, the back-propagation NNs used are composed of one input layer of N neurons, one hidden layer of K neurons and one output layer of N neurons [4], as shown on Fig. 3. Such a network achieves a compression ratio of N/K:1.

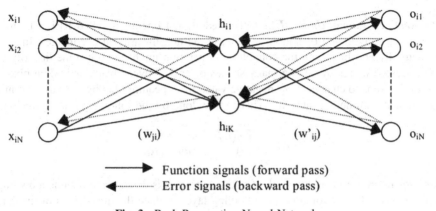

Fig. 3. Back-Propagation Neural Network

2.2   Convolutional Neural Networks

Deep learning models have achieved remarkable results in computer vision, so they become a new tendency in image recognition and classification. In this context appears our used CNN algorithm. As we can see from Fig. 4, the CNN is divided into 4 steps which are Convolution, Non Linearity (ReLU), Pooling or Sub-Sampling and Classification (Fully Connected Layer). These operations are crucial to build a CNN system.

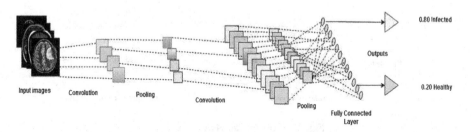

Fig. 4. CNN architecture with 2 convolution and pooling layers

Convolution: linear filtering is mathematically a convolution operation giving by:

$$g = f * h \tag{2}$$

Where g is the new image, h is the original image and f represents the used filter (window). More precisely, at each pixel (i, j), the convolved feature is:

$$g(i,j) = \sum_u \sum_v h(u,v)f(i-u,j-v) \tag{3}$$

Significantly, the convolution layer is composed of a set of filters. Convolution considers image as a combination of multiple matrix h, every matrix will be multiplied by a filter f to extract features from this image. Convolution is sweeping the whole image to extract features. The output matrix is called the convolved feature or the Feature Map.

The Rectified Linear Unit (RELU): This additional operation called RELU is used after every convolution operation to increase the non-linearity in our images. Images are naturally non-linear but the convolution operation might impose some linearity to the processed image by adding many shades of gray between black and white pixels. The objective is to change every negative value from Feature Map by Zero to keep just the element with height intensity. This can be done by the following transformation:

$$h(i,j) = \begin{cases} h(i,j) & \text{if } h(i,j) > 0, \\ 0 & \text{Otherwise.} \end{cases} \tag{4}$$

Pooling: In order to avoid the risk of over-learning, it is desirable to include a pooling layer between the convolution ones. Pooling layers reduce the dimensions of the data by combining the outputs of neuron clusters at one layer into a single neuron in the next layer. Typically, pooling may compute a max or an average. We choose to perform a Max Pooling where *3 × 3* clusters is represented by the height element from the new feature map after RELU, as shown in Fig. 5. It is a sub-sampling making an image rate compression of 9 to 1.

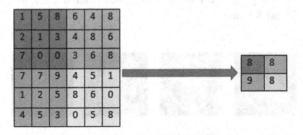

Fig. 5. Pooling by a 2 × 2 filter

Fully Connected Layer: Neurons in a fully connected layer have connections to all activations in the previous layer. The activations can be computed as an affine transformation. This layer basically takes an input volume (Convolved Feature or Max Pooling or RELU value) called Weight. CNN gives the result based on the weight calculated in the last Max-Pooling step. Figure 6 shows the functioning of this step.

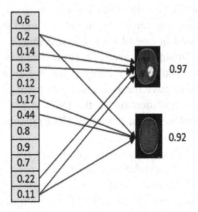

Fig. 6. Fully Connected Layer output

Obviously, every medical image will have some common weights with our training set and test set output. These weights differ from an image to another. By adding these common weights, our CNN chooses the highest value and decides, based on this value, to which class will belong our image.

3 Experiments

Our dataset of brain images is composed with samples from two classes, healthy brain and brain with Tumor. This dataset was downloaded from Kaggle (Platform for predictive modeling and analytics competitions) and from the Cancer Imaging Archive (TCIA) generated by the National Cancer Institute Clinical Proteomic Tumor Analysis Consortium (CPTAC) [19]. We choose 1000 axial MRI images in our test as it is shown in Figs. 7 and 8 below.

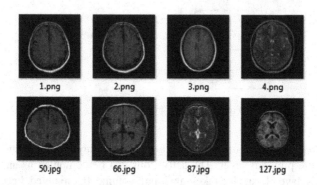

Fig. 7. Examples of healthy MRI Brain images

As it's mentioned before, we pre-process images before the recognition step to reduce the amount of data. To constitute our PNN training set, a 2D brain image, used as input data, was manually segmented to provide a target image. Each pixel of the training image was classified in one of three classes: image background, brain tissue and other head structures (mainly fat tissue, bone and muscles). Then, the PNN was designed using 1000 input and target training pairs chosen equally among the three classes. This training set size gave the best results in terms of classification precision and computing time. After classification by the PNN in the 3 classes, only pixels in brain tissue were considered as region of interest (ROI) pixels, so that the output brain image is a binary image.

For the compression purpose, input and ouput layers are composed of 9 neurons to process (3×3) successive non-overlapping blocks. For nearly lossless compression of ROI blocks, K is equal to 5 neurons, leading to a compression ratio of 1.8:1 for these areas. For lossy compression out of ROIs, K has been chosen as small as 1 neuron, leading to a compression ratio of 9:1.

For both networks, the transfer functions used in hidden and output layers were linear functions. In fact, linear back-propagation networks for image compression have been already proven to outperform non-linear networks which use sigmoid transfer functions [6]. We have experienced this point, and the use of sigmoid transfer functions provided slower convergence and higher mean square error during network training than linear transfer functions.

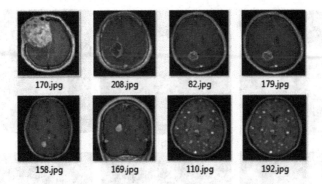

170.jpg 208.jpg 82.jpg 179.jpg

158.jpg 169.jpg 110.jpg 192.jpg

Fig. 8. Examples of Tumoral MRI Brain images

After the preprocessing step, our CNN extracts features using the four steps as mentioned before. To compute the loss, we implemented the support vector machine (SVM) instead of the conventional softmax function with the cross entropy function. The SVM objective is to find the optimal hyperplane to separate two classes in a given dataset. The weight parameters are then learned using three different optimizer functions: Stochastic Gradient Descent (SGD), Adaptive Moment Optimization (Adam) and Root Mean Square Propagation (RMSprop). These optimizers perform a parameter update for each training example. The following section presents and discusses the obtained results of our approach.

Experiments were conducted on HP computer with i7 core processors. Our program is developed using Python Programming Language, and using Keras and Tensorflow Libraries which are dedicated to the CNN programming.

4 Results and Discussion

For image segmentation, the PNN training was processed as the network is designed, which allows a fast training time of about 1 min. For image low-ratio compression, a training set of about 3500 (3×3) pixel patches taken exclusively in the brain tissue area was used. The performance goal for the back-propagation NN was set to 5.10^{-4}, with an adaptive learning rate. The goal was achieved after about 10 min. For image high-ratio compression, a low performance goal of $1.4.10^{-2}$ was found to be sufficient, using 2000 pixel patches taken in the background for training. This last training took less than 1 min.

Figure 9 shows the compression results obtained on 3 different slices from the dataset. After classification of every pixel in the image, a low-ratio compression was applied to every (3×3) block containing at least 5 pixels belonging to ROI, and a high-ratio compression was applied to other blocks. This threshold of 5 pixels was chosen empirically, as it gave the best results in terms of distortion and compression ratio achieved.

One can observe on the reconstructed image that the regions out of the brain area (non ROIs) appear blurred as every (3×3) block is compressed with one gray level.

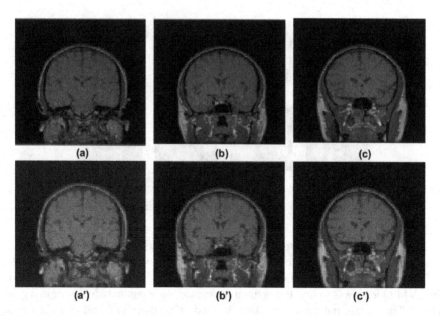

Fig. 9. Original images on top (a), (b), (c) and bottom their corresponding reconstructed images (a'), (b') and (c').

Concerning the brain area, the major features of medical interest (gray matter, brain sulci and ventricles) seen on the original image are all preserved on the decompressed image.

More quantitatively, distortion was measured on each image by calculating the peak signal-to-noise ratio (PSNR) values in the brain tissue area. Distortion results are shown on Table 1. The PSNR values obtained are very acceptable, considering that the original MRI images are quite noisy (the signal-to-noise ratio is about 15 dB).

Table 1. Distortion PSNR values

Images	PSNR (dB)
Image (a)	28,22
Image (b)	27,84
Image (c)	28,41

The compression ratio achieved with this method is slightly variable for each brain image, as it is dependent on the size of the brain area relatively to the size of the whole image. For the 3 different images presented here, the average compression ratio was equal to 6.6:1, which is a high compression ratio when dealing with medical images.

These compressed brain images were then presented as an input to the CNN-SVM system. In this test, we used the RMSprop optimizer [22] and mean squared error distance. In every test, we change the number of epochs when an entire dataset is passed forward and backward through the network. The training accuracy and loss of CNN-SVM when epoch is fixed on 50 are shown on Fig. 10. For the accuracy and loss, we followed the definition given in Keras. The learning rate increases and the value lost decreases steadily and faster when the number of epochs increases. This is because increasing the epoch's number implies weights updating in the neural network. Thus, as much as we train the network, it would memorize the desired outputs for the training set inputs.

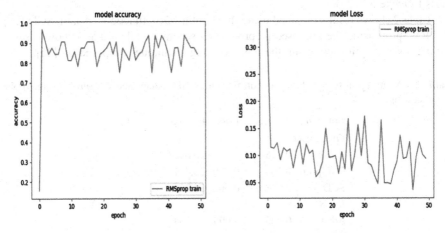

Fig. 10. Accuracy and Loss vs. epochs (=50)

Figure 11 shows the execution time for every epoch of our program. As we can see, as much as we increase epoch number, which is the number of iterations, the execution time becomes higher and higher. In this figure, we can notice that the execution time can be almost represented by an increasing linear function.

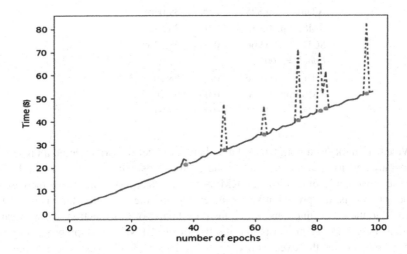

Fig. 11. Execution Time versus number of epochs

There are some exceptions, however, which are represented by red dots. These abrupt changes in the execution time are due to the machine performances. In normal case, we use GPU to compile this kind of programs, because CNN needs higher performances to give results in minimal time. But in our case and due to materiel limitations, we used only CPU to run it which justify the long time that the program takes to make a decision.

Table 2 shows results obtained using the 3 optimizer's functions, Adam, SGD [23] and RMSprop using the proposed preprocessing scheme, while Table 3 shows results for the 3 same optimizers using the preprocessing techniques proposed on [25].

Table 2. Accuracy, loss and the execution time for SGD, Adam and *RMSprop* using *BPNN* preprocessing

Optimizer	Accuracy	Loss	Execution time (S)
Epoch = 80			
Adam	0,925	0,075	30,042
RMSprop	0,964	0,036	28,421
SGD	0,938	0,062	28,231
Epoch = 100			
Adam	0,905	0,095	38,164
RMSprop	0,966	0,035	37,2546
SGD	0,910	0,090	38,8561

Table 3. Accuracy, loss and the execution time for SGD, Adam and RMSprop using other preprocessing techniques

Optimizer	Accuracy	Loss	Execution time (S)
Epoch = 80			
Adam	0,875	0,0996	39,0468
RMSprop	0,932	0,071	38,532
SGD	0,968	0,049	38,3302
Epoch = 100			
Adam	0,876	0,107	58,2037
RMSprop	0,906	0,0071	57,7669
SGD	0,901	0,099	58,0477

We can remark from both tables that Adam optimizer did not undergo a big change in accuracy and loss, and compared to the 2 others, its execution time is the highest one. The most stable function is the RMSprop optimizer. As more as we increase the number of epochs, the precision keeps increasing and the execution time is the lowest compared to the other functions, which justifies the use of this function in our research. But more interesting to notice is that the use of the BPNN in the preprocessing step reduces dramatically the execution time about 10 s with 80 epochs and about 20 s while using 100 epochs. Our preprocessing scheme increases also the accuracy for the 3 used optimizers.

5 Conclusion and Future Work

We have presented in this paper an automatic system to classify MRI brain images. We developed and implemented an algorithm based on BPNN and adapted CNN. We gave more importance to the pre-processing step and this part helped us to build a stronger model and thus to obtain better results in accuracy and execution time. It provides a fully automatic algorithm, as the medical ROIs in the image are detected using a selective class of Neural Networks, so that there is no need for a manual segmentation of these ROIs. Considering both the average compression ratio and the distortion error this technique appears to be an efficient way for the specific compression and classification of MRI brain tumor images. The challenges faced in this work, is to select the best existing classifier especially in a huge brain tumor dataset. In future work, we can extend this classification to a large number of classes and generalize the program to be applicable on 3D MRI images which is a big challenge since there are lacks of data.

References

1. Jiang, W.W., Kiang, S.Z., Hakim, N.Z., Meadows, H.E.: Lossless compression for medical imaging systems using linear/non-linear prediction and arithmetic coding. In: Proceedings of the IEEE International Symposium on Circuits and Systems, vol. 1, pp. 283–286 (1993)
2. Panagiotidis, N.G., Kalogeras, D., Kollias, S.D., Stafylopatis, A.: Neural network-assisted effective lossy compression of medical images. Proc. IEEE **84**(10), 283–286 (1996)
3. Li, X., Bhide, S., Kabuka, M.R.: Labeling of MR brain images using Boolean neural network. IEEE Trans. Med. Imaging **15**(5), 628–638 (1996)
4. Jiang, J.: Image compression with neural networks: a survey. Sig. Process. Image Commun. **14**, 737–760 (1999)
5. Specht, D.F.: Probabilistic neural networks. Neural Networks **3**, 109–118 (1990)
6. Mougeot, M., Azencott, R., Angeniol, B.: Image compression with back-propagation: improvement of the visual restoration using different cost functions. Neural Networks **4**(4), 467–476 (1991)
7. Mcculloch, W.S., Pitts, W.: A logical calculus of the ideas immanent in nervous activity. Bull. Math. Biophys. **5**(4), 115–133 (1943)
8. Hu, M.K.: Visual pattern recognition by moment invariant. IRE Trans. Info. Theory **8**(2), 179–187 (1962)
9. Gordillo, N., Montseny, E., Sobrevilla, P.: State of the art survey on MRI brain tumor segmentation. Magn. Reson. Imaging **31**(8), 1426–1438 (2013)
10. Dimitrovski, I., Kocev, D., Kitanovski, I., Loskovska, S., Dzeroski, S.: Improved medical image modality classification using a combination of visual and textual features. Comput. Med. Imaging Graph. **39**, 14–26 (2014)
11. Erickson, B.J., Korfiatis, P., Akkus, Z., Kline, T.L.: Machine learning for medical imaging. In: RSNA Annual Meeting, November 2016
12. Affonso, C., Rossi, A.L., Vieira, F., Carvalho, A.: Deep learning for biological image classification. Expert Syst. Appl. **85**, 114–122 (2017)
13. R. Haralick, K. Shanmugam, and I. Dinstein "Textural features for image classification". IEEE Trans. (1973)
14. Tang, Q., Liu, Y., Liu, H.: Medical image classification via multiscale representation learning. Artif. Intell. Med. **79**, 71–78 (2017)

15. Le, Q.V.: Building High-Level Features Using Large Scale Unsupervised Learning. Google Inc., USA (2012)
16. Mohan, G., Subashini, M.: MRI Based Medical Image Analysis: Survey on brain tumor grade classification. Biomed. Sig. Process. Control **39**, 139–161 (2017)
17. Descombes, X., et al.: Vascular network segmentation: an unsupervised approach. In: IEEE 9th International Symposium of Biomedical Imaging (ISBI), vol. 0, pp. 1248–1251 (2012)
18. Descombes, X., et al.: Brain tumor vascular network segmentation from micro-tomography. In: IEEE 8th International Symposium of Biomedical Imaging (ISBI), vol. 0, pp. 1113–1116 (2011)
19. El Boustani, A., Kinsner, W.: Selective compression of MRI brain images using two classes of neural networks. In: Proceedings of the International Conference on Image and Signal Processing, ICISP01, vol. 1 of 2, pp. 216–220 (2001)
20. Kheradpisheh, S.R., Ganjtabesh, M., Thorpe, S.J., Masquelier, T.: STDP-based spiking deep convolutional neural networks for object recognition. Neural Networks **99**, 56–67 (2017)
21. Clark, K., et al.: Cancer Imaging Archive (TCIA): maintaining and operating a public information repository. J. Digit. Imaging **26**(6), 1045–1057 (2013)
22. Mukkamala, M.C., Hein, M.: Variants of RMSProp and adagrad with logarithmic regret bounds. In: International Conference on Machine Learning, Sydney, Australia (2017)
23. Kingma, D.P., Ba, J.: Adam: a method for stochastic optimization. In: ICLR 2015 (2015)
24. Roy, S., Das, N., Kundu, M., Nasipuri, M.: Handwritten Isolated Bangla Compound Character Recognition: a new benchmark using a novel deep learning approach. Pattern Recogn. Lett. **90**, 15–21 (2017)
25. El Boustani, A., Aatila, M., El Bachari, E., El Oirrak, A.: MRI brain images classification using convolutional neural networks. In: Attiogbe, C., et al. (eds.) MEDI 2019, Workshops, CCIS 1085, pp. x-y, 2019. Springer, Cham (2019)

Overview on HEVC Inter Frame Video Coding's Impact on the Energy Consumption for Next Generation WVSNs

Achraf Ait-Beni-Ifit[1]([✉])(iD), Othmane Alaoui-Fdili[1,3], Patrick Corlay[2], François-Xavier Coudoux[2], and Mohammed El Hassouni[1]

[1] LRIT-CNRST URAC29, Faculty of Sciences,
Mohammed V University in Rabat, Rabat, Morocco
mr.ifit@gmail.com
[2] IEMN UMR 8520, Department OAE, UPHF, Valenciennes, France
[3] LAPSSII, Ecole Supérieure de Technologie de Safi,
Université Cadi Ayyad, Safi, Morocco

Abstract. With the advent of the High Efficiency Video Coding HEVC standard, wireless transmission of video data consumes more and more energy, a major concern in the field of Wireless Video Sensor Networks (WVSNs). The energy resources are limited, consisting only in the battery of the sensor nodes that determines their lifetime. In this paper, we propose an empirical parametric model to predict the energy consumption of an HEVC based video encoder in its inter prediction mode, used in the context of the next generation WVSNs. Such a model is of great interest to minimize the waste of energy of the encoding phase, while meeting the required video quality. The proposed model predicts energy consumption, considering the adopted Number of P frames (NP). A Raspberry Pi 2 card based video sensor node is used for modelling and validation, considering different configurations. The obtained results demonstrate that the proposed model describes well the occurred energy dissipation during the video encoding phase, with an average prediction error of 1.6%.

Keywords: Inter prediction · Energy efficiency · Video compression · H.265/HEVC · Next generation wireless video sensor network · Raspberry Pi 2

1 Introduction

The advent of the High Efficiency Video Coding H265/HEVC standard has allowed a revolution in the field of mobile video communication. A technological advance that led to a new generation of Wireless Video Sensor Networks (WVSN). Each node in a WVSN can capture still or moving pictures from the environment, processes them, then routes them towards the destination.

© Springer Nature Switzerland AG 2019
C. Attiogbé et al. (Eds.): MEDI 2019 Workshops, CCIS 1085, pp. 135–145, 2019.
https://doi.org/10.1007/978-3-030-32213-7_10

The standard reflects the experience of about four decades of research and three decades of international standardization of the technology of encoding digital video. HEVC is still adopting a hybrid coding scheme, however, existing coding tools were significantly enhanced and some new tools have been introduced. HEVC is today the state of the art of video compression with a reduction of bitrate of 50% compared with its predecessor H 264/AVC standard [1].

Inter prediction plays an important role in HEVC to attain this outstanding improvement. In HEVC, the inter prediction of the current block is obtained by straightly repeating or interpolating a block from the reference frame. However, it was proved that inter coding consumes quite ten times the energy drained by intra coding [2,3]. Therefore to deploy an HEVC video encoder supporting inter GOPs (Group of Pictures), using P frames, at an energy constrained wireless sensor node, we need to study the behaviour of the energy consumption according to the number of these frames.

One can intuitively say that the energy increase with the increasing of P frames (NP). However, the main question that we are trying to answer is how does energy increase when inter coding is used? The answer will allow us, in fact, to give an insight into the real impact of inter coding on energy consumption.

In this paper, we propose an empirical model describing the impact of the Number of NP on the energy consumption during the video encoding of an HEVC-based sensor video node.

The rest of this paper is organized as follows: in Sect. 2, a brief overview of the previous works given on the subject is presented. In Section 3, we presented a study of the impact of the inter prediction phase on the consumed energy during video compression. In Sect. 4, the proposed mathematical models describing the behaviour of the consumed energy during the video compression as a function of NP under different QP configurations are derived. Section 5 validate the proposed models. Finally, Sect. 6 concludes the paper.

2   Related Works

In the literature in fact, many works were directed towards the study of the Intra-only mode of the HEVC video encoder, given its energy efficiency compared to the inter modes. In a previous study [4], we propose an empirical parametric model to predict the energy consumption of an HEVC based video encoder in its intra-only mode, used in the context of the next generation WVSNs. The proposed model predicts the energy consumption, considering the adopted Quantization Parameter (QP) and the Frame Rate parameter (FR). A Raspberry Pi 2 card based video sensor node was used for modelling and validation, considering different configurations and spatial resolutions. The obtained results demonstrate that the proposed model describes well the occurred energy dissipation during the video encoding phase, with an average prediction error of 4.5%.

In [5], Alaoui-Fdili et al. propose an optimal solution for the problem of minimizing the energy consumed by an H264/AVC video encoder, deployed on a WVSN to encode and transmit video stream under a specified video distortion. Actually, empirical models were proposed in order to define the behaviour of both the energy and the distortion consumed during the encoding and the transmitting processes, considering only the FR and the QP parameters. On the other hand, the proposed models led to the proposal of a framework allowing the adaptive selection of the QP and FR parameters in order to solve the problem under consideration. However, inter coding was not considered.

Several other studies have proposed efficient mode decision schemes for HEVC inter prediction, Vanne et al. analyse in [6] the rate-distortion-complexity characteristics of the HEVC inter prediction as a function of different block partition structures and puts the analysis results into practice by developing optimized mode decision schemes for the HEVC encoder. experiments show that the proposed schemes are able to cut the average complexity of the HEVC reference encoder by 31%–51% at a cost of 0.2%–1.3% bit rate increase under the random access coding configuration.

In [7], considering the hierarchical structure of the HEVC encoder (CU-based structure), Zhang et al. explore the relationship between the impossible modes and the distribution of the distortions to help the encoder skip checking the unnecessary modes. Besides, since the residual values can reflect the prediction result directly, they propose a method to skip some motion estimation operations according to the distribution of the residuals.Experimental results show that the proposed method can save about 77% of encoding time with only about a 4.1% bit-rate increase compared with HM16.4 anchor.

3   The Impact of the Inter Prediction Phase

While the previous compression standards used macroblocks of 16×16 luminance size and two 8×8 chrominance blocks, HEVC introduces the so-called CTUs (Coding Tree Unit), with a size selected by the encoder according to the degree of motion. A CTU consists of a luminance coding tree block (CTB) and the two corresponding chrominance CTBs, of size $L \times L$ such as $L = 16, 32$ or 64. Large CTU sizes generally provide better compression efficiency, but can also increase the complexity of the compression process. HEVC uses a tree partitioning structure. CTU is partitioned into CUs (Coding Units), of size form 8×8 to 32×32, each CU contain eventually a CB (Coding Block) of luminance and two CBs of chrominance. During the inter prediction process, a single motion data may not optimally represents the prediction of the CU in terms of RD cost as objects within this CU may have different motion vectors. CUs are therefore split into PUs to more accurately reflect the different motion vectors within the single block of pixels. In order to determine the best PU configuration, an intensive Motion Estimation (ME) process is undertaken. HEVC has to theoretically search through all the possible blocks in the search window which is commonly known as the full search algorithm so as to reach the best match in terms of minimum distortion and low number of bits to represent the encoded region. The inter prediction is done at the GOP level. As shown in the Fig. 1, a GOP contains an intra-encoded I frame followed by a varying number of P and B frames, the P frames are predicted unidirectionally from the previous frame and

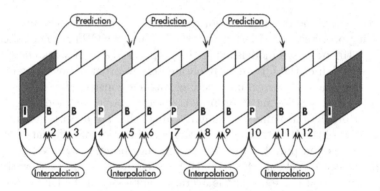

Fig. 1. A GOP containing I,P and B frames

the B frames are bidirectionally predicted from the previous frame and the one that follows. In this work, we have considered GOPs containing just P frames, started by an I frame as shown in the Fig. 2, the fact that the B frames are extremely expensive in terms of complexity.

Therefore, The main purpose of this study is to estimate the number of clock cycles consumed during video encoding by the inter prediction phase while varying the NP.

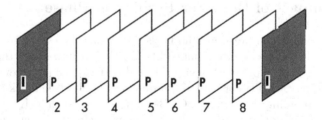

Fig. 2. The considered GOP

In fact, we adopt the approach that is based on profiling the HEVC using Valgrind Profiling Tool [8,9] in a Raspberry Pi 2 (RPI2) Card, Fig. 3 illustrate the video node used. Valgrind is a powerful profiling tool dedicated to Linux systems. The Valgrind tool provides the ability to compute the number of clock cycles consumed for each function executed by the CPU.

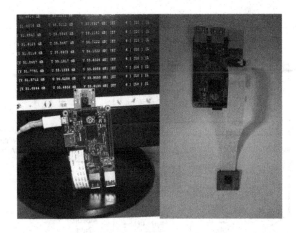

Fig. 3. Raspberry Pi 2 Card and the camera module

Such an approach will provide us an accurate overview of the number of the consumed clock cycles for each encoding phase of the HEVC Encoder. Then, according to Dai et al. [10], the energy consumed could be approached by:

$$E(N) = N * C * V_{dd}^2 + V_{dd} * (I_0 e^{\frac{V_{dd}}{nV_T}} (\frac{N}{f})) \tag{1}$$

Where N is the number of clock cycles, C is the average capacitance switched per cycle, V_{dd} is the supply voltage, I_0 is the leakage current, f is the clock speed, V_T is the thermal voltage and n a processor dependent constant.

In order to derive accurate results, we have carried out several compression operations considering five values of NP $(1, 3, 5, 7, 9)$, respectively under $QP = 10$ (Quantization Parameter) using the video sequence Akiyo in QCIF spacial resolution at 30 fps. We consider the HM-11.0 implementation to carry out encoding process under this configuration:

- **Partitioning:** Max CU size is 64×64 and Max Partition Depth is 4
- **Motion Search:** Fast Search algorithm is activated, Search Range is 64, Hardmard Motion Estimation is activated, Fast Decision for Merge RD (Rate-Distortion) cost (FDM) is activated

The configuration used can be optimized by considering Search Range (SR) as modelling parameter, which is in fact our ongoing investigations.

Profiling is achieved through the Valgrind tool under RPI2 Card to estimate the total number of clock cycles. With the use of Valgrind, we managed to gather the exact number of cycles of each type of operation in all functions of HEVC Encoder. Figure 4 presents the encoder's structure (i.e. prediction, transformation, quantization and entropy coding).

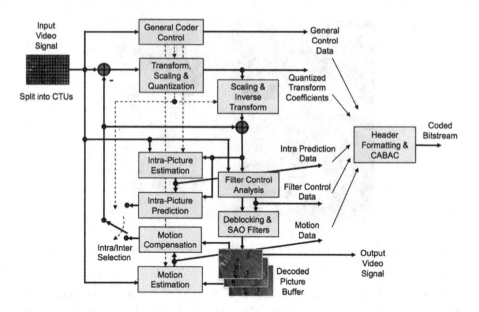

Fig. 4. HEVC Encoder Block diagram

Figure 5 shows the clock cycles consumption rate of the inter prediction phase, relative to the overall consumption of the encoder for each NP value. As could be seen, the rate varies between 21% and 24% for NP = 1 and NP = 9, an obvious variation since the increase in the number of P frames automatically generates an increase in the compression ratio and therefore an impact on the number of cycles consumed. On the other hand, we note that the rate stabilizes between NP = 5 and NP = 9, a rather interesting observation confirmed also by another sequence that will allow us to study the overall behaviour of the energy consumption of a HEVC encoder by considering the inter prediction with an average NP of 5.

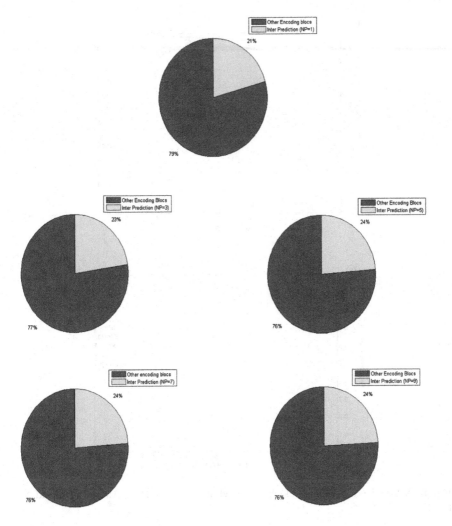

Fig. 5. The consumption rate of the number of clock cycles of the prediction phase

4   Modelling the Global Consumed Energy as a Function of NP

In this section, we performed several tests this time on the overall energy consumption of the HEVC encoder by always varying NP (1, 3, 5, 7, 9) and QP (10, 20, 30, 40, 50). The video sequences considered are: Akyio of QCIF spatial resolution and News of CIF spatial resolution at 30 fps.

Figure 6 illustrates the behaviour of the normalized consumed cycles during the video compression of the tested video sequences. We can notice that the number of clock cycles and thus the energy consumed, increases with the increase of the number of P frames. Indeed, the addition of a frame P to the GOP

(a)

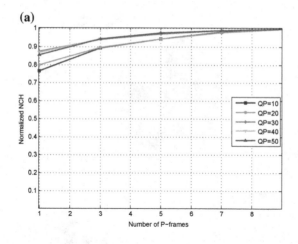

(b)

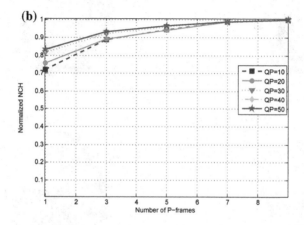

Fig. 6. Normalized number of clock cycles while varying NP for Akiyo Fig A and News Fig B

generates more complexity in the prediction, the fact that in each frame P, the Prediction Blocks (PB) seek to find the MV between the current block and the corresponding block, an operation which obviously leads to an increase in complexity. We also note that the number of clock cycles has exactly the same behaviour for each value of QP of the two video sequences.

Table 1. a and b values for each sequence and each QP value

Seq	Akiyo QCIF					News CIF				
QP	10	20	30	40	50	10	20	30	40	50
a & b values	a = 0.77	a = 0.79	a = 0.87	a = 0.87	a = 0.86	a = 0.73	a = 0.76	a = 0.82	a = 0.83	a = 0.84
	b = 0.12	b = 0.10	b = 0.06	b = 0.06	b = 0.07	b = 0.14	b = 0.12	b = 0.09	b = 0.08	b = 0.08

Figure 7 shows the behaviour of an increasing factor dependent on NP for each QP value of the video sequence Akiyo (due to the lack of space we didn't add figures for the Sequence News), we call it $\gamma(NP)$. This factor increases exponentially the consumed energy E, which reach its minimal at $NP = 1$ and its maximal at $NP = 9$ in this present work. Based on all the above mentioned arguments, we propose to model $\gamma(.)$ as follows:

$$\gamma(NP) = a * NP^b \tag{2}$$

Where a and b are coefficients dependent on the content obtained by minimizing the Root Mean Squared Error (RMSE) between the measured and the predicted

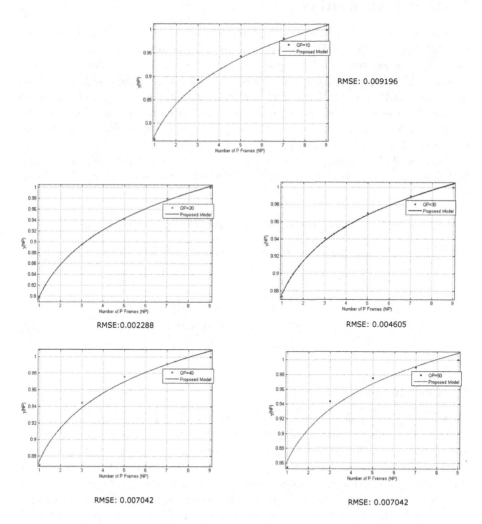

Fig. 7. Measured data and its approximation using the proposed model of Eq. 2 for Akiyo

data. In fact, RMSE is a quadratic scoring rule that also measures the average magnitude of the error. It's the square root of the average of squared differences between prediction and actual observation. The proposed model describe well the behaviour of the adopted configuration.

The corresponding values of a and b in Eq. 2 for each sequence and each QP value, is determined by curve fitting optimisation [11]. The results of this operation are reported by Fig. 7 and a and b values for each sequence are reported in Table 1. Points are the measured coefficients and the curves are the predicted ones by the proposed model of Eq. 2. As can be seen, the proposed model describes well the behaviour of the measured coefficients.

5   Model Application

In this section, we apply the proposed model on another video sequence using five different values of QP and NP. The model parameters a and b values of each sequence are set, as a first approach in this paper, to the average value for each QP. We report in Table 2 the Measured Value (MV), the Predicted Value (PV) and the Prediction Error (PE) for each configuration. MV is obtained by normalizing the measured number of clock cycles for each configuration in terms of QP and NP. PV is obtained using the proposed model in Eq. 2, for each of the pairs (QP, NP) listed in Table 2. As can be seen, the PE varies from 1% for to 3%, even if the model parameters values are not the optimal ones. As shown in Table 2, the average prediction error of the proposed model in Eq. 2 is about 1.6%.

Table 2. The tests results considering different configurations

Sequence	QP	NP	a	b	MV	PV	PE
Tennis CIF	10	5	0.75	0.13	0.93	0.94	1%
	40	7	0.85	0.07	0.97	0.98	1%
	30	3	0.82	0.08	0.90	0.88	2%
	20	7	0.77	0.11	0.95	0.98	3%
	30	5	0.82	0.08	0.93	0.94	1%

6   Conclusion

In this paper, we presented first a study of the impact of the number of P frames (NP) on the energy consumption of the inter prediction phase considering the HEVC video encoding standard, used in an energy constrained context such as the WVSN, independently of the QP parameter. We deduce, that from certain NP values the consumption rate stabilizes at 24% of the total energy budget. We proposed then an empirical parametric model to predict the overall energy consumed by the encoding phase, as function for NP. Finally, the proposed model was validated and applied considering another video sequence and proved its accuracy.

References

1. Sullivan, G.J., Ohm, J.-R., Han, W.-J., Wiegand, T.: Overview of the high efficiency video coding (hevc) standard. IEEE Trans. Circuits Syst. Video Technol. **22**(12), 1649–1668 (2012)
2. Alaoui-Fdili, O., Fakhri, Y., Corlay, P., Coudoux, F.-X., Aboutajdine, D.: Energy consumption analysis and modelling of a h. 264/avc intra-only based encoder dedicated to WVSNS. In: 2014 IEEE International Conference on Image Processing (ICIP), pp. 1189–1193. IEEE (2014)
3. Ahmad, J.J., Khan, H.A., Khayam,S.A.: Energy efficient video compression for wireless sensor networks. In: 2009 43rd Annual Conference on Information Sciences and Systems, pp. 629–634. IEEE (2009)
4. Ait-Beni-Ifit, A., Alaoui-Fdili, O., Corlay, P., Coudoux, F.-X., Aboutajdine, D.: Profiling and modelling of HEVC intra video encoder's energy consumption for next generation WVSNS. In: El Abbadi, A., Garbinato, B. (eds.) NETYS 2017. LNCS, vol. 10299, pp. 472–482. Springer, Cham (2017). https://doi.org/10.1007/978-3-319-59647-1_34
5. Alaoui-Fdili, O., Coudoux, F.-X., Fakhri, Y., Corlay, P., Aboutajdine, D.: Video sensor node energy preservation through dynamic adaptive video encoding parameters' values selection. Sustain. Comput. Inf. Syst. **18**, 34–44 (2018)
6. Vanne, J., Viitanen, M., Hämäläinen, T.D.: Efficient mode decision schemes for HEVC inter prediction. IEEE Trans. Circ. Syst. Video Technol. **24**(9), 1579–1593 (2014)
7. Zhang, J., Li, B., Li, H.: An efficient fast mode decision method for inter prediction in HEVC. IEEE Trans. Circuits Syst. Video Technol. **26**(8), 1502–1515 (2015)
8. Saab, F., Elhajj, I.H., Kayssi, A., Chehab, A.: Profiling of HEVC encoder. Electron. Lett. **50**(15), 1061–1063 (2014)
9. Seward, J., Nethercote, N., Weidendorfer, J.: Valgrind 3.3-Advanced Debugging and Profiling for GNU/Linux Applications. Network Theory Ltd., Bristol (2008)
10. Dai, R., Wang, P., Akyildiz, I.F.: Correlation-aware qos routing with differential coding for wireless video sensor networks. IEEE Trans. Multimedia **14**(5), 1469–1479 (2012)
11. Paul. Pilotte. Curve fitting toolbox, 17 December 2015

TPM Based Schema for Reinforcing Security in IBE's Key Manager

Zakaria Igarramen[1(✉)], Ahmed Bentajer[2], and Mustapha Hedabou[1,3]

[1] Cadi Ayyad University, ENSA of Safi, Safi, Morocco
z.igarramen@gmail.com, m.hedabou@gmail.com
[2] SIGL Laboratory, Abdelmalek Essaadi University,
ENSA of Tetouan, Tetouan, Morocco
a.bentajer@gmail.com
[3] University Mohammed VI Polytechnique, Benguerir, Morocco

Abstract. Confidentiality and secure deletion are among the most important security concerns about public cloud storage. Client-side cryptography is widely recognized as a robust approach for addressing these issues. However, managing keys related to encrypted files and their policies is a very challenging task for cloud storage's users. Studies have shown that even the most achieved solution, namely FADE design, suffers from a leak of cryptographic key due to authentication mechanism and a heavy key management infrastructure. In this paper, we propose a new design that brings the use of Identity Based Encryption (IBE) and Trusted Platform Module (TPM) together. The use of the IBE leads to ease the key management since the security of the entire system is mainly based only on one master key that will be in turn stored and managed securely trough the TPM facilities. The analysis of the prototype implementation of our design have demonstrated that it offers a significant value-added of security with a negligible overhead amount of computing time.

Keywords: TPM · IBE · Security · Confidentiality · Trusted computing

1 Introduction

In the last decade, the use of cloud-based services gained an expanding interest. For the general public, the cloud is materialized using storage solutions for storing, sharing and massive computation of data. Outsourcing sensitive data to a Cloud Service Provider (CSP) removes the burden of maintaining internal infrastructures. Customers only need to pay the allocated resources.

Therefore, outsourcing sensitive data storage to a third party manager raises many security issues [1–3]. It is commonly agreed that client-side cryptography is a good alternative to reduce the risk of data confidentiality leakage [1, 4, 10, 14]. However, it is the client who must securely manage the security decryption key.

© Springer Nature Switzerland AG 2019
C. Attiogbé et al. (Eds.): MEDI 2019 Workshops, CCIS 1085, pp. 146–153, 2019.
https://doi.org/10.1007/978-3-030-32213-7_11

Therefore, when data need to be shared with a group of users, maintaining the security of decryption keys become more difficult even if a key manager system (KMS) is set up [12].

Using ID-based cryptography (IBE) leverage this issue since the Private Key Generator (PKG) compute the corresponding private key (d_{ID}) each time the user needs it for decryption process [1,8]. As, the PKG knows all privates keys it may allow a global key escrow if it is compromised. Thus, this requires more trust to the PKG since the confidentiality of data is based on the secret of the master secret (msk) key used to compute the d_{ID}.

In this paper, we describe a model based on the use of Trusted Platform Module (TPM) for improving the security of PKG and its msk. Our model relies on a decentralized PKG used in conjunction with TPM for managing the security of the msk.

The originality of our model is double benefits. First, it increases the confidentiality of the msk, since it remains encrypted when it is not used by the PKG. Second, processes that need to secure secrets, such as digital signing, can be made more secure with a TPM. For example, if at boot time it is determined that the server is not trustworthy because of unexpected changes in configuration, access to the msk can be blocked until the issue is remedied. Besides the prototype can work atop any cloud storage solution since no engineering changes are needed on the CSP side.

The reminder of this paper is as follow. The second section presents a background of key management security issues in cloud storage and IBE. The third section presents TPM. In the fourth section, we present our design, which will be discussed in the fifth section. Finally, we come-up with our conclusions and assumptions.

2 Background

Cloud storage confidentiality issues have been discussed in many research articles [1,3,4,14], the problem is that when customers outsource their data they lose control over them. Many cryptographic solutions have been proposed to bypass this issue, most of them are client-side encryption based [1,3,4]. The aim is to encrypt data before outsourcing them and delegate the cryptographic keys to a trusted third party. Perlman [14] proposed the Ephemerizer that securely delete data after an expiration time through ephemeral key. Data are encrypted by an ephemeral key managed by the Ephemerizer which destroy it at time expiration, as a result data remain unreadable. Tang et al. [10] extend the Ephemerizer solution, in FADE each key corresponds to a combination, using logical OR/AND, of atomic policies that can be revoked.

However, FADE focused more on secure deletion operations on cloud and the PKG's security has been almost not discussed. Ranjan et al. [5] proved that the PKG can present key escrow. A malicious user may intercept a policy P_i and its corresponding private key.

2.1   ID-Based Encryption

IBE is a public key cryptosystem that does not rely on a Certificate Authority (CA). The idea was first proposed by Adi Shamir in 1984 [6]. The system enables any pair of users to communicate securely with no need for certificates and CA deployment. This means that each entity, which has access to public parameters of the system, may generate a public key generated from publicly identifiable information denoted (ID) in order to simplify cryptographic key management. To get the d_{ID}, the user must authenticates him self to PKG through his ID. In 2001, Boneh and Franklin [8] proposed a full scheme that achieve IBE based on bi-linear function defined in elliptic curves such as Weil and Tate Pairing [7].

The IBE scheme as proposed by Boneh and Franklin uses four algorithm:

- **Setup:** Run once by the PKG to generate the whole system parameters (msk, the Master Public Key (mpk) and $params$). While $params$ and mpk are made available for the public the msk is kept secret and used to compute d_{ID}
- **KeyGen:** Used by the PKG in order to compute the d_{ID}
- **Encrypt:** Used by the entity willing to encrypt data using its ID
- **Decrypt:** Used by the entity willing to decrypt data using the d_{ID}

Boneh and Franklin scheme is based on a bilinear pairing e on G_1, G_T and two hash function $H_1 : 0, 1^* \rightarrow G_1 \setminus \{\infty\}$ and $G_T \rightarrow \{0, 1\}^l$ where l is the bi-length of plain text. The PBC is a free portable C [9] library allowing the rapid prototyping of Pairing-Based Cryptosystems. It is designed to be the backbone of implementations of PBC providing elliptic curve generation, elliptic curve arithmetic and pairing computation.

Nowadays, IBE is widely implemented in different applications including emails, due to its simplified key management. A commercial implementation of IBE is published by Voltage Security to enable enterprises to send and receive secure communications.

2.2   Trsuted Platform Module

TPM is a cryptoprocessor promoted by the Trusted Computing Group (TCG) to promote Trusted Computing Platform (TCP). Computers that incorporate TPM can provide cryptographic-based function. TPM (Fig. 1) is a chip that contain a cryptographic co-processor, secure memory, I/O components and other components. It also implements a validated FIPS key size generation for computing digital signature key (512 to 2024 bits). The TPM chip becomes part of new released PC motherboard. The chip is able to store an Endorsement Key (EK) that identify the TPM (Thus device authentication). The chip is tamper resistant through its multiple physical security mechanism. Besides, the chip enables platform integrity, this is done during the boot process, the firmware and operating system components (integrity measurement) are measured and stored in the TPM $\rightarrow$ BIOS $\rightarrow$ BootLoader $\rightarrow$ OS $\rightarrow$ Application. The integrity measurements can be used as evidence for how a system started. Once we need to attest the platform, a trusted third party sends a token to the platform. The platform takes both the ML and token encrypted by the TPM's EK and send the encrypted information to the third party which decrypt it using EK's corresponding public key (thus ensuring authentication) and checks the integrity of data (ML and Token) to verify that the configuration it deems trusted.

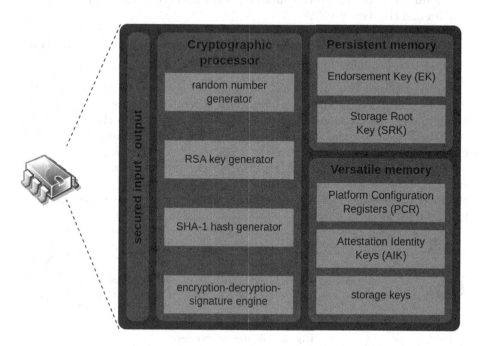

Fig. 1. Components of a Trusted Platform Module complying with the TPM version 1.2 standard

3 Proposed Design

In this section, we present our design for secure deletion and secure key management through IBE and TPM. To encrypt a file the user generates a data key (AES-256 CBC mode) and uses his ID as a public key to encrypt it. For the PKG, once the **Setup** algorithm executed, the msk is encrypted by the TPM and kept secret until a user ask for a d_{ID}. The fully IBE client-side cryptography is described in [1]. In this paper we focus more on PKG security and its interaction with TPM (Fig. 3).

We note that we are still developing the code based on *TrouSerS's C API* [11]. In order to test our design, we have used an embedded Linux platform with TPM chip. We wrote small Bash files in order to enable the PKG interact with the TPM.

3.1 Architectural Solution

In this section, we present our secure deletion model based on IBE. Each file is associated to the ID of the user. The file is encrypted with a data key

(256-bit AES key), and the data key is further encrypted by IBE mechanism. The components of our design are:

- **Cloud user:** Generates the data key, performs cryptographic operations on data and the data key.
- **Cloud storage service:** A non-trusted third party storage provider
- **PKG:** A server with TPM integrated. It generates the d_{ID} and performs cryptographic operation through TPM for the msk

In the **Upload** (Fig. 2) process, the user does not need to interact with the PKG, he executes the **POST** function which generates the data key K and IBE public key D_{id}. **At a second stage, the function encrypts the file F with K ($Enc\{F\}_K$) then the K with D_{id} ($Enc\{F\}D_{id}$) and upload data to the cloud storage.**

For the **Download** process (Fig. 3), the user get the data from the cloud storage, authenticates himself at the PKG and asks for the d_{ID}. At this stage, the PKG will ask the TPM to unseal the msk in order to compute the d_{ID} then it will be resealed.

Fig. 2. File upload process

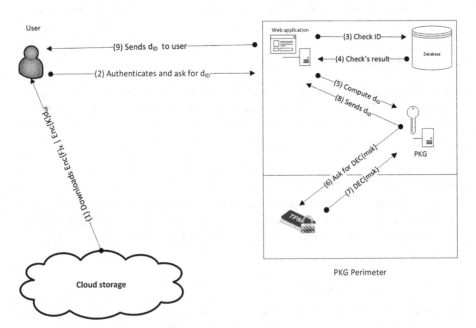

Fig. 3. File download process

3.2   Securing the Msk

In upload process, the user does not need to interact with the PKG (Fig. 2). In Download process, the user authenticates him self at the PKG which verify the authorization and grant access to a computation of d_{ID}. At this stage, PKG asks the TPM to unseal the *msk* then it will be resealed once the computation done:

```
# tpm_unsealdata −i  msk.enc −o  msk −z
```

Experiments has been conducted to measure the running time of plain upload/download and cryptographic operations between the TPM and the PKG. We dropped the overhead cost time of cryptographic operations between TPM and PKG since it was almost zero. The only overhead cost time is related to client-side cryptography using IBE mechanism.

4   Discussion

First, we talk about prerequisites that we have used to test our design. The **tcsd** daemon from the *trouSerS* API must be running and *tpm-tools* installed in Linux distribution. We used a well-known password (20 bytes of 0s) for owner and Storage Root Key (SRK) in order to facilitate the test environment (so that it can be non-interactive), for this purpose the command **tpm_takeownership -y -z** is used. However, other password should be used in production environment. For IBE client-side cryptography we used the same design as described in [1].

Tests are conducted using a computer with an i5 1.6 GHZ processor and 16 GB RAM. Experiments are performed on files of the following sizes: 10 KB, 1 MB, 5MB, 10 MB and 15 MB.

Once the Setup algorithm executed and global parameters generated the *msk* is sealed by TPM:

```
# tpm_sealdata −i  msk −o  msk.enc −z
```

We measured the overhead cost time of our design for download (Table 1) operations on files of different sizes (Upload operation measurements have been dropped since they do not require interactions with TPM). The measurements concerns the cryptographic operations using IBE design and operations for unsealing the *msk*. For sealing operation we dropped the measurements since it does not affect our system.

The experiment have proved that the overhead cost time of our IBE design with TPM does not imply a remarkable overload time, and that the transfer of the plains files remains a dominant factor. Also, the design enable to reinforce the PKG security with a zero-time cost. Our model leverage the burden of key management infrastructure and reinforce the confidentiality of the IBE PKG. By using the TPM we add a new security layer with a zero overhead cost time. Also, the use of TPM enables more trust in the service of PKG and resists to software attacks.

Table 1. Proposed design download operation

File size	Plain download	Design download	Decryption	Key generation	TPM unseal	Overhead
100 KB	1.339	1.3929	0.0454	0.0085	≈0.0	4.03%
1 MB	2.417	2.4728	0.0473	0.0085	≈0.0	2.31%
5 MB	7.334	7.4504	0.1079	0.0085	≈0.0	1.59%
10 MB	13.152	13.3608	0.2003	0.0085	≈0.0	1.59%
15 MB	21.089	21.3842	0.2867	0.0085	≈0.0	1.40%

Security: Our model makes it possible to keep the confidentiality of the outsourced data, since they are encrypted on the client side. So, it is difficult for malicious users or the storage service provider to have access to these data even in case of a data leak or system disaster. The nature of hardware-based cryptography ensures that the information stored in hardware is better protected from external software attacks [13].

Besides, our model addresses the problem tied to Key Management by using the TPM to seal the *msk*, using hardware cryptography the performance is increased because the host system does not support encryption operations. Also, it protects against the most common risks, such as startup attacks, malicious code and force attacks. Unlike software security that shares host resources and it is vulnerable to force attack since malicious users can access the memory of the host and reset the counter of decryption attempts.

5   Conclusion and Perspectives

In this paper we surveyed the security concerns of PKG in IBE. We proposed a design for reinforcing the security of PKG. Compared to traditional PKI, the use of IBE does not imply a repository of public keys and simplify the key managements and there is no need to request certificate of the public key every time for an establishment of connection. Our solution takes benefits from the use of TPM that protect the *msk* from corruption and unauthorized access by sealing it when it is not used by the PKG, also it enables the authentication capabilities inherent to TPM, so only the PKG is able to get the unsealed *msk*.

As a perspective, we aim to continue the development of our design with *TrouSerS's C API*. Also we aim to enable the integrity check function provided by the TPM through setting up a model for Root of Trust Reporting (RTR).

References

1. Bentajer, A., Hedabou, M., Abouelmehdi, K., Igarramen, Z., El Fezazi, S.: An IBE-based design for assured deletion in cloud storage. Cryptologia 1–12 (2019). https://doi.org/10.1080/01611194.2018.1549123
2. Wheeler, A., Winburn, M.: Privacy challenges. In: Wheeler, A., Winburn, M. (eds.) (Cloud Storage Security) Computer Science Reviews and Trends 2015, Chap. 3, pp. 57–74. Elsevier, Boston (2015). https://doi.org/10.1016/B978-0-12-802930-5.00003-4

3. Sun, X.: Critical security issues in cloud computing: a survey. In: 2018 IEEE 4th International Conference on Big Data Security on Cloud (BigDataSecurity), IEEE International Conference on High Performance and Smart Computing, (HPSC) and IEEE International Conference on Intelligent Data and Security (IDS), Omaha, pp. 216–221. IEEE (2018) https://doi.org/10.1109/BDS/HPSC/IDS18.2018.00053

4. Rajeswari, S., Kalaiselvi, R.: Survey of data and storage security in cloud computing. In: IEEE International Conference on Circuits and Systems (ICCS), Thiruvananthapuram, pp. 76–81. IEEE (2017). https://doi.org/10.1109/ICCS1.2017.8325966

5. Ranjan, A. K., Kumar, V., Hussain, M.: Security analysis of cloud storage with access control and file assured deletion (FADE). In: Second International Conference on Advances in Computing and Communication Engineering, Dehradun, pp. 453–458. IEEE (2015). https://doi.org/10.1109/ICACCE.2015.10

6. Shamir, A.: Identity-based cryptosystems and signature schemes. In: Blakley, G.R., Chaum, D. (eds.) CRYPTO 1984. LNCS, vol. 196, pp. 47–53. Springer, Heidelberg (1985). https://doi.org/10.1007/3-540-39568-7_5

7. Hankerson, D., Menezes, A.J., Vanstone, S.: Guide to Elliptic Curve Cryptography, 1st edn. Springer, New York (2004). https://doi.org/10.1007/b97644

8. Boneh, D., Franklin, M.: Identity-based encryption from the Weil pairing. In: Kilian, J. (ed.) CRYPTO 2001. LNCS, vol. 2139, pp. 213–229. Springer, Heidelberg (2001). https://doi.org/10.1007/3-540-44647-8_13

9. PBC Library. https://crypto.stanford.edu/pbc/about.html. Accessed 2 Mar 2019

10. Tang, Y., Lee, P.P.C., Lui, J.C.S., Perlman, R.: FADE: secure overlay cloud storage with file assured deletion. In: Jajodia, S., Zhou, J. (eds.) SecureComm 2010. LNICST, vol. 50, pp. 380–397. Springer, Heidelberg (2010). https://doi.org/10.1007/978-3-642-16161-2_22

11. The open-source TCG Software Stack. http://trousers.sourceforge.net/. Accessed 24 Feb 2019

12. Barker, E., Barker, W., Burr, W., Polk, W., Smid, M.: Recommendation for Key Management, Part 2: Best Practices for Key Management Organization. NIST Special Publication. NIST (2005). https://doi.org/10.6028/NIST.SP.800-57p2

13. Regenscheid, A.: Platform Firmware Resiliency Guidelines. NIST Special Publication 800-193. NIST (2018). https://doi.org/10.6028/NIST.SP.800-193

14. Perlman, P.: The Ephemerizer: making data disappear. Technical report. Sun Microsystems, Inc., Mountain View (2005)

Towards Distributed Learning in Internet of Things. Air Quality Monitoring Use Case

Lazrak Noussair[1(✉)], Jesualdo Tomás Fernández Breis[2], Jihad Zahir[1],
and Hajar Mousannif[1]

[1] Computer Systems Engineering Laboratory (LISI),
Faculty of Science Semlalia, Cadi Ayyad University, Marrakesh, Morocco
lazrak.noussair@gmail.com
[2] Department of Informatics and Systems, Faculty of Computer Science,
Campus de Espinardo, University of Murcia, Murcia, Spain

Abstract. The Internet of Things (IoT) is becoming a buzz word due to the extensive application of it. It can be found anywhere nowadays, Healthcare, Smart cities, Smart energy, smart buildings and so on. The internet of thing has been a subject of improvement in terms of the price, size and persistence, but one of the main challenges in understanding IoT is in dealing with the device and data heterogeneities and establishing the interoperability between devices, information, and services built on top of it. Therefore, Ontologies can bring the change we are aiming in establishing a standard inter-devices communication and enable interoperability in m2m communication that allows data and data semantics to be described in application-independent ways.

Keywords: Ontologies · Machine learning · Distributed discovery · Internet of Things · Interoperability

1 Introduction

The world nowadays knows an unprecedented use of IoT devices as a manner of getting the right information at the right moment, this particular field have known various changes, innovation in terms of size, price, accuracy and efficiency. Nowadays we talk about billions of sensors all around the globe thanks to the emergence of the low-cost sensors. Therefore, designing and manufacturing low-cost sensors is an urgency, ranging in types from stationary to portable ones. However, the accuracy and completeness of their data is under questioning. At best, low-cost sensors can provide air quality monitoring of specific pollutants. Yet, without the ability to conduct deeper air quality data analysis and advanced analysis, the accuracy of the low-cost air quality sensors pollutant readings cannot be relied in general. There is also no promise that low-cost air quality sensors (as an example) can distinguish between the different types of key air pollutants, which is just as critical as having the ability to provide the accurate levels of each air pollutant. For instance, an overall AQI is good but it's not that good if you take a deeper look into the AQI components. if fine particulate matter (PM) is monitored but not ozone (O3), and O3 is high but the sensor says everything

© Springer Nature Switzerland AG 2019
C. Attiogbé et al. (Eds.): MEDI 2019 Workshops, CCIS 1085, pp. 154–159, 2019.
https://doi.org/10.1007/978-3-030-32213-7_12

(PM) is ok, then there can be unexpected health issues, especially for those already sensitive to ozone, like children.

In this paper, we suggest that sensors can be inter-connected to reach a level of understanding, sharing knowledge between entities and provide better data.

IoT have surly marked a big change in our modern-day life, since they are the middle ware between real and virtual world as they convert the physical world to more digital one. Its impact is mostly noticeable in the case of demotics, where the home can be equipped with multiple low-power devices to provide new services. But in this paper, we will focus more on environmental sensing devices, for instance, Air quality index. In fact, there have been several efforts on environmental monitoring using Wireless Sensor Network (WSN). The initial efforts of using ICT based technology for climate moni-toring system that monitors parameters like temperature and humidity on a mobile device is discussed in [1]. The deployment and networking and routing issues for similar microclimate monitoring systems is discussed in [2]. In an earlier work, we reviewed different challenges and opportunities that are facing the internet of things in environ-mental monitoring process [3], in [4], authors discuss the importance of technologies and architecture for urban IoT and a proof of concept monitoring system for a smart city.

But as good as it sounds, it still faces tremendous challenges when it comes to the data processing and data storage. As we go throughout the applications of IoT we notice that they serve the same purpose but they have widely different architectures, different services and different technologies. Many applications interacting with the sensors, store their data in their own proprietary format. In other words, making their own application isolated from others and cannot directly interact with each other. Variances in the data format lead to interoperability issues between the IoT architec-tures. But still, the reason it to keep track of environmental conditions and provide the right information at the right moment. Hence, if we have a common ground for the monitoring process, it will absolutely increase the pertinence and efficiently of the monitoring. Much work has to be done in order to ensure the compatibility and enable reuse of architecture, and, reuse of knowledge.

One way to establish this interoperability is using a semantic-based technology to annotate all the information shared by the different platforms. In this paper, we suggest a full-fledged ontology that spans across the necessities for the observations produced by resources in an Air Quality Monitoring Application. We aim to create an ontology that globalize the needs of every IoT device. We include also machine learning parameters for a better knowledge sharing experience. We stress out that this is an extension of our work on Air Quality Monitoring using machine learning and statistical methods.

2   Related Work

Research initiatives and standardization activities in areas allied to the IoT vision have mainly focused on sensor descriptions and observation data modeling. For instance, The Semantic Sensor Network (SSN) ontology, created by W3C delivers a standard for modeling sensor devices, sensor platforms, knowledge of the environment and observations [5, 6]. SSN allows storing and archiving and establishing a common ground of inter-connected IoT devices. Also, Semantic Sensor Observation Service lvl

(SemSOS) provides a rich semantic knowledge ground while retaining the standard SOS specifications/service interactions. This standard goes far in offering interoperability between repositories of heterogeneous sensor data and applications that use this data. Many of these applications, however, are ill equipped at handling raw sensor data as provided by SOS and require actionable knowledge of the environment in order to be practically useful [7].

The Smart Appliances REFerence (SAREF) ontology[1] have gone far in solving the interoperability between IoT devices, it could be found in home automation project as well as energy efficiency-based projects, it is built over the concept of the device – function – command. Each device offers functions through associated commands. A function is presented to the network through a Service, which specifies the input and output parameters.

Even if the use of these standards can deliver a "shared-ground" oriented approach in IoT inter-communication, but the interoperability is far from being solved and a semantic IoT architecture is required to provide interoperability between connected IoT systems.

3   Proposed Architecture

Our aim is to establish a common model structure that detail various concepts and provide abstractions of the components and their attributes. This section defines the main abstractions and concepts that underlies the IoT domain and describes the relationships between them.

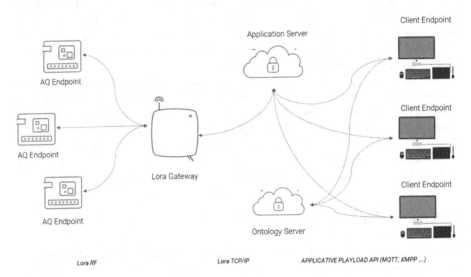

Fig. 1. Proposed IoT architecture with Semantic Gateway

---

[1] http://saref.linkeddata.es.

Figure 1 illustrates our proposed architecture in which we provide a semantic gateway. For the inter IoT communication, Low-power wide area networking technology offers long-range communication between IoT devices, which enables new types of services. LoRaWAN is arguably the most adopted. It promises ubiquitous connectivity in outdoor IoT applications, while keeping network structures and management simple [8]. We use two servers, one for data storage and data preprocessing, and the other one for the ontology. We adopted a distributed architecture for processing optimization and collective performance. In this paper, we will focus more on the ontology and machine learning part.

To enable shared knowledge in our IoT project, we suggest a set of ontologies that model entity, resources and IoT services. These ontologies will represent a high-level model that references and builds upon existing vocabularies. The concepts related to other relevant domains, such as sensors, observation and measurement and location, can be included from other ontologies. Where appropriate, properties are included to allow linking the proposed ontologies to external ontologies; for example, the meaning of retrieved measurement, in our case, the AQI (Air Quality Index). Also, other external ontologies like the global Geo Names ontology where the given location is more fully described. This enables reusability of ontologies and fosters modularity.

4 Device Model

Our Device Model have certain aspects that need to be taken into consideration. For example, when one needs to know about the location of a device or the features of interest that data is available for. The OWL-DL representation has been used to define the entity model. The entity ontology is available at https://noussair.com/ontologies/DeviceModel.owl. A diagram of the main attributes in the device model is shown in Fig. 2.

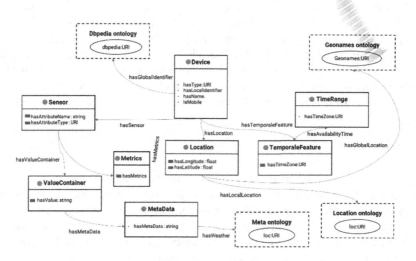

Fig. 2. Device Model

As shown is Fig. 2 above, a device entity can have certain features, which include TimeFeatures, Location and sensors which is a subclass of the device. A sensor also has its own features including value container in which we will store all features of interests which the sensor can provide. Each value container has the literal value specification (value), which is connected to metadata information. The metadata information can, for instance, be used to specify the units of measurement for the value, its timestamp or a notion of its quality. Also Metrics Feature is used for machine learning reasons, to be more specific, storing the metrics from the batching learning process that have been calculated by other devices, so the metrics and parameters are communicated with other (new) sensors. The main prediction model used in this study is Random forest. In a previous work, we reviewed machine learning models in air quality index prediction based on some of the AQI features provided by the device (NO2, SO2, O3, PM10). And the results show that Random Forests (RF) performed well on our 2 years data set compared to the other prediction models shown in the table below (Table 1):

Table 1. Prediction models performance

Method	MSE	RMSE	MAE	R2
KNN	302.413	17.390	8.285	0.764
SVM	1833.860	42.824	32.566	−0.433
RF	*60.147*	*7.775*	*4.197*	*0.953*
ANN	477.616	21.854	13.445	0.627
MLR	587.216	24.233	16.221	0.541

The results of Temporal features are specified through time zone and through object properties to the time range (in terms of start and end time) and date range (start and end date) concepts. The location is defined in terms of the geographical coordinates (hasLatitude, hasLongitude, has Altitude). The location concept also connects our ontology with another external one (hasGlobalLocation) and local location (hasLocalLocation) ontologies. The local location ontology is used mainly to track also inside the buildings, streets and places that are not covered by the global location which links the entity to existing high level location ontologies such as GeoNames, which provides toponyms or place names for cities, districts, countries and universities.

5   Conclusion

In this work, we presented an approach enabling the distributed discovery in IoT using ontologies and machine learning. We proposed a set of ontologies to represent a standardization in D2D interoperability and information exchange.

As shown in Fig. 3, the ontology allows us to get better insight within the data communicated by the device, including Air Quality Index insights, as well as providing other insights about the location, features, prediction metrics.

Fig. 3. Final results

This paper introduces a modular IoT ontology designed to enable the interoperability between IoT devices. After a presentation of its modules, an instantiation of our ontology is presented in an air quality monitoring use case. The main IoT core domain is also connected to two other ontologies to enrich the knowledge discovery within the data retrieved by the device. For instance, Air Quality Index ontology provides the meaning of the observation retrieved from the sensors. Also, Geonames ontology provides more insights about the location of the device based on GPS coordinates.

The main reason behind using ontologies and distributed machine learning is reusing the machine learning model's parameters and extracting more insights from the data provided by a single device. Although initial results are promising, our proposed ontology still need to be improved to include more device features, services, actuators. It will be a subject of improvement if our future work.

References

1. Ito, M., Katagiri, Y., Ishikawa, M., Tokuda, H.: Airy notes: an experiment of microclimate monitoring in shinjuku gyoen garden. In: 4th International Conference on Networked Sensing Systems, INSS (2007)
2. Díaz, M., Martín, C., Rubio, B.: State-of-the-art, challenges, and open issues in the integration. J. Network Comput. Appl. **67**, 99–117 (2016)
3. Noussair, L., Jihad, Z., Hajar, M.: Responsive cities and data gathering: challenges and opportunities. In: Conference: The 3rd International Conference in Smart Cities Applications, Tetouan (2018)
4. Zanella, A., Bui, N., Castellani, A., Vangelista, L., Zorzi, M.: Internet of things for smart cities. IEEE Internet Things J. **1**(1), 22–32 (2014)
5. Lefort, L., et al.: Semantic Sensor Network XG Final Report. w3c (2011)
6. Comptona, M., et al.: Web semantics: science, services and agents. J. Web Semant. **17**, 25–32 (2012)
7. Sheth, A., Henson, C.A., Pschorr, J.K., Sheth, A., Thirunarayan, K.: Collaborative Technologies and Systems (2009)
8. Adelantado, F., et al.: Understanding the limits of LoRaWAN. IEEE Commun. Mag. **55**(9), 34–40 (2017)

Workshop on Security and Privacy
in Models and Data

Workshop on securiTy and pRivacy in moDEls aNd daTa (TRIDENT)

Workshop Description

Nowadays, security and privacy are two relevant aspects for every system relying on software, constantly gaining momentum in an overwhelming set of domains, such as healthcare. Several domains are increasingly adopting cloud-based applications as core business, becoming more and more complex and generating federated architectures. In this sense, several technological challenges related to security and privacy are stemming from these domains; while some of these challenges have been discovered and solved, others are evolving, such as the traditional securing applications [1], the insider threat problem [2], or new legislations.

From a software development point of view, new approaches such as Privacy By Design [3] or Blockchains are gaining momentum, providing benefits but also implying trade-offs. Along these lines, the analysis on how these technologies are solving specific issues and the benefits that they provide is an ongoing debate at research level.

From a legal point of view, legislations are seen as optional by several software developers, even though their business impact is increasing.

This TRIDENT workshop is focused on security and privacy in models and data, and the overall aim of this workshop is to address a broad range of issues related to security and privacy issues within models and data in a broad range of domains.

Organization

TRIDENT Chairs

Xabier Larrucea	Tecnalia, Spain
Muhammad Barham	IBM Research Labs Haifa, Israel

International Program Committee

Cristina Alcaraz	University of Malaga, Spain
Eunate Arana	Biocruces, Spain
Muhammad Barham	IBM Research Labs Haifa, Israel
Alberto Berreteaga	Tecnalia, Spain
Ilio Catallo	FCSR Fondazione Centro San Raffaele, Spain
Gareth Howells	Metrarc, UK
Xabier Larrucea	Tecnalia, Spain
Borja López	Biocruces, Spain
Andrea Micheletti	HSR, Italy

Klaus McDonald-Maier   Metrarc, UK
Juri Papay   IT Innovation, University of Southampton, UK
Brian Pickering   IT Innovation, University of Southampton, UK
Matthias Pocs   Stelar, Germany
Tony Schaffel   Lancs, Spain
Mike Surridge   IT Innovation, University of Southampton, UK

Semi-real-time Hash Comparison for Detecting Intrusions Using Blockchain

Oscar Lage Serrano$^{(\boxtimes)}$ ⓘ, Santiago de Diego de Diego$^{(\boxtimes)}$ ⓘ,
Iñaki Seco$^{(\boxtimes)}$ ⓘ, and Xabier Larrucea$^{(\boxtimes)}$ ⓘ

Tecnalia, Parque tecnologico de Bizkaia, Derio, Spain
{oscar.lage, santiago.dediego, inaki.seco,
xabier.larrucea}@tecnalia.com

Abstract. This paper proposes an extensible Blockchain-Based Industrial Anomaly Detection (BIAD) system for industrial scenarios. This approach is to use Blockchain to prevent a set of attacks at semi-real time by comparing logs. Besides, this solution regards attacker firmware modifications following the same comparison principle within the same infrastructure.

Keywords: Blockchain · Intrusion detection system · Critical infrastructure · Industrial systems

1 Introduction

The proliferation of the smart world which is being currently experienced, using thousands of smart devices, has not been achieved exempt from a price. Smart 'things' make our lives much easier, but this concept comes with a frightening and continuous consideration: what the impact would be when the smart devices are hacked. Term 'When' implies that each smart device is either not yet hacked or is already hacked. Therefore, the important is the impact of the attack and how it can be reduced, or even eliminate it, to the minimum possible.

Cyber-attacks are carried out mainly using Internet, as is shown in [1]. Some malicious software and programs such as viruses and worms are used by cyber-attackers for targeting public, national, private and individual points of interest. Years ago, fears in addressing cyber-attacks entailed the prevention of website hacking. However, nowadays, a cyber-attack may cost human lives, if for example a Critical INfrastructure (CIN) collapses following a stealthy cyber-attack.

Once the society is becoming increasingly reliant on CIN, new technologies are needed to increase detection and response capabilities. Detecting and responding to cyber-attacks by a highly motivated, trained and well-funded attacker has been proven highly challenging. One of the most vulnerable and high-impact CIN is the Smart Grid since the collapse of an energy production utility may cause human lives, millions of euros, denial of a very important and common good such as energy and days or even months of recovering.

Smart Grid is considered as the next-generation power system, which promises resilience, sustainability and efficiency to the energy CIN, as is written in [2]. As soon

© Springer Nature Switzerland AG 2019
C. Attiogbé et al. (Eds.): MEDI 2019 Workshops, CCIS 1085, pp. 165–179, 2019.
https://doi.org/10.1007/978-3-030-32213-7_13

as the smart grid paradigm is reaching every house and building, the potential of attracting cyber-attackers towards getting access to the underlying systems and networks is getting considerably larger.

According to the European Network and Information Security Agency (ENISA) [3] "A cyber security incident to power grids could be defined as any adverse event that can impact the confidentiality, integrity or availability of the Information and Communication Technology (ICT) systems supporting the different processes of the organisations involved in the well-functioning of the power system, including all its domains (e.g., markets, operation of the distribution or transmission grid, customers, etc.)". In the light of the aforementioned incidents it is apparent that the Smart Grid concept brings big challenges and initiatives across both industry and academia, in which the security topic emerges to be a critical concern.

Europe is developing new strategies to confront today's sophisticated cyber-attacks in Smart Grid infrastructure. Recently, cyber-attack incidents have been dangerously perpetrated, like in December 2015, when a Ukraine power grid was attacked and electricity knocked out for 225,000 people, as described in [4]. Most of the current security solutions, which are focused on early detection, neglect the power that analytics and visualisation could bring in the today's Smart Grid arsenal. In addition, advanced forensics, subject to preserve user privacy, are being developed but the trade-off between forensic effectiveness and user privacy has not yet been addressed. Besides, current forensic tools may suffer from several attacks in their log and event files, making the forensic investigation unreliable infeasible. Consequently, an attacker is able to launch an attack, erase his logs and escape without leaving any traces. Effective solutions in capturing attacks traces and so ensuring forensic investigation content are still required. To make it worse, recent cyber security incidents have been recorded in Smart Grids all over the world, but the exact technical details of these attacks are still not clear by all Smart Grid operators. For instance, the malware Stuxnet [5] was categorised as an Advanced Persistent Threat (APT) which proposed to exploit zero-day vulnerabilities in Smart Grid control systems known as Supervisory Control And Data Acquisition (SCADA). Nevertheless, the details of the attack are not still known to most of the energy operators, although they could encounter similar attacks in the future. The main problem of the consortia and the organisations, gathered to become a common source of information, is the lack of trust [6].

This paper is the result of applying Blockchain to an industrial environment in order to provide additional functionalities to the original system. Blockchain is a very suitable infrastructure to achieve several security requirements, which are almost impossible to meet with traditional systems. These security requirements are confidentiality, integrity, availability, non-repudiation and traceability, as well as a solid access control. Having a single infrastructure able to preserve natively these requirements is, without any doubt, promising.

This approach uses Blockchain as a distributed industrial anomaly detection (BIAD) which allows us to detect incoming attacks efficiently. One of the advantages of this approach is that it enables the detection of new attacks at the same time they take place, while common IDS are not able to reach this ratio of detection. In addition, they have other additional drawbacks, being one of these that they constitute a Single Point of Failure (SPoF), unless you apply proper redundancy, which is not always simple, considering that these IDS systems would need to be constantly synchronized. Guaranteeing integrity, non-repudiation and traceability of different events is quite complicated with traditional IDS. However, Blockchain overcomes these availability issues by default as well as keeping traceability and non-repudiation of these events. Another benefit is the use of ciphers over the data, so the events are kept confidential. Furthermore, it is crucial to reach a single view of the data in these scenarios, which is one the strong points of Blockchain infrastructures.

Additionally, as it is said before, Blockchain represents an anti-tampering infrastructure, so considering that the first step for an attacker when breaking into a system is to delete every evidence of presence, it is necessary a backup trusted ledger where it possible verify what is happening.

All these additional functionalities are going to be fully discussed in the subsequent sections, but focusing on Blockchain as a detection tool, Smart Contracts are able to perform semi-real-time analysis to detect real-time attacks if being able to define accurate alerts for different attack vectors. In the next section, different alerts will be presented, which can allow us to achieve this objective, all of them using Smart Contracts.

Another important aspect comes with forensics. By using Blockchain in an industrial environment, sysadmins are getting a useful forensic tool which can help them to understand what happened if there was an attack. In this way, IDS and forensic capabilities have been combined within the same infrastructure.

Differently from other works proposing Blockchain as an IDS, like the ones further explained in the State of the Art, this solution is completely focused on a Smart Grid scenario. It solves a particular problem while other works only scratch the surface, presenting general only-theoretical solutions, which can be applied in a many different scenarios. Smart Grid environments are quite different from other traditional scenarios, so a tailored solution is needed.

2   Related Work

Since the emergence of IDS forty years ago, it has been the most widely used security tool dedicated to detecting anomalous incidents and behaviours in a particular computer network, whose main target is to record information and generate alerts. Over the years this evolved into CIDS, which consist of collaborative intrusion detection mechanism, usually by means of distributed systems, through which to exchange information about the attacks, and thus prevent and protect the associated equipment. However, there is still a vulnerability in the face of attacks from within the network, as it will be seen in the following lines, which commits the entities involved and hinders the transfer of information.

After analysing the attacks as they were happening, it is pretended to protect the information from these attacks by improving the network. [7] studies the vulnerabilities that the Collaborative Intrusion Detection Networks (CIDN) may have, related to attacks produced from inside the network itself, as well as the security measures and responses that are currently obtained in collaborative environments. Its concluded that, although a network may be apparently protected against internal attacks, in real world applications many mechanisms are based on supposedly safe concepts, but in the end, they are still susceptible to cyber-attacks.

Therefore, there is still a need and a margin for improvement in this sector, even considering the high number of attacks and the creativity to elaborate them. Focusing on electrical infrastructures, they are specified by common standards (IEC61850, IEC60870, DNP…) but that do not specify any security measures, so it is possible to inject malicious messages to make undesired operations, fooling an IED to trust this fake message [8]. There is another attack vector, even more dangerous, which can affect a whole Smart Grid network. It is possible to perform synchronized attacks to different devices to break down the whole infrastructure, as also described in [6]. These kinds of attacks are extremely dangerous because they can change the actual state of the network completely.

Related to intrusion detection, there are some research works such as [9] where authors study different methods to analyse traffic and propose different solutions to apply monitoring techniques on SCADA systems. This work focuses on the headers in protocols and traffic streams, group the data and extract important information using data mining algorithms. An IDS design is shown in [10], based on models of sensor networks used in SCPs, being able to identify different communication patterns (master to slave, network admin to field devices, HMI to master…). However, this solution has some drawbacks, being the most important one that it needs attack-free learning data to work properly, which is not always simple. However, [11] and [12] are focused on inspecting packets to obtain useful data, similarly to what is done in [9] and they do not need attack-free learning data. [13] proposes to generate communication patterns and present an anomaly-based IDS for SCPs by working with IP-port combinations. Last but not least, [14] shows an IDS for AMI (Advanced Metering Infrastructure) in the Smart Grid.

Traditional intrusion detection systems have their own drawbacks when it comes to Smart Grid scenarios. First, NIDS (Network Intrusion Detection Systems) are not prepared to work properly in the Smart Grid, where latency is a serious issue. Besides, there is not public databases with effective rules for these environments, so it complicates the process of detecting incoming attacks. HIDS (Host Intrusion Detection Systems) don't offer a much better alternative, because they usually need much resources to work properly, being completely unsuitable for being deployed in RTU devices, due to the lack of computational power of these devices.

In addition, the aforementioned research works are not offering a solution for availability issues. Due to its functionality related to detect attacks, an IDS is commonly a target for an attacker breaking into a network, so it is crucial to achieve availability in this system. A simple solution is to deploy several IDS, getting availability through redundancy, but this approach has some issues. The most serious one is synchronisation, because it is complicated to synchronise several IDS to work together, since all the them need to have a single view of the data. Consequently, some authors propose Blockchain-based alternatives to traditional IDS. Due to the recent appearance of new ways of managing data based on Blockchain technologies, several solutions have arisen that avoid the need to trust in a third part, as it is analysed in [15]. This simplifies the collaboration and distribution of information between previously defined entities and speeds up the procedures and processes that this information depends on, such as the detection of an anomaly in a foreign computer.

Since this is about extremely sensitive information, there are many studies about the security that Bitcoin, as the main and pioneer Blockchain, has provided to the world. In general, there is a certain scepticism to believe in a new born technology, especially if it is continually being put in evidence, as in the cases of study [16] and [17]. However, the reality is completely different, because up to now, it has proved to have a lot of potential in terms of information security.

Following this same topic, there are some proposals suggesting the implementation of Blockchain as a mean to guarantee the source and veracity of the data in an industrial security environment. One of these proposals is described in [18], in where, supported by a network of distributed nodes, a set of events is monitored, analysed, ciphered and recorded in an independent Blockchain.

Compared to the solutions seen above, this last one describes in a more precise way how an IDS, based on a collaborative and distributed platform, would work. It has several similarities with the one described in this document, but it shows a very theoretical approach, only presenting a comparison between the two different types of Blockchain: permissioned and permissionless, analysing advantages and disadvantages of both configurations. In other words, it reaches a very valid but broad conclusion, which does not solve the problem. However, he introduces us the possibilities of this new technology, Blockchain, could have in the industrial security environment. This document further deepens the problem and specifies a real solution, using a specific tool what is also tested.

Related to monitoring activities, there are some studies which try to apply Blockchain to enhance logging systems. Several proposals refer to the Blockchain technology to support the storage, sometimes massive, of the logs from many computers. One of the first examples [19] written by some members of the University of La Sapienza in Rome and the University of Southampton. It tries to find a solution to the European project Sunfish based on a distributed and serverless database which provides integrity and stability to the data, analyses the advantages and disadvantages of using this tool by implementing cloud computing, but they don't come any further because of the immaturity of technology.

During 2018, Nokia Bell Labs published a small report [20] in which, unlike the previous one, it proposes to make use of private and permissioned blockchains instead of public ones to manage the logs, in this case focused on information related to banks, and therefore extremely sensitive, but it does not extend excessively. Later that same year, two experts from the University of Toronto expanded the information with another proposal [21]. In this case it raises, in a more technical but imprecise way, the possibilities and potential uses of Blockchain to store and verify logs, although for mere uses of providing integrity and privacy, without getting to performance the information. Immutability of logs has been widely discussed in the past, being represented in [22] with a MAC-based anti-tampering system. Blockchain already uses its own anti-tampering system based on cryptographically signed blocks, which is quite similar to this approach.

Currently, some projects have already been launched with the goal of storing information related to computer data logs, such as Guardtime [23] and LogSentinel [24]. The first of these, among other things, is based on the Blockchain technology to audit the type of movements and records that are made between organizations, including secure hash algorithms or hash trees, in order to understand the client security and scalability needs, albeit unilaterally to him. LogSentinel, following the same approach, analyses the requirements and advises on decision making as far as data security is concerned, and makes use of a distributed database of computer records to protect information and provide an infrastructure that simplifies its use to its customers

3 Architecture of the Solution

In this section, the chosen architecture for implementing the proof of concept is presented, using Hyperledger Fabric as a Blockchain network.

In order to prove the suitability of this solution, a real RTU device has been used. It's important to consider that, due to confidentiality issues with the manufacturer, it has been necessary to omit the details about the specific aspects of this device, such as model or kind of device. Anyway, one relevant aspect is that this device uses a VxWork operating system, which is a common kind-of Linux distribution for embedded systems. Some modifications have been made over this device in order to perform the communication with the Blockchain. As shown in the diagram devices act as Blockchain users communicating with a BaaS (Blockchain as a Service) through an API node, which is Peer3 in this case.

As it is shown in Fig. 1, one of the advantages of this design is its modularity. Only the left part of the diagram (orange rectangle) has been implemented because there is yet only one Chaincode running in the peers. This Chaincode is the one which implements all the different defined alerts as well as the rest of the functions in the BIAD.

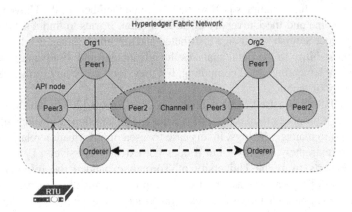

Fig. 1. Arquitecture of the solution

However, Hyperledger Fabric allows the combination of different Chaincodes (Fabric Smart Contracts) in the same peers, allowing for different separated and non-related functionalities in the same Blockchain infrastructure. This design allows to implement further modifications in the distributed alert system by adding new organisations with their own peers. It is possible to setup a new channel grouping several peers from different organisations to achieve privacy of the data within this channel. That is why this design has been proposed for the BIAD, because it is quite easy to add new nodes and organisations the system to adapt it to different needs.

In terms of scalability, as many nodes as it is required can be added, so any level of availability can be reached. For this use case, three nodes plus the ordering nodes have been deployed, which are more than enough for this testing purposes. Ordering nodes are special nodes used in Hyperledger Fabric networks and do not offer extra availability, but they are the ones who coordinate the communication within the infrastructure.

3.1 Hyperledger Fabric as Chosen Technology

There are many reasons why it has been decided to use the Hyperledger Blockchain platform, starting with the privacy of the data. The information managed on the network is sensitive and private, and therefore only certain users should be able to have access to it, Fabric is a permissioned network that manages users unlike public networks, managing their permissions according to some predefined roles, and with the ability to identify all the users that interact with it. More considerations about the suitability of public against private blockchains can be found in [17].

At the enterprise level, the storage required by a public Blockchain is not practical given the amount of information that it contains, so it has been discarded for the proof of concept. By privatizing the Blockchain, the obtained distributed database limits the access to the appropriate entities, thus the stored data will be minimized up to the point that is required. Considering the number of users, a public CIDS would be very useful for his enrichment of information, to the detriment of confidentiality and quality of it, but one of the main drawbacks of most public blockchains is the need of a transaction tax payment, which would hinder it from thriving.

In addition, related to the deployment of smart contracts, they are immutable on platforms like Ethereum once they are mined. In the case of use that is exposed here is fundamental to consider updating the chaincode as it is used, in order to optimize and avoid errors that may arise, of course, with the consent of all parties and corresponding record of the mentioned update, which is not an issue with Hyperledger Fabric.

Last but not least, we must consider the possibility with Hyperledger Fabric of easily including additional nodes that participate in the network, providing simple and rapid scalability. It is also important to notice that the consensus algorithm in a private Blockchain network is programmable, so it can be adapted to the requirements of the use case and is semi-centralized over a specific type of nodes to avoid excess energy consumption during the processing of transaction performed, unlike other types of networks such as public ones, which need an absolute peer consensus to work correctly.

3.2   Identity Management

One of the advantages in using Blockchain is that it provides a solid Identity Management. Hyperledger Fabric implements a stable mechanism to achieve this particular requirement. Hyperledger Fabric is compatible with traditional identity schemes, like CAs architectures or X.509 certificates. It is possible to define a new CA tree using root and intermediate CAs for using it with this solution but is even possible to attach an existing CA infrastructure to the Blockchain, so existing defined identities can be used.

In this use case, each device interacting with the BIAD has its own X.509 certificate with a private-public keypair. Hyperledger Fabric, as a permissioned Blockchain network, checks the identity of each device before accepting any transaction from this device and, besides, a login system has been implemented, using these certificates to authenticate other devices, like the sysadmin computer. This avoids any identity theft by an attacker because he will not be able to get the original certificate of the device, as is done in traditional systems.

As well as it is done with Blockchain users, this identity management can be done with the rest of elements of the infrastructure. Each organisation belonging to the Blockchain is identified by its own certificate, as well as every node in the system. In other words, every single element in the Blockchain has an identity, so it is protected from being supplanted.

Hyperledger Fabric is also compatible with CRLs (Certificate Revocation Lists) schemes, being possible to revoke old or compromised certificates directly from the Blockchain. This is crucial and supposes a step forward from previous architectures, because now the IDS is the one who perform all these operations, including revoking and assigning certificates. Someone can think this is too risky, because it adds much responsibility in a single device, compromising availability, but an anti-SPoF IDS have been designed, so there are not availability issues with it.

4   User-Defined Alerts

In this section it is show three different alerts that have been implemented in the BIAD. Rather than three alerts, they are actually two specific alerts plus several connectivity tests. As it is shown in "SmartContracting it" subsection, it is possible to actually add as many rules or alerts as it is needed, because of the flexibility of the Smart Contracts. These three rules will be shown to teach how Blockchain can be used to prevent attacks.

4.1   Log Comparison

First of all, when referring to log comparison, it is not about storing logs in the Blockchain, which is the typical approach of several other solutions, such as the ones previously discussed (see [19–22]). However, there is no doubt that storing logs is the first step to perform this log comparison, because it is obviously needed to store different kind of logs in Blockchain before any kind of analysis can be done. For clarification sake, logs are not stored directly to the Blockchain, rather than their hash.

First, considering a finite number of devices n, defining for each device d $s.t.$ $1 \leq d \leq n$, $L^d = (L_1, \ldots, L_i)^d \subset \mathbb{N}$ as the set of all logs of the device d. $L = \bigcup_{d=1}^{n} L^d$ can also be defined as the set containing all logs.

Noting i as the number of logs of device d, defining $L_k^d \subset L^d$ $\forall d$ $s.t.$ $1 \leq d \leq n$, with $L_k^d \subset L^d$ as the log k of the device d, being k $s.t.$ $1 \leq k \leq i$

Calculating $H(L_k^d)$ $\forall L_k^d \in L \subset \mathbb{N}$, being $H()$ a SHA3-256 hash function applied over the log. Next step is to store safely this log in the BIAD, using an HTTPS connection.

Finally, noting $(L_k^d)_b$ as the log k of the device d stored in the Blockchain, calculating $H((L_k^d)_b) \forall L_k^d \in L \subset \mathbb{N}$

It is only needed to check if (Table 1):

$$H((L_k^d)_b) = H(L_k^d) \; \forall L_k^d \in L \subset \mathbb{N} \tag{1}$$

Table 1. Important log files

Log file	Content	Pre-processing
.ssh/authorized_keys	SSH public keys granted to access the system	No
.ssh/known_hosts	Known host which have accessed to the host in the past	No
/var/log/apache2/access. log	Log information for Apache	Yes
/etc./passwd	List of users in the system	No
/var/log/auth.log	System access logs, including failed attempts	Yes

It is important to notice that a log storing is not the main goal, as has been done in previous works, but doing a real time log comparison embedded into the whole infrastructure, which actually works as a distributed IDS, being some steps further to previous works in the area.

In this industrial scenario, the focus is on different kind of logs, especially the ones which allows to know if someone has just broken into the system. Because of that, the focus has been, amongst other, on login history, which can be founded in an /var/log/ *auth.log* file in most distributions. It's important to remember that targets are RTU devices, which usually are built using an embedded Linux distribution, so these files can present different names depending on the kind of studied device. For clarification sake, some other files, which are liable to be monitored, are shown in Fig. 1. It is important to mention that these files are specific for this RTU, so they are expected to change in another system. Working with different RTUs, it has been discovered that most of them have similar file systems, having the same files as the ones written in the table below, which are also commonly seen in normal systems.

Once these files are located, a really simple python script has been developed, *hash_logs.py*, which systematically looks for these files in the filesystem and hashes them. Once this hash has been calculated, the next step is to submit it to the Blockchain and perform the comparison as it has been previously discussed. If the hashes are not the same, it automatically generates an alert which is sent to the SIEM for further treatment.

4.2 Firmware Comparison

Another user-defined rule has been created in the BIAD. This rule is related with the firmware of the device. First of all, is necessary to hash the original firmware in each device. In the desktop search no related work as the one proposed in the paper has been identified. To achieve this goal, as well as previously done in the log comparison rule, another simple python script called *hash_firmware.py* has been created. This script searches for the device firmware and hash it, and after doing this, it submits this hash to the Blockchain.

For both the log comparison and the firmware comparison, a SHA3-256 hash has been used to ensure not dealing with security issues related to insecure or obsolete algorithms during the hashing process. In this case, considering F^d the firmware of device d so calculating $H(F^d)$ being again $H()$ the same hash function as explained before. The rest of the comparison process is similar to the one explained in the log comparison subsection, just considering that now the focus are firmwares instead of log files. Because of that, now the mathematical model is simplified, not dealing with more than one file per device. In this case, the comparison is as follows.

Defining $F = \bigcup_{d=1}^{n} F^d$ as the set of all firmwares. Following the same notation, and checking (2) equation:

$$H(F^d)_b) = H(F^d) \, \forall F^d \in F \subset \mathbb{N} \tag{2}$$

Once it is done, it's time to check periodically the hash stored in the Blockchain with the hash within the device. Similarly to log files, different hash values indicate alteration in the firmware, which is an anomaly and must be reported.

4.3 Anomaly-Based Versus Rule-Based

Unlike common detection techniques based on rules, this solution is rather based on anomalies, which has some advantages against rules. Mainly, anomaly-based solutions are able to detect zero-day attacks and not-discovered attack vectors, which is completely impossible for rule-based solutions.

However, dealing with many false positives is a serious drawback. Each time a log changes, his hash is changed, so it can generate many false alerts to the SIEM. To prevent this situation, pre-processing techniques are performed before submitting hashes to the Blockchain. Some logs like, for example, *.ssh/authorized_keys*, do not change with each login, so no pre-processing is needed, but others do. The table shows which ones need to be pre-processed due to these constant changes when a legitim user enters in the device.

This issue can be solved using a user-made script which erases new lines in these log files almost at the same time they are written. As there is only a reduced list of authorised users, it is feasible to check if a login has been made with a known user and consequently erase this line. It can be made by choosing a small periodicity than in the Blockchain refresh. Considering λ_b as the periodicity in sending the information to the Blockchain, it is only necessary to choose $\lambda_e < \lambda_b$ as the periodicity in which erasing is done. In addition, λ_b must be really small, typically a few seconds, avoiding an attacker removing his fingerprints before the hash is submitted to the Blockchain.

4.4 Proof of Conectivity

Another functionality implemented in the BIAD is the ability to check the availability of the different devices. Blockchain is not able to launch periodic tests against the different devices to check connectivity. However, it is possible to configure Blockchain to launch any test if an authorised user sends the proper request. Blockchain exposes an API Node, which is listening for incoming request. Sysadmins can perform an HTTP request to the Blockchain to launch the connectivity testing.

It can be done as simple as a *ping* validation or can be implemented as a complete stress testing. It must be sure that the chosen Blockchain technology supports this kind of integration with the operative system. In the discussion about the most suitable Blockchain technology for this use case, this will be a crucial aspect to consider.

The BIAD uses different proofs of connectivity to check the actual state of the different devices. First of all, a simple *ping* mechanism has been implemented. A simulation of a sysadmin computer has been used, launching requests with periodicity λ to check if the device is running. This periodicity must be scheduled considering the network latency, as well as the number of devices, being equal to 20 s in this case. The recommendation for production environment even shorter periods of time, in order to detect DoS attacks more quickly.

In addition, additional stress tests have been implemented, which provide information about the state of the device. It is not appropriate to launch periodically stress tests in a production environment due to performance issues, so the process has not been automatized. Anyway, it is possible from this external computer to call the Blockchain to perform this operation using a simple API REST call as before, so a sysadmin can perform a stress test whenever he needs. *Hping* can be used as a simple CLI software to perform these kind of stress tests. It is possible for an attacker to break into the network and use this functionality to launch DoS attacks against systems in there, so to prevent these DoS attacks a user-management system has been implemented within the BIAD. Using X.509 certificates it is possible to identify the different computers which will have read and write rights to the BIAD. More details about this aspect can be checked in the "Identity Management" subsection.

4.5 SmartContracting It

Smart Contracts are the brain of the whole Blockchain infrastructure. When a new hash is submitted, the code running into the Blockchain stores this hash safely and properly to perform further analysis.

Operations are integrated into the same infrastructure, which is fully synchronised. It is also possible to represent in the diagram the availability probe, in which a sysadmin calls the correspondent function and the Blockchain checks the availability status of the device. In this schematic diagram, three nodes are represented, but this basic design can be extended to as many nodes as it is needed. Focusing on Hyperledger Fabric Blockchain technology, further details about how this extension can be done can be read in previous sections.

In the Fig. 2 it is observed how Smart Contracts perform all the operations without intervention of any user, excepting the availability probes, which are launched by the sysadmin from the sysadmin computer:

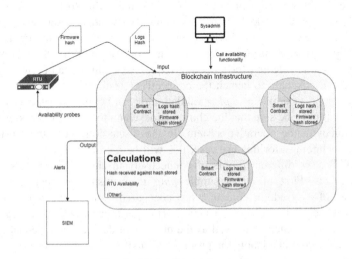

Fig. 2. Smart Contracts scheme

Each node has access to the same information, so all of them have a single view of the data, which, as mentioned before, is crucial to reach consensus. As it is shown, there is a substantial difference between inputs and outputs. In inputs, the Blockchain exposes a single API node, and it changes transparently depending on the availability of this node, but calculations are done in every single node in the Blockchain and the results are passed to an external SIEM system, which will be able to generate intelligence using this information.

One of the advantages of the Smart Contracts is the ability to be programmable. At the end, a Smart Contract is, at the end, a piece of code. That means that it is possible to program every desired functionality in the same way it can be done in a normal software. The only difference when dealing with Smart Contracts is to be aware that this code will work in several nodes at the same time. Because of that, it is possible to implement new alerts or adapt the existent ones depending on the use case, just changing the Smart Contract. As it is discussed later, some Blockchain technologies don't allow these modifications, so the Blockchain technology must be chosen carefully before going into any implementation stage.

Once many people are interested in the BIAD concept, more complex rules can be defined as is actually being done with traditional IDS, like Snort, being even possible in the future to download them directly from different repositories. Due to the flexibility of the solution, it is possible to incorporate rules to the system as easily as updating the Smart Contracts issuing a new transaction.

5 Conclusion

This approach presented within this paper is based on the use of a Blockchain in order to replace traditional IDS. These intrusion detection systems have a set of weaknesses and the use of a blockchain based architecture and the definition of a set of rules prevent attacks where traditional IDS are not covering *per se*. In fact, a blockchain architecture has been adapted to an industrial system which contains a set of RTUs, and a set of rules have been defined. In this sense, IDS capabilities have been enhanced by using Blockchain technology, gaining extra functionalities against traditional systems and the final result is a prototype of a Blockchain IDS for industrial systems with the BIAD. The proof of concept is still very limited, but it can be updated with new functionalities and user-defined alerts as soon as they are developed in the future. In other words, the result is the backbone of what can be the next generation IDS.

From a log comparison point of view, this approach does not store logs. However, this architecture stores the generated hashes. From the Identity Management point of view, blockchain provides a solid Identity Management, and Hyperledger Fabric implements a stable mechanism to achieve this particular requirement. In fact, this approach is based on X.509 certificates, and the RTUs contain these certificates. As stated before, a firmware comparison has been performed, with devices connected within this industrial system. This step is required for doing the log comparison as well. In this sense, a python script called *hash_firmware.py* has been implemented, who searches for the device's firmware, it hashes it, and it submits it to the Blockchain. In addition, there is another advantage with respect to the anomaly-based versus rule-based detection approach. In fact, there are just a reduced list of authorised users, it is easy to check if a login has been made with a known user and consequently erase this line. Finally, for its use in industrial systems might be useful to work with shorter periods of time, in order to detect DoS attacks more quickly.

References

1. http://www.nec.com/en/global/solutions/safety/info_management/cyberattack.html. Accessed 08 Nov 2018
2. Tan, S., De, D., Song, W.Z., Yang, J., Das, S.K.: Survey of security advances in smart grid: a data driven approach. IEEE Commun. Surv. Tutor. 19(1), 397–422 (2017)
3. European Network and Information Security Agency (ENISA) "Annex II. Security aspects of the smart grid" (2012). https://www.enisa.europa.eu/topics/critical-information-infrastructures-and-services/smart-grids/smart-grids-and-smart-metering

4. McCarthy, J., et al.: Situational Awareness For Electric Utilities. NIST Special Publication 1800-7, February 2017
5. D'Antonio, S., Oliviero, F., Setola, R.: High-speed intrusion detection in support of critical infrastructure protection. In: Lopez, J. (ed.) CRITIS 2006. LNCS, vol. 4347, pp. 222–234. Springer, Heidelberg (2006). https://doi.org/10.1007/11962977_18
6. Wang, W., Lu, Z.: Cyber security in the smart grid: survey and challenges. Comput. Netw. **57**, 1344–1371 (2013)
7. Li, W., Meng, W., Kwok, L.-F., Ip, H.H.S.: PMFA: toward passive message fingerprint attacks on challenge-based collaborative intrusion detection networks. In: Chen, J., Piuri, V., Su, C., Yung, M. (eds.) NSS 2016. LNCS, vol. 9955, pp. 433–449. Springer, Cham (2016). https://doi.org/10.1007/978-3-319-46298-1_28
8. Yu, D.Y., Ranganathan, A., Locher, T., Capkun, S., Basin, D.: Short paper: detection of GPS spoofing attacks in power grids. In: Proceedings of the 2014 ACM Conference on Security and Privacy in Wireless & Mobile Networks, WiSec 2014, pp. 99–104 (2014)
9. Mahmood, A.N., Leckie, C., Hu, J., Tari, Z., Atiquzzaman, M.: Network traffic analysis and SCADA security. In: Stavroulakis, P., Stamp, M. (eds.) Handbook of Information and Communication Security, pp. 383–405. Springer, Heidelberg (2010). https://doi.org/10.1007/978-3-642-04117-4_20
10. Roosta, T., Nilsson, D.K., Lindqvist, U., Valdes, A.: An intrusión detection system for wireless process control systems. In: 5th IEEE International Conference on Mobile Ad Hoc and Sensor Systems, MASS 2008, pp. 866–872. IEEE (2008)
11. Cheung, S., Dutertre, B., Fong, M., Lindqvist, U., Skinner, K., Valdes, A.: Using model-based intrusion detection for scada networks. In: Actas de SCADA Security Scientific Symposium (2006)
12. Düssel, P., Gehl, C., Laskov, P., Bußer, J.-U., Störmann, C., Kästner, J.: Cyber-critical infrastructure protection using real-time payload-based anomaly detection. In: Rome, E., Bloomfield, R. (eds.) CRITIS 2009. LNCS, vol. 6027, pp. 85–97. Springer, Heidelberg (2010). https://doi.org/10.1007/978-3-642-14379-3_8
13. Valdes, A., Cheung, S.: Communication pattern anomaly detection in process control systems. In: IEEE Conference on Technologies for Homeland Security, HST 2009, pp. 22–29. IEEE (2009)
14. Faisal, M.A., Aung, Z., Williams, J.R., Sanchez, A.: Data-stream-based intrusion detection system for advanced metering infrastructure in smart grid: a feasibility study. IEEE Syst. J. **9**, 31–44 (2015)
15. Meng, W., Tischhauser, E.W., Wang, Q., Wang, Y., Han, J.: When intrusion detection meets blockchain technology: a review. IEEE Access **6**, 10179–10188 (2018)
16. Giechaskiel, I., Cremers, C., Rasmussen, K.B.: On bitcoin security in the presence of broken cryptographic primitives. In: Askoxylakis, I., Ioannidis, S., Katsikas, S., Meadows, C. (eds.) ESORICS 2016. LNCS, vol. 9879, pp. 201–222. Springer, Cham (2016). https://doi.org/10.1007/978-3-319-45741-3_11
17. Pham, T., Lee, S.: Anomaly detection in the bitcoin system - a network perspective (2016)
18. Alexopoulos, N., Vasilomanolakis, E., Ivánkó, N.R., Mühlhäuser, M.: Towards blockchain-based collaborative intrusion detection systems. In: D'Agostino, G., Scala, A. (eds.) CRITIS 2017. LNCS, vol. 10707, pp. 107–118. Springer, Cham (2018). https://doi.org/10.1007/978-3-319-99843-5_10
19. Gaetani, E., Aniello, L., Baldoni, R., Lombardi, F., Margheri, A., Sassone, V.: Blockchain-based database to ensure data integrity in cloud computing environments (2017)
20. Shekhtman, L.M., Waisbard, E.: Securing log files through blockchain technology. In: Proceedings of the 11th ACM International Systems and Storage Conference (SYSTOR 2018), p. 131. ACM, New York

21. Pourmajidi, W., Miranskyy, A.: Logchain: blockchain-assisted log storage, pp. 978–982 (2018). https://doi.org/10.1109/CLOUD.2018.00150
22. Cucurull, J., Puiggalí, J.: Distributed immutabilization of secure logs. In: Barthe, G., Markatos, E., Samarati, P. (eds.) STM 2016. LNCS, vol. 9871, pp. 122–137. Springer, Cham (2016). https://doi.org/10.1007/978-3-319-46598-2_9
23. https://guardtime.com/. Accessed 15 Feb 2019
24. https://logsentinel.com/. Accessed 16 Feb 2019

Modelling Compliance Threats and Security Analysis of Cross Border Health Data Exchange

Mike Surridge[✉][iD], Ken Meacham, Juri Papay,
Stephen C. Phillips[iD], J. Brian Pickering[iD], Ardavan Shafiee,
and Toby Wilkinson[iD]

University of Southampton, IT Innovation Centre, Southampton, UK
{ms, kem, jp, scp, jbp, ash, stw}@it-innovation.soton.ac.uk

Abstract. Digital health data is created, stored and processed in healthcare IT infrastructures. These infrastructures are the target of large-scale cyber-attacks and are found to be vulnerable, primarily for two main reasons: the heterogeneity of infrastructure and the numerous stakeholders (medical staff, managers, patients, regulators etc.). Furthermore, the stakeholders have different attitudes, skills, awareness and data handling practices that offer many opportunities for malicious activities. Healthcare in general is characterised by a multitude of regulations and adherence to them is essential to the functioning of the system. Compliance management is usually described in terms of risks and involves activities such as risk identification, assessment and treatment. Our paper conceptualises the notion of a "compliance threat" and discusses the security of cross-border health data exchange. The paper presents the architecture of the System Security Modeller and illustrates the security risk assessment of the "break glass" scenario which requires health data communication in an emergency situation.

Keywords: Health data · Compliance · GDPR · Security · Modelling

1 Introduction

Businesses and organisations have to operate in an environment with ever increasing numbers of regulations. Compliance management assumes adherence to regulations and standards and can be described by activities such as risk identification, risk assessment and treatment. The regulations are not static: government and industrial bodies tend to make changes. This, along with frequent changes to a business and its infrastructure, results in a need for regular compliance audits. Achieving full compliance with all regulations may even be impossible, especially considering that the requirements can be conflicting and also involve stakeholders with different interests.

In this environment it is becoming difficult for organisations to identify, prioritise and respond to regulatory demands that impact their business. Non-compliance may result not only in financial penalties but can threaten the functioning and the very existence of the business. As the number and complexity of regulations increases, the

© Springer Nature Switzerland AG 2019
C. Attiogbé et al. (Eds.): MEDI 2019 Workshops, CCIS 1085, pp. 180–189, 2019.
https://doi.org/10.1007/978-3-030-32213-7_14

cost of demonstrating compliance also grows. Therefore, automating compliance checking could help reduce cost, avoid duplication and allow companies to react quickly to the deficiencies identified by auditing.

The paper introduces a methodology for modelling compliance in the context of threat analysis. It presents the System Security Modeller (SSM) tool which allows automated identification of end-to-end security risks and compliance issues during system design. It also calculates the impact of non-compliance for the overall system architecture. The application of the SSM is illustrated on a use case scenario involving the exchange of medical records across national boundaries within the EU.

Section 2 provides a short survey of related work. Section 3 introduces the architecture of System Security Modeler, which can be used for security threat analysis and compliance assessment. Section 4 describes non-compliance as a threat and provides examples. Section 5 describes the "break glass" scenario illustrating the security aspects of health data exchange across national boundaries. Section 6 summarises the paper.

2   Related Work

2.1   Compliance Management

Compliance management is a risk-based optimisation problem aiming to reduce the cost of audits, and the identification and resolution of non-compliance issues. The approach uses dynamic programming to find the balance between the need to satisfy the multitude of regulatory requirements and the available resources [1].

The CORAS framework is based on the ISO 31000 [2] standard and incorporates the method, formal compliance specification language and risk analysis tool [3]. The CORAS language contains elements such as assets, threats, risks and controls. The compliance risks are calculated based on the probability of occurrence and the consequence of incidents. The CORAS methodology was applied in various domains for example, oil and gas exploration [3, 4] and for the analysis of legal documents [5].

Finding a suitable graphical representation can significantly reduce the complexity of compliance management. This allows change of regulations to be monitored as well as the status of compliance within an organisation [6].

For compliance modelling it is important to identify the stakeholders who need to take actions to ensure that the system is compliant with the regulations. This assumes the existence of trust-relations and the distribution of work between stakeholders who manage compliance risks [7].

Document and model-based approaches to compliance management were compared in [8] according to the effort required for modelling, interpreting, documenting and monitoring the status of compliance. The paper presented a model of a hospital using three different notations: User Requirements Notation (URN), Goal-oriented Requirement Language (GRL) and Use Case Maps (UCM). These notations provided the means to capture the goals, assets, actors and tasks required for achieving data privacy compliance. The paper concludes that using a mixture of document and model-based approaches offers the best trade-off.

One of the issues is understanding legal documents and translating them into models and policies that can be followed by an organisation in order to achieve compliance. Breaux *et al.* suggested to use Semantic Parametrisation to help with the disambiguation of documents for extracting the rights and obligations of stakeholders that impact their privacy and security requirements [9].

The objectives, processes and policies required for building a compliance management system are described in the ISO 19600 standard [10]. Understanding the operation of an organisation is one of the key elements of this standard. This involves analysing all compliance obligations and the possible risks. The standard also outlines the role and responsibilities of stakeholders in planning, implementation and operation of processes that ensure an organisation's compliance with the regulations [11].

Recently several GRC (Governance Risk Compliance) platforms have been developed that allow adherence to standards and regulations to be tracked [12, 13]. Although businesses are aware of the importance of GRC, in practice this task is often handled by different units which use different methods and tools. As a result, the information about compliance is scattered in separate spreadsheets, text documents and even emails which makes auditing difficult. The main purpose of GRC platforms is to automate business processes, to integrate the information produced by different units and provide a real time picture about the GRC status.

2.2   Threat Modelling

Over the years numerous methods have been developed for identifying and analysing threats in ICT systems. In threat modelling we can distinguish four stages, these are: system design, threat identification, threat addressing, and validation [14]. Threat modelling and analysis tools in general terms can be classified as: asset, attacker and software centric tools.

Software centric tools, for example VsRisk [15], Threat Modeling Tool [16] and ThreatModeler [17] are based on vulnerability databases such as OWASP [18]. These tools mainly address software related threats; however they find it difficult to identify threats related to human factors or inappropriate use of the system.

Attacker centric tools such as SeaMonster [19] and securiCAD [20] are better suited for modelling human behaviour, which depends on expert knowledge of the techniques used by the attacker. One of the difficulties is to relate the attacks to system resources and to identify appropriate countermeasures.

Asset centric methods are based on standards ISO 27005 [21] and ISO 31010 [22]. They capture the relationship between threats and system components. These methods assume the involvement of a security expert with extensive knowledge of the types of threats that can affect the system. Manual analysis to identify threats and appropriate responses takes a long time and it is an error prone process.

3   System Security Modeller

The SSM enables automated security risk analysis and identification of counter measures to address security threats. Based on the information in a knowledge base the primary and secondary threats for the given system model are automatically generated for each asset, along with corresponding candidate control strategies. Primary threats are caused by system faults or malicious activity. Secondary threats represent the propagation of threats through the system This detailed information helps users to understand what measures are required to counter the threats. Compliance threats (described below) are also detected.

The architecture of SSM follows a layered pattern with a clear separation between the Presentation, Access Control, Service and Persistence layers (Fig. 1). The browser provides a graphical user interface, written in JavaScript and HTML5. The server side is accessed via a REST Controller which forwards requests to functional modules. System Model Designer provides for the construction of system models by connecting assets. The Model Validator checks and enhances the initial model by generating inferred assets and relations. The Model Querier provides a set of predefined queries for retrieving different parts of the model. The User & Model Management module provides an API for the database which contains Model Metadata and user-related information.

The Persistence layer uses two databases. The Triple store contains the Core Model, Domain Model(s) and System Model(s). The Core Model is an ontology which defines the vocabulary and the relationships between its terms. Domain Models (installed by an administrator) define asset types, permitted relationships, threats and controls relevant to a particular domain. Each System Model (created by a user) uses the elements of a Domain Model to represent the system that the user is modelling: a network of assets and their relationships along with the associated threats and controls (see examples in Figs. 2 and 3). The User & Model database stores Model Metadata and User details.

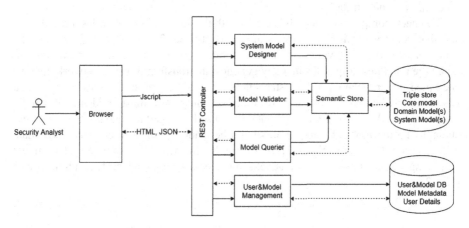

Fig. 1. The main building blocks of the System Security Modeller. The full arrows represent controls and the dashed arrows data flows.

4   Non-compliance as a Threat

The SSM conceptualises non-compliance as a special class of threat. Security threats in our models have the potential to cause misbehaviour (an undesirable effect) in an asset as a result of external causes. Compliance threats differ in that they themselves cause no misbehaviours and have no external causes: they are inherent to the configuration of the system. Security threats also have an associated risk level whereas compliance threats are either present or not. Due to the fact that regulations tend to mandate processes or controls which will mitigate certain classes of threat, there is often an overlap between the security threats found in our models and the compliance threats: controlling for one will often resolve the other. Thus, non-compliance can have security implications by making the system vulnerable to malicious attacks. For example, regulations can mandate that all sensitive personal data must be encrypted and communicated via secure channels. The regulations may stipulate which patterns of interactions between the assets (human and technological) are permitted and which are prohibited. Compliance threats are usually caused by faulty design or misconfiguration rather than malicious activity. To address compliance threats multiple measures often need to applied, for example changing the network of assets (adding/removing assets and relations), using data masking or consent management tools, etc.

To illustrate compliance threats, two examples are provided. The first illustrates country-specific rules for the access and storage of genetic data and the second describes SHiELD best-practice requirements for cross-border health data communication. The GDPR standard mandates that all personal data must be collected and processed lawfully and fairly. The regulations stipulate the type of data that is allowed be communicated and what transformations (i.e. data masking, anonymisation) the data must undergo. In addition to the general GDPR rules, individual countries can also introduce regulations regarding special categories of data such as health data. For example, they may also introduce specific rules mandating patient's consent prior to accessing any health data.

To check compliance, we validate that both the standard GDPR rules are followed and that country-specific regulations are also satisfied. These requirements state the conditions for data encryption, communication, storage and access. For example, in Spain the regulation stipulates that any genetic data transferred over a network must be encrypted. The regulation in Italy states that access to the space where the genetic data is stored must be restricted to authorised persons only, who must be identified using a biometric key. Access to the genetic data must also be logged to keep track of all access attempts. Furthermore, the audit trail should be made available to citizens whose data was accessed (the data subject). This case can be illustrated by a simple system model consisting of a database server, genetic data, data centre and system administrator (Fig. 2).

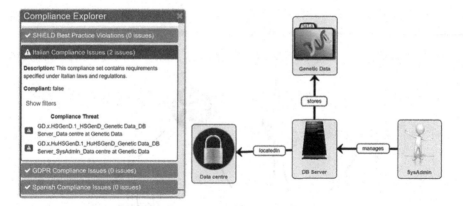

Fig. 2. Compliance with the national regulations concerning access to genetic data.

The Compliance Explorer of SSM indicates two threats for the Italian regulations, that can be resolved by selecting all three controls: Access Control at Data Centre, Biometric ID Verifier at the Data Centre and Logging at DB Server.

5 Break Glass Scenario

Tourism in Europe is one of the most important industries: about 10% of the GDP can be linked directly or indirectly to tourism. According to estimates from the World Tourism Organisation in 2016, 37.6 million tourists visited the UK alone, with 27.9 million from Europe [23]. This mass movement of people also has health implications as visitors from abroad might need emergency medical treatment. In this case access to health data may well be essential. The technology for the exchange of health data is already available, however there are security, legal and compliance issues related to cross border data traffic.

The following "break glass" scenario (also found in [24]) illustrates how health data requirements affect system design. This scenario is illustrated in Fig. 3 and can be described as follows. An Italian tourist while on holiday in Spain suffers a medical emergency that requires urgent treatment. The Spanish doctor at the hospital's emergency department contacts Italy via the NCP (National Contact Point) requesting emergency non-consensual access to the patient's records. The storage and access to health data is governed by the jurisdiction of corresponding countries. The process flow is shown along the top line of the Figure ("Web browser" to "Health record database") and the various hosts and network infrastructure to convey the messages are shown lower down the figure. All the hosts (including network routers) are linked to specific jurisdictions. The key relationships to the health record are also shown: that the data relates to a human, that it is stored on a server in Italy and received by the "Web browser" in a different jurisdiction.

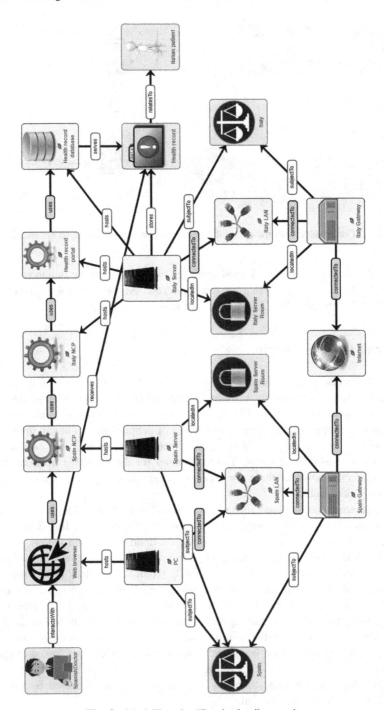

Fig. 3. Modelling the "Break-glass" scenario.

The system model consists of just 20 assets placed by the user but the SSM identifies 306 primary and 164 secondary security threats (many similar). The SSM supports an iterative process for applying controls and recomputing the number of active threats. For illustration purposes we consider the effect of software patching control. Applying only software patching to the servers, gateways and the PC resolves 129 threats.

The compliance threat analysis shows there are three GDPR compliance issues, one Spanish regulatory compliance issue, and one SHIELD best practice compliance issue. Figure 4 shows the SHiELD best practice compliance threat diagram for cross-jurisdictional data transfer which is matched to the elements in Fig. 3 and thus identified as present in this scenario.

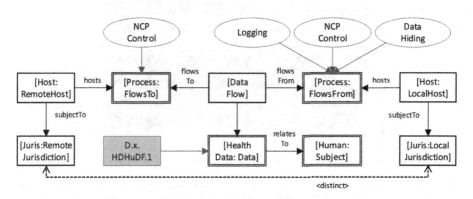

Fig. 4. Cross-jurisdictional data transfer threat.

Figure 5 is the dialogue box shown to the user to explain this compliance threat. The compliance threat relates to health data being transferred between two jurisdictions (Italy and Spain here). To be compliant, the software processes on either side of the border ("Italy NCP" and "Spain NCP" in Fig. 3 and shown as "<distinct>" in Fig. 4) must be NCP-regulated exchange processes and data hiding and logging controls should also be used.

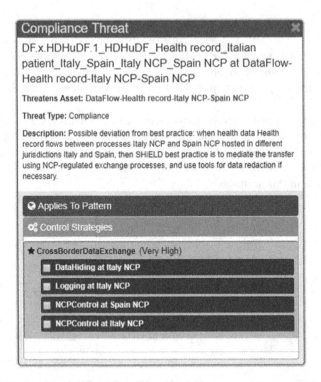

Fig. 5. The SSM identifies a compliance threat (defined as best practice by the SHiELD project) relating to cross-jurisdiction data exchange and proposes the necessary controls.

6   Summary

This paper interpreted non-compliance as a threat and investigated the security issues of cross border health data exchange. Compliance threats are not security threats and they have no effect on the confidentiality, integrity or availability of data but on the interpretation of local (or national) regulation. In this case the threat is that the system would be non-compliant with the corresponding regulation. The issue of national regulatory compliance was illustrated using the example of genetic data. Genetic data is one of the types of data listed in the GDPR Article 9(4) under which member states may enact their own regulations.

The paper then demonstrated the use of the SSM for security and compliance analysis of a "break glass" scenario illustrating cross border health data exchange. The SSM identifies the potential weaknesses of the system model, automatically generates threat definitions, computes any cascading effects and proposes controls for the mitigation of threats. The security expertise in SSM is encoded in a Domain Model (an ontology) that can be reused for the inference and diagnosis of threats in ICT systems covering both design and run-time. SSM uses semantic and machine reasoning technologies for creating models of systems and associated security properties.

Acknowledgement. The work presented in this paper was funded by the European Union's H2020 research and innovation programme under grant agreement No. 727301 (SHiELD).

References

1. Muller, S., Supatgiat, C.: A quantitative optimization model for dynamic risk-based compliance management. IBM J. Res. Dev. **51**(3.4), 295–307 (2007)
2. ISO 31000. https://www.iso.org/iso-31000-risk-management.html
3. Refsdal, A., Solhaug, B., Stølen, K.: Security risk analysis of system changes exemplified within the oil and gas domain. Int. J. Softw. Tools Technol. Transfer **17**(3), 251–266 (2015)
4. Solhaug, B., Seehusen, F.: Model-driven risk analysis of evolving critical infrastructures. J. Ambient Intell. Humaniz. Comput. **5**(2), 187–204 (2014)
5. Mahler, T.: Tool-supported legal risk management: a roadmap. Eur. J. Legal Stud. **2**, 146 (2008)
6. Bellamy, R.K., et al.: Seeing is believing: designing visualizations for managing risk and compliance. IBM Syst. J. **46**(2), 205–218 (2007)
7. Surridge, M., et al.: Trust modelling in 5G mobile networks. In: SecSoN 2018: Proceedings of the 2018 Workshop on Security in Softwarized Networks: Prospects and Challenges. ACM SIGCOMM 2018 Workshop on Security in Softwarized Networks: Prospects and Challenges, 24 August 18, pp. 14–19. ACM, New York (2018). https://doi.org/10.1145/3229616.3229621
8. Ghanavati, S., Amyot, D., Peyton, L.: Comparative analysis between document-based and model-based compliance management approaches. In: 2008 Requirements Engineering and Law, pp. 35–39. IEEE, September 2008
9. Breaux, T.D., Vail, M.W., Anton, A.I.: Towards regulatory compliance: extracting rights and obligations to align requirements with regulations. In: 14th IEEE International Requirements Engineering Conference, RE 2006, pp. 49–58. IEEE, September 2006
10. ISO 19600:2014 - Compliance management systems – Guidelines. https://www.iso.org/standard/62342.html
11. Bleker, S., Hortensius, D.: ISO 19600: The development of a global standard on compliance management. Bus. Compl. **2**, 1–12 (2014)
12. RSA. https://www.rsa.com/en-us/products/integrated-risk-management/archer-platform
13. CURA. https://www.curasoftware.com
14. Shostack, A.: Threat Modeling: Designing for Security. Wiley, Indianapolis (2014)
15. VsRISK. https://www.vigilantsoftware.co.uk/
16. Threat Modeling Tool. Microsoft. https://www.microsoft.com/en-us/securityengineering/sdl/threatmodeling
17. Threat Modeler. http://threatmodeler.com
18. OWASP. https://www.owasp.org/index.php/Category:OWASP_Top_Ten_Project
19. Meland, P.H., Spampinato, D.G., Hagen, E., Baadshaug, E.T., Krister, K.M., Velle, K.S.: SeaMonster: providing tool support for security modeling. Norsk informasjonssikkerhetskonferanse, NISK (2008)
20. securiCAD. https://www.foreseeti.com/
21. ISO/IEC. ISO 27005: Information technology – Security techniques – Information security risk management (2011)
22. ISO/IEC. ISO 31010: Risk management – Risk assessment techniques (2009)
23. World Tourist Organization. http://www2.unwto.org/
24. Larrucea, X., Santamaria, I., Colomo-Palacios, R.: Assessing source code vulnerabilities in a cloud-based system for health systems: OpenNCP. IET Softw. **13**(3), 195–202 (2019)

Resolving Stakeholder Tussles in Healthcare Systems: Ethical Challenges to Data Protection

Brian Pickering[1]([📧]) [ID], Giuliana Faiella[2] [ID], and Fabrizio Clemente[2,3]

[1] University of Southampton, Southampton SO16 7NS, UK
j.b.pickering@soton.ac.uk
[2] Fondazione Santobono Pausilipon Onlus, Naples, Italy
guiliana.faiella@gmail.com
[3] Institute of Cristallography CNR, Rome, Italy
fabrizio.clemente@ic.cnr.it

Abstract. For cross-border collaborative healthcare delivery, data protection legislation seems to be increasingly obstructive. In extreme cases, this may compromise the quality of care a patient receives and at the same time prevent clinicians practicing and developing their medical skills to their full potential. A dilemma develops whereby the fundamental rights of patient and clinician are constrained by the very legal instruments designed to make delivery of healthcare easier. The contention between patient and clinician expectations, or *tussles*, may pose a threat to future healthcare delivery. Compromising healthcare delivery in this way has wider implications for community trust. The concept of tussles in technology infrastructures suggests an actor-network approach involving the patient and clinician relationship within the context of community response to their interactions to offer an innovative perspective on the problem of tussles in healthcare. In this paper, we develop such an approach and discuss an initial validation based on cross-border healthcare scenarios illustrating the contention between fundamental ethical rights and actor-network compliance.

Keywords: Ethics · Privacy · Regulation · Trust · Proportionality · Healthcare · Actor networks

1 Introduction

To discipline the digital economy and facilitate the easy movement of people between member states, the European Commission introduced the General Data Protection Regulation [1]. Harmonizing the treatment of personal data across states, it was hoped, would benefit private citizens not only commercially but also for their care. A tourist (a potential patient) could therefore expect appropriate treatment regardless of host country, with clinicians able to access their health records wherever needed. But in complex networks, like the infrastructures required for the secure transfer of personal and special category data between member states [2], the needs and expectations of different stakeholders may well conflict [3]. This is particularly important within healthcare since failure to gain access to health data could put the data subject (the patient) at risk. Innovative health services tend to focus on privacy and security.

C. Attiogbé et al. (Eds.): MEDI 2019 Workshops, CCIS 1085, pp. 190–201, 2019.
https://doi.org/10.1007/978-3-030-32213-7_15

In consequence, they often introduce many additional challenges regarding legal and ethical concerns that need to be addressed to provide healthcare professionals and developers with regulations and guidance [4, 5]. What is more, unless the patient is unconscious and unable to give explicit consent where vital interests might be used as a lawful basis for processing, the clinician may be prevented from accessing the information they need to treat the patient effectively and in accordance with the ethical principles of their profession. In this paper, we explore the ethical and legal tussles which different stakeholders face who depend on healthcare socio-technical systems. With the GDPR in place, it is assumed that all technology developers need to do is handle data such as health records securely, including appropriate access control. But earlier work by [6] provides a multi-disciplinary perspective of how the information society affects individuals as well as society as a whole, concluding that human choice is paramount. Yet the drive for digitalization, not least of patient health records, is increasingly difficult to resist [7]. Li [8], by contrast, and the failure of the ICT-enabled healthcare system described by Dyb and Halford [9] illustrate a complicated interaction between human choice, policy and the socio-technical context where technology is deployed. It is hardly surprising, therefore, that the adoption of ICT into healthcare environments is known to depend on multiple factors beyond the technical functionality of the technology itself [10, 11]. There is clearly a need to revisit factors beyond regulation and consider 'human choice' as it relates to different agents within a complex network. Based on work by Liyanage, Faiella and their colleagues [12–14], we present an ethical framework designed to identify potential tussles within cross-border, coordinated healthcare. Extending the initial attempt to balance societal and individual interests in making health data available [13] to explore contention between the rights and concerns of multiple stakeholders, the framework presents ways in which the ethical and regulatory tussles of those stakeholders around the network may be evaluated.

1.1 Tussles

The concept of tussles for cyber-physical networks was originally coined in regard to resource contention [3]. For example, net neutrality dictates that all information is treated equally when transmitted across the network. We think that fair. Yet in emergencies, priority should be given to the most significant information packets, such as from emergency services. Contention arises between treating everyone with equanimity and contextual demands. Further, unless the emergency services use specific routing, all packets must be inspected compromising privacy to identify which are a priority. But even here the monetization of personal data suggests multiple standards [15]. So, tussles represent conflicts between stakeholder interests. Therefore, this paper explores the contention between the ethical expectations of actors within a healthcare actor network and professional or regulatory requirements for operational security.

1.2 Tussles in Healthcare

Consent is a common lawful basis whereby the data subject agrees their data may be collected and used for specific purposes such as healthcare (Art. 6 & Art. 9) [1].

Consent must be explicit (it must be auditable) and informed (the data subject must understand why and how their data are to be used). Other legal bases are possible, though may conflict with a data subject's expectation of privacy.

Taking cross-border travel to illustrate the problem, consider several different scenarios as listed in Table 1. Each brings to light different potential contention.

Table 1. Sample scenarios to validate the proposed approach

Scenario	Description
1	A businessman travelling abroad who has a known medical condition travels for work to another EU country. Because of the pre-existing condition he has provided *explicit and informed consent* for access to his medical records as it relates to this specific problem. While away, he feels unwell and is taken to a local hospital for treatment
2	An Italian lawyer has gone to Brussels to attend a workshop on e-Privacy. She has no known medical condition. She is taken ill at the workshop and has to be taken to hospital urgently
3	While on vacation from home in Hamburg to Spain, a mother and son are involved in a serious accident. They are rushed to a hospital emergency department unconscious
4	A young student is on an exchange study tour. He is a member of a religious community which is subject to violent opposition. During clashes in the street, he is injured and needs hospital treatment

In the first scenario, since the patient (the data subject) has provided explicit consent for a specific condition, the clinician in the host country may access the personal/special category data. However, there may be contention if the current episode is not directly or solely related to the pre-existing condition. If the patient has been specific and explicit about the data which can be shared, then there may be other factors which the host clinician is not allowed to see. This may include religious belief (see below) or a relevant comorbid condition. The clinician may not therefore be able to treat the patient appropriately: they cannot necessarily avoid harm or exercise their own professional autonomy.

Provided the lawyer in the second scenario is conscious, local clinicians can attempt a diagnosis by discussing symptoms with her. The problem might arise if they feel they need additional information which she is unable or refuses to provide. As above, the clinician is prevented treating her to the best of their ability. But for the data subject (the patient) herself, she may have legitimate reason not to want to disclose certain information: she is legally not medically trained and may not, therefore, be competent to make a fully informed decision. As with the previous example, it may not be possible to request only relevant data to be transferred.

In the third example, vital interests may be used if both mother and child are unconscious. Even if conscious, the child cannot give consent in most member states. Further, if the father is present or easily contactable, he can provide consent for the child. But only *in extremis* can he do the same for his partner. The clinician may be delayed in accessing relevant data which may compromise appropriate treatment. This could also undermine the patients' chances of complete recovery depending on their condition.

In the final scenario, the patient needs to give consent, of course, but may be reluctant to disclose their religious beliefs for fear of discrimination. In so doing, however, they may be treated using medication or some other procedure which is against their religious conviction. The clinician may therefore inadvertently contradict the wishes of their patient; they will do emotional if not physical harm.

All four scenarios present issues not only for the clinician being able to practice to their best ability and satisfaction, but also for the patient in that they may not receive the most appropriate treatment and may be obliged to disclose more than they would like. Trying to resolve contention between patient and client might, for instance, use a different lawful basis for processing. But if the home medical institution uses consent, it is unclear how a different lawful basis might override the original basis. There is clearly a need to think of healthcare from a different perspective.

1.3   The Socio-technical Context of Healthcare

Healthcare is not only about the treatment of patients. Sitting & Singh [16] describe a complex layered socio-technical system, including the clinical context as well as operational workflows. For our purposes, this may be simplified to a broader socio-technical dimension: patients are treated by clinicians within a community. The agents form a simple actor network [17, 18], with the community bystanders who alternately benefit from the successful treatment of patients through increased medical knowledge and expertise (clinicians *inform*), but also monitor the overall acceptability of what is being done in terms of patient care and medical research (the community sees what happens and so patient and community *protect* one another). A schematic is shown in Fig. 1.

The actors rely on a socio-technical system with multiple technology and infrastructure components as Sitting & Singh describe [16] but also broadcast and social media supporting information exchange and community building [19, 20]. So, *community* are not directly involved in the treatment of patients as previously explained and yet play an important moderating role in the actor network. The most significant feature of the network though is the focus on activity – interaction between patient and clinician, and observation by the community – as well as structure. Contention between the rights both of patient and of clinician would have a directly negative effect for the community in reducing trust, but also perhaps indirectly in constraining the medical experience and information which might add to and improve future knowledge. The clinicians may find themselves criticized for being unwilling to take the risk to try and access the information they require. Over time, trust in the operation of the network would decline.

1.4   Ethical and Regulatory Context for Health Data

With that in mind, we next consider actor behavior and how it relates to structure. De Lusignan, Liyange and their colleagues undertook a systematic literature review on the use of healthcare data [12]. This led to the identification of fourteen ethical principles and the same number of privacy principles [12]. They extended the approach to identify a further set of seven ethical and eight privacy guidelines [13]. The principles and guidelines were then validated in a 3-round Delphi study by a cohort of healthcare and informatics professionals, finding unambiguous agreement on nine each of the ethical and privacy principles, three ethical guidelines, and all nine privacy guidelines. Notwithstanding reported difficulties in interpretation of the principles, interestingly they found no agreement on the ethical principles that clinical judgement should be respected, whether the lawfulness bases might be ignored, and on the privacy principles that data subject (patient) consent should be respected and the purpose of processing limited [13]. Important for establishing agreement on a set of principles, perhaps, are failures to reach consensus. Although their aim was to look at the use of healthcare data in research, the results might inform perceptions of ethical treatment around health data for actual patient engagement.

Based on De Lusignan et al.'s work [12], Faiella et al. [14] sought to use the ethical and privacy principles in order to identify a set of design principles for developing technology to support the secure curation of healthcare data in real life healthcare contexts. They identified six basic principles: trust, privacy & security, related alternately to consent and data subject rights on the one hand and to data management methods; ownership & control; equity; and dignity. Extending this provides the starting point for the present study. We suggest a modified approach as their original, technology-focused framework is extended to the socio-technical, actor network.

2 Approach

In each of the four scenarios described above, ethical principles such as autonomy and the expectation to be able to give and receive effective treatment conflict with legal considerations around data protection. In this section, we develop an approach to validate fundamental ethical principles in the context of trust and proportionality to handle tussles in healthcare.

2.1 Ethical Principles

Lacking consensus from domain experts [13], our initial approach is based on one regulatory principle and three fundamental ethical values. One difference between the GDPR [1] and the previous Directive [31] was the more formal definition of data subject rights. This gives the onus back to the data subject, to some degree, even though they may be unsure of how to exploit or the consequences of asserting those rights [32].

As a high priority item [12, 14] and as part of the concept of data ownership and control [14], we will consider *autonomy* as a fundamental right and therefore as an ethical consideration. Autonomy, in the sense of personal control over data, was part of the motivation for the data subject rights encoded in the GDPR. Beyond that, the European Convention on Human Rights [30] includes articles on life itself (Article 2), privacy (Article 8), and to have individual beliefs respected (Article 9). These are summarized in Table 2 along with an explanation of how they apply to patient and clinician.

Table 2. Basic ethical principles based on rights as they relate to patients and clinicians in the network

Ethical Principle	Actor	
	Patient	Clinician
Autonomy	The right to determine what should happen	The right to use their skills to the best of their ability
Privacy	The right for personal information not to be disclosed	The right to act as a professional rather than pursued as an individual
Beliefs/Values	The right to have convictions respected	The right to follow their own beliefs and convictions in doing their job
Life/Benefit	The right to be given whatever treatment is necessary to preserve life	The right to provide treatment to their patients to preserve lives

2.2   Trust and Proportionality

Fig. 1. Schematic view of a healthcare actor network

Trust in a socio-psychological sense is the willingness to expose oneself to vulnerability [21–23]. In an actor network therefore, trust is less about reliance on regulatory control but rather on how the trustor interacts with the trustee. Where technology is involved, trust may be mediated by self-efficacy and agency [24–26]. Trust becomes an "organizing principle" [27] which underlies both the activity across a socio-technical network (between patient and clinician) as well as how it is perceived (by the community) [28, 29]. So in the present discussion, we extend our concept of trust from what Faiella and her colleagues mean [14] to the socio-psychological construct based on these trustworthiness indicators [21]: *Benevolence* or the belief that the trustee (the clinician) is motivated to do the best they can for the trustor (the patient); *Competence* or the belief that the clinician has the necessary skill to treat the patient; and *Integrity* or the belief that the clinician will use their skill appropriately.

Faiella et al. [14] also introduced the concept of proportionality. As they define it, this refers to the balance between excessive security and pragmatic data governance. Since this is a socio-technical system, we take proportionality to refer to the actions of the clinicians as well as structural elements in delivering treatment as part of the network. So here, we take proportionality for our healthcare actor network to refer both to physical measures (*security* and reduction of inadvertent *disclosure risk*) and behaviors (the clinician operates to the best of their ability to *avoid harm*). *Proportionality* in this sense refers to the physical infrastructure *and* the measures taken to maintain its security whilst the clinician attempts to execute their duties to ensure the best possible outcome for the patient.

As shown in Fig. 1. *trust* facilitates the mutually beneficial operation of the network: the willingness of the patient to expose themselves to vulnerability as the original definition suggests [21–23] provides some leeway for the clinician to achieve their aims. In so doing, the community at large appreciates (and thereby trusts) that the network functions well. The appropriate balance of skill, human activity and physical security measures – *proportionality* – allows this trusting stance to develop and be maintained.

3 Validation

The ethical principles selected (see Sect. 2.1) may now be used to gauge the effectiveness of the healthcare actor network. The assumed benefit of respecting ethical principles can be used as an indication of how this contributes to *trust* while respecting the challenges associated with *proportionality*.

Table 3. Ethical principles versus *Trust* and *Proportionality* from the Patient's perspective

Ethical principle	Trust			Proportionality		
	Benevolence	Competence	Integrity	Security	Risk reduction	Avoid harm
Autonomy	+			+	+	
Privacy	+		+	+	+	
Beliefs/Values	+			+		+
Life/Benefit	+	+	+			+

Table 3 shows an example from the perspective of a patient. Each plus sign (+) indicates a positive contribution to trust or to maintaining appropriate balance in the system. For example, respecting the patient's *autonomy* – their ability to decide for themselves what information is and is not disclosed (see Scenario 1 above, for instance) – may lead to the patient's perception of benevolence but nothing else. If the clinician fails to treat them appropriately, they will not recover satisfactorily and therefore competence and integrity would be undermined.

Similarly, when their privacy is respected, the patient will assume clinician benevolence and integrity, as well as a secure network and reduced risk of disclosure. If the clinician is unable to access a complete medical record, then this may compromise their ability to carry out their professional duties (their *competence*) and to avoid harm.

Respecting beliefs would again lead to a perception of benevolence, in not using treatment which might contravene those beliefs this would allow the clinician to avoid emotional harm (though not necessarily physical harm). This may also lead to perceptions that network security is good. Finally, focusing only on a patient's right to life (getting the best possible treatment) would optimize trust across the clinician's benevolence, competence and integrity, as well as allow the clinician to avoid harm. However, there may be concerns about security and the avoidance of risk of data disclosure.

Table 4. Ethical principles versus *Trust* and *Proportionality* from the Clinician's perspective

Ethical principle	Trust			Proportionality		
	Benevolence	Competence	Integrity	Security	Risk reduction	Avoid harm
Autonomy	+	+	+			+
Privacy			+	+	+	
Beliefs/Values			+	+		+
Life/Benefit	+	+	+			+

Following similar reasoning for the clinician would lead to a different perspective on trust and proportionality in Table 4. To encourage trustworthiness in their skill and experience, clinicians want to project *benevolence* (they have the patient's best interests at heart), their *competence* (they have the ability to treat correctly) and their *integrity* (they act appropriately). They are less interested in operational issues such as infrastructure security and possible data breaches, but they do want to avoid harm with their treatment. All these indicators relate to their autonomy – their right to determine how they treat their patients. Remembering that the rights in the far-left column (*privacy, beliefs/values* and *benefit*) are from the clinician's perspective allows the table to be completed. For instance, the beliefs/values right for the clinician may refer to their religious or philosophical beliefs but equally to their professionalism.

Comparing patient and clinician matrices of rights related to trust and proportionality in the actor network results in the summary shown in Table 5. Here, a plus sign (+) shows where there is agreement between the two actors (each from their own perspective), a minus sign (−) indicates a disagreement (one but not both of the actors), and a blank that neither agrees nor disagrees.

Of the twenty-four cells in the table, where individual rights can be supported by the construct of trust and the operational characteristics of the network, there are ten cases of agreement (+) and eight cases of disagreement (−); and six cases (blank) where neither shows a possible relationship between their rights and trust or proportionality. Across all possible relationships in the network, therefore, there are 8/24 (a third of cases) where the perspective of patient and the clinician treating them are at odds. Excluding the 6 cases where neither is affected, the level of contention increases to 8/18 discrepancies. Tussles between patient and clinician perspectives occur for almost half of the cases, therefore.

Table 5. Differences between expectations of Patients and Clinicians

Ethical principle	Trust			Proportionality		
	Benevolence	Competence	Integrity	Security	Risk reduction	Avoid harm
Autonomy	+	−	−	−	−	−
Privacy	−		+	+	+	
Beliefs/Values	−		−	+		+
Life/Benefit	+	+	+			+

Since little consensus on respect for clinical judgement, consent, legal compliance and the use of personal data [13] found, Table 6 attempts to summarize a community perspective of the effectiveness of the healthcare actor network. For example, *autonomy* applied both to patient and clinician assumes that treatment would be effective (avoiding harm) and therefore trust would be maintained (i.e., the perception of benevolence, competence and integrity); privacy, by contrast, relates only to physical security and awareness of it ("integrity"). To respect beliefs and values, and preserving life and maximizing benefit, would reflect a perfectly operational actor network in which trust is developed and continued. Interestingly, the privacy line seems to reflect only the robustness of the infrastructure and its perceived security that are appreciated. Trust is only developed in conjunction with treatment outcomes (avoiding harm).

Table 6. Ethical principles versus *Trust* and *Proportionality* from a Community perspective

Ethical principle	Trust			Proportionality		
	Benevolence	Competence	Integrity	Security	Risk reduction	Avoid harm
Autonomy	+	+	+			+
Privacy		+	+	+		
Beliefs/Values	+	+	+	+	+	+
Life/Benefit	+	+	+	+	+	+

4 Discussion

In seeing the healthcare delivery socio-technical system in terms of an actor network introduces the perspective of interactional relationships. Deadlock around the contention between patient and clinician is not so much a reflection of inconsistencies between data protection legislation and the ethical rights and expectations of the data subject, but rather what the community at large regards as best for the whole community. The ethical design principles which apply to the technology elements [14] of an actor network are relevant for individual actors to perceive the effective delivery of care. However, human-to-human interactions also rely on interpersonal and organizational trust [21, 22, 27]. Developing and maintaining trust is a continual negotiation [28] which may be hampered by expectations around privacy and technical security. Whilst patient and clinician develop this trust, it may well be that independent bystander perceptions from the broader community need to shape the implementation of privacy.

If this community perspective could be separately validated, then this would offer a solution to the contention between patient and clinician expectations. In a healthcare actor network, the expectations of the generic community of bystanders in the network may override those of individual actors. Trust as an "organizing principle" [27] develops and is maintained only when compromise occurs: data subject consent, as evidenced by Liyanage et al. [13], is not the final arbiter. For healthcare delivery to be seen to be effective and thereby trusted, there must be cooperation between patient and clinician. The former must be prepared to accept vulnerability [21, 23], whilst the latter should perhaps be guided by other factors such as data subject beliefs and convictions. The clinician's judgement may not unequivocally determine the course of action [13] but be subject to community scrutiny. This in turn would allow for culturally divergent perspectives [33].

This exploratory study focuses on healthcare as a socio-technical actor network. Specifically, we have considered not only the physical security of the infrastructure, but also its trustworthy operation. We have looked from the different actors' perspectives to identify the possible source of contention between the expectations of those actors (i.e., stakeholder tussles). This contention is exacerbated in cross-broader collaborative healthcare where different legal bases at different cross-border locations may be incompatible. To resolve these tussles, looking at the effectiveness of the healthcare actor network in terms of the relationship between ethical principles and the maintenance of trust and proportionality, introduces a third actor: the community at large.

5 Future Research

The panel of experts in the Liyanage et al. [13] studies failed to reach consensus on all the ethical and privacy principles or guidelines they identified from their original systematic literature review. Our proposed re-examination of healthcare socio-technical systems suggests that the community at large – those who benefit from advances in healthcare as well as monitor how it is delivered – may be able to resolve the patient-clinician tussle. Using the design principles which Faiella et al. [14] propose we have attempted to review the different actor perspectives within the context of features of patient-clinician interactions (trust) and of the operation of the socio-technical healthcare delivery system (proportionality). To validate this, we now intend to develop quantitative instruments to investigate the attitudes of private citizens to the resolution of tussles that the analytical tables above suggest.

Acknowledgements. The research reported in this paper was supported with funding from the European Union's Horizon 2020 research and innovation programme under grant agreement 727528 (the KONFIDO project) and 727301 (the SHiELD project).

References

1. European Commission: Regulation (EU) 2016/679 of the European Parliament and of the Council of 27 April 2016 (2016)
2. Nalin, M., et al.: The European cross-border health data exchange roadmap: Case study in the Italian setting. J. Biomed. Inform. **94**, 103–183 (2019). https://doi.org/10.1016/j.jbi. 2019.103183
3. Clark, D.D., et al.: Tussle in cyberspace: defining tomorrow's internet. IEEE/ACM Trans. Networking (ToN) **13**(3), 462–475 (2005). https://doi.org/10.1109/TNET.2005.850224
4. Natsiavas, P., et al.: Comprehensive user requirements engineering methodology for secure and interoperable health data exchange. BMC Med. Inform. Decis. Mak. **18**(1), 85 (2018). https://doi.org/10.1186/s12911-018-0664-0
5. Larrucea, X., et al.: Assessing source code vulnerabilities in a cloud-based system for health systems: OpenNCP. IET Software **13**(3), 195–202 (2019). https://doi.org/10.1049/iet-sen. 2018.5294
6. Collste, G., Duquenoy, P., George, C., Hedström, K., Kimppa, K., Mordini, E.: ICT in medicine and health care: assessing social, ethical and legal issues. In: Berleur, J., Nurminen, M.I., Impagliazzo, J. (eds.) HCC 2006. IIFIP, vol. 223, pp. 297–308. Springer, Boston, MA (2006). https://doi.org/10.1007/978-0-387-37876-3_24
7. Halford, S., et al.: Beyond implementation and resistance: how the delivery of ICT policy is reshaping healthcare. Policy Polit. **37**(1), 113–128 (2009). https://doi.org/10.1332/ 030557308X313714
8. Li, J.: A sociotechnical approach to evaluating the impact of ICT on clinical care environments. Open Med. Inform. J. **4**, 202–205 (2010). https://doi.org/10.2174/ 1874431101004010202
9. Dyb, K., Halford, S.: Placing globalizing technologies: telemedicine and the making of difference. Sociology **43**(2), 232–249 (2009). https://doi.org/10.1177/0038038508101163
10. Sanson-Fisher, R.W.: Diffusion of innovation theory for clinical change. Med. J. Aust. **180**, S55–S56 (2004)
11. Yarbrough, A.K., Smith, T.B.: Technology acceptance among physicians: a new take on TAM. Med. Care Res. Rev. **64**(6), 650–672 (2007). https://doi.org/10.1177/ 1077558707305942
12. De Lusignan, S., et al.: Using routinely collected health data for surveillance, quality improvement and research: framework and key questions to assess ethics, privacy and data access. J. Innov. Health Inform. **22**(4), 426–432 (2016). https://doi.org/10.14236/jhi.v22i4. 845
13. Liyanage, H., et al.: Building a privacy, ethics, and data access framework for real world computerised medical record system data: a delphi study. Yearbook Med. Inform. **25**(01), 138–145 (2016). https://doi.org/10.15265/IY-2016-035
14. Faiella, G., et al.: Building an ethical framework for cross-border applications: the KONFIDO project. In: Gelenbe, E., et al. (eds.) Euro-CYBERSEC 2018. CCIS, vol. 821, pp. 38–45. Springer, Cham (2018). https://doi.org/10.1007/978-3-319-95189-8_4
15. Erramilli, V.: The tussle around online privacy. IEEE Internet Comput. **16**(4), 69–71 (2012). https://doi.org/10.1109/MIC.2012.92
16. Sittig, D.F., Singh, H.: A new socio-technical model for studying health information technology in complex adaptive healthcare systems. In: Patel, V.L., Kannampallil, T.G., Kaufman, D.R. (eds.) Cognitive Informatics for Biomedicine. HI, pp. 59–80. Springer, Cham (2015). https://doi.org/10.1007/978-3-319-17272-9_4

17. Kaghan, W.N., Bowker, G.C.: Out of machine age?: complexity, sociotechnical systems and actor network theory. J. Eng. Technol. Manag. **18**, 253–269 (2001). https://doi.org/10.1016/S0923-4748(01)00037-6

18. Law, J.: Notes on the theory of the actor-network: ordering, strategy, and heterogeneity. Syst. Pract. **5**(4), 379–393 (1992). https://doi.org/10.1007/BF01059830

19. Newman, N.: The rise of social media and its impact on mainstream journalism (2009)

20. Gunton, L., Davis, K.: Beyond broadcasting: customer service, community and information experience in the Twittersphere. Reference Serv. Rev. **40**(2), 224–227 (2012). https://doi.org/10.1108/00907321211228282

21. Mayer, R.C., et al.: An integrative model of organizational trust. Acad. Manag. Rev. **20**(3), 709–734 (1995). https://doi.org/10.5465/AMR.1995.9508080335

22. Schoorman, F.D., et al.: An integrative model of organizational trust: past, present, and future. Acad. Manag. Rev. **32**(2), 344–354 (2007). https://doi.org/10.5465/AMR.2007.24348410

23. Rousseau, D.M., et al.: Not so different after all: a cross-discipline view of trust. Acad. Manag. Rev. **23**(3), 393–404 (1998). https://doi.org/10.5465/AMR.1998.926617

24. Thatcher, J.B., et al.: The role of trust in postadoption IT exploration: an empirical examination of knowledge management systems. IEEE Trans. Eng. Manag. **58**(1), 56–70 (2011). https://doi.org/10.1109/TEM.2009.2028320

25. McKnight, D.H., et al.: Trust in a specific technology: an investigation of its components and measures. ACM Trans. Manag. Inf. Syst. (TMIS) **2**(2), 12 (2011). https://doi.org/10.1145/1985347.1985353

26. Pickering, B., et al.: The Interplay between Human and Machine Agency. In: HCII 2017, Toronto, Canada (2017). https://doi.org/10.1007/978-3-319-58071-5_4

27. McEvily, B., et al.: Trust as an organizing principle. Organ. Sci. **14**(1), 91–103 (2003). https://doi.org/10.1287/orsc.14.1.91.12814

28. Lewicki, R.J., Wiethoff, C.: Trust, trust development, and trust repair. Handbook Conflict Resolut. Theory Pract. **1**(1), 86–107 (2000)

29. Sparks, B.A., Browning, V.: The impact of online reviews on hotel booking intentions and perception of trust. Tour. Manag. **32**(6), 1310–1323 (2011). https://doi.org/10.1016/j.tourman.2010.12.011

30. Council of Europe: European Convention for the Protection of Human Rights and Fundamental Freedoms, as amended by Protocols Nos. 11 and 14, E. C. o. H. Rights

31. European Commission: Directive 95/46/EC of the European Parliament And Of The Council (1995)

32. Acquisti, A., et al.: Privacy and human behavior in the age of information. Science **347**(6221), 509–514 (2015). https://doi.org/10.1126/science.aaa1465

33. Hofstede, G., et al.: Cultures and Organizations: Software of the Mind. McGraw-Hill, New York (2010)

Multi-value Classification of Ambiguous Personal Data

Sigal Assaf$^{(\boxtimes)}$, Ariel Farkash, and Micha Moffie

IBM Haifa Research Labs, Haifa, Israel
{sigalasa, arielf, moffie}@il.ibm.com

Abstract. Addressing privacy regulation such as GDPR requires organizations to find and classify sensitive and personal data in their datastores. First, data discovery tools are applied to identify the data. Then, data classification tools are applied on the data that was discovered. Organizations must classify the data into concrete categories to manage data appropriately. In this paper we focus on multi-value classification, where the classifier provides a category to set of values all from the same category. Traditional classifiers usually apply single-value classification methods to a multi-value data set. However, in many cases this resulting an incorrect classification when, for example, domain categories overlap. In this paper, we address this scenario and provide two methods to overcome this problem.

Keywords: Classification · Data discovery · Relational database

1 Introduction

Organizations are now required to support various privacy regulations such as the EU GDPR [1]. As a result, organization need to discover the personal data in the organization datastores, categorize the data, and finally apply appropriate methods to protect the data. For example, the GDPR defines special categories such as racial and health data. A company must have a legitimate and lawful reason for collecting, storing, transmitting, or processing this data.

Sensitive data may be found in both structured and unstructured data repositories. For operational and management purposes it is rather common that the organization group data into sets of values, where the values of each set belong to a category. The trivial example is a relational database where all column values belong to the same category and can construct such a set. Multiple value sets can also be extracted from semi-structured documents. For example, given a set of JSON documents on different individuals, the organization can extract all values at a specific JSON path to construct a set of values to be categorized.

Traditionally, a naïve approach was used to classify multiple values – simply run a set of predefined single value classifiers, referred as *naïve classifier*. Each single value classifier is configured to check if a value belongs to a specific category. The score for each category is a value between 0.0 to 1.0 representing the proportion of values matching the category. Finally, the multiple value set would be classified with the category with the highest overall score.

© Springer Nature Switzerland AG 2019
C. Attiogbé et al. (Eds.): MEDI 2019 Workshops, CCIS 1085, pp. 202–208, 2019.
https://doi.org/10.1007/978-3-030-32213-7_16

There are many known solutions to implement a single value classifier. First, a classifier can check if a value belongs to a regular expression, sometimes with additional restrictions implemented in code. For example, a credit-card number classifier would validate that the value is composed out of 8 to 19 digits (optionally separated by spaces or dashes) by checking if the value satisfies a regular expression. In addition, the classifier would validate the checksum - the value's last digit implements the Luhn Algorithm [2]. Another example of a traditional classifier is to check if the value belongs to a predefined dictionary of values belonging to the category. For example, city dictionary, nationality dictionary and name dictionary.

Furthermore, a classifier (single value or multi-value) may also consider the context from which the values have been extracted. For example, the metadata in relational database, or column name, can provide additional information for the classification [3] and the JSON Path in JSON documents provides a label that may hint on the data category. For example, the label "Address" in the pair "Address": "17 Ashton Street" helps classify the field correctly.

In this paper, we discuss and present solutions to complex classification cases where the existing approaches (e.g. naïve classifier) incorrectly classify multi-value sets. The remainder of the paper is organized as follows: Sects. 2 and 3 present two methods that address this problem: Sect. 2 discusses pattern categories and their related restrictions and Sect. 3 presents a solution based on category value statistic distribution. Section 4 concludes the paper.

2 Multi Value Pattern-Based Classifier

A single value pattern-based classifier checks if a value belongs to some category by validating if the data satisfies the category restrictions. A restriction can be regular expression, range of values, or special restrictions such as Luhn checksum. A multi value naïve pattern-based classifier uses the single value pattern-based classifier to classify a set of values. We extend the pattern-based classifier and support differentiating values that from an initial look, i.e., from the string pattern, and for untrained eyes, may belong to two or more different data categories.

Consider for example the following classifiers each one addressing one of the following values: Foreign County Id (eight digits followed by Luhn Checksum [2]), Social Security Number (SSN) [5] and a 9-digits Patient Id. Assume the following value – a 9-digit sequence 427356720 - is to be classified. This value will be classified as both a Foreign Country Id, an SSN and a Patient Id. Now, consider a set of values, each 9 digits long. In such a case, the Patient Id classifier will always provide the patient-id category a score of 1.0, given that it has no restrictions other than being 9 digits. For a set of Foreign Id values which contains no errors, both the Patient-Id and Foreign-Id will get the highest score. However, if the data contains errors (e.g., typos) while the Patient-Id category will still get the score 1.0, the Foreign-Id category will get a lower score as the typo values will not satisfy the Luhn checksum requirement.

Given a set of categories, all relate to the same basic domain (in our example, 9-digit strings $d_9d_8d_7d_6d_5d_4d_3d_2d_1$), we suggest differentiating between the categories by comparing the expected randomness behavior of the category restrictions. A restriction is any special requirement of the category beyond the basic domain format. Table 1 displays the restrictions in our example. The last column – Random Satisfaction fraction (*rs*) displays the expected fraction of values that satisfy the restriction given values that have been generated randomly from the basic domain. Our solution uses these restrictions and their corresponding *rs* values to enhance the scoring provided by the naïve classifier.

Table 1. Category restriction example

Category	Restriction name	Description	*rs*
Foreign Country id	Luhn checksum	Last digit satisfies the Luhn checksum	0.1
SSN	Area code	$d_9d_8d_7 \neq 000$ and $d_9d_8d_7 \neq 666$ and $d_9d_8d_7 < 900$	0.898
	Group number	$d_6d_5 \neq 00$	0.99
	Serial number	$d_4d_3d_2d_1! = 0000$	0.999
Patient Id		No special restrictions	1.0

Given n random values and a restriction r, if n and rs satisfies Eq. 1 we can transform the distribution of the number of values that satisfy restriction r to normal distribution, where μ and σ^2 values are as described in Eqs. 2 and 3 [6].

$$n * rs \geq 5 \, and \, n * (1 - rs) \geq 5 \tag{1}$$

$$\mu = n * rs \tag{2}$$

$$\sigma^2 = n * rs * (1 - rs) \tag{3}$$

For example, given 1000 random 9-digit strings, we would expect that about 100 strings would match the Luhn checksum restriction ($\mu = 100$, $\sigma = 9.48$) (see Fig. 1).

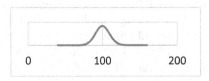

0	100	200

Fig. 1. Expected distribution for matching Luhn checksum

Given category sample values and considering the expected random satisfaction fraction we make two observations: (1) The number of values that match the correct category's restrictions is much above each restriction μ value; (2) The number of values that match other (incorrect) category restrictions is close to the restriction μ value. Based on this insight, our classifier first calculates the percent of values that satisfy the category restrictions. Then, the score is adjusted (reduced) if the matches for other category restrictions are significantly higher than the expected on random values.

2.1 Detailed Algorithm

Figure 2 shows pseudo-code for the concept we discussed. In lines 6 and 7 we calculate the restriction mean and *sd*. Line 8 calculates a factor which will be used later when scoring a category. The factor is a value between 0.0 to 1.0. It is zero when the number of matches equals to the restriction's random mean. The value increases when the number of matches increases. Line 17 shows how we use this factor to update the scoring.

Input: 1) Sample values s 2) Basic domain d;
     3) List of restrictions $r_1, r_2, ...$ 4) List of categories $c_1, c_2, ...$

Preparation step:

```
(1)      exponent ← 2
(2)      distance ← 4
(3)      d.matches ← number values in s that are in d
(4)      for each restriction rᵢ
(5)          rᵢ.matches ← number values in s that matches rᵢ
```

   (6) $r_i.mean \leftarrow d.matches * r_i.rs$

   (7) $r_i.sd \leftarrow \sqrt{d.matches * r_i.rs * (1 - r_i.rs)}$

   (8) $r_i.factor \leftarrow error\_function((\frac{r_i.matches - r_i.mean}{distance * r_i.sd})^{exponent})$

Category score calculation:

```
(9)      for each category cᵢ
(10)         cᵢ.matches ← number values in s that satisfy cᵢ
(11)         factors ← Φ
(12)         for each restriction rᵢ
(13)             if (cᵢ requires rᵢ)
```

   (14)   factors $\leftarrow$ factors $\cup$ $r_i.factor$

```
(15)             else
```

   (16)   factors $\leftarrow$ factors $\cup$ $(1 - r_i.factor)$

   (17) $c_i = min(factors) * c_i.matches$

Fig. 2. Pattern based classifier pseudo-code

2.2 Results

We implemented and ran the classifier on three datasets. Each dataset contains 1000 values for each category: SSN, Foreign Id and Patient-Id. The difference between the data set is the error rate – the percent of values that don't match the corresponding category. Table 2 displays the results – a score calculated for each category. The pattern-based classifier differentiates correctly between the categories.

Table 2. Classifier result

	SSN values	Foreign Id values	Patient ID values
No errors			
SSN score	0.98	0	0.04
Foreign Id score	0	0.96	0
Patient Id score	0	0	0.94
2% errors			
SSN score	0.97	0	0.05
Foreign Id score	0	0.95	0
Patient Id score	0	0	0.96
5% errors			
SSN score	0.92	0	0.01
Foreign Id score	0	0.93	0
Patient Id score	0	0	0.96

3 Statistic Classifiers

In Sect. 2, we presented a method to differentiate between categories based on category restrictions. In this section, we exploit category distribution information for the same purpose. For example, High Density Lipoprotein (HDL), Low Density Lipoprotein (LDL), High Blood Pressure and Low Blood Pressure are all categories which are very difficult to correctly classify without accounting for each category's unique statistical value distribution. The categories value range may overlap. For example, the numeric range for Ammonia level in blood is 15–50 μmol/L and the numeric range for Ceruloplasmin is 15–60 mg/dL. All Ammonia level values are also Ceruloplasmin, and most Ceruloplasmin values are also valid Ammonia values. Similarly, number of school years and number of smoked cigarettes are hard to differentiate. These categories can be distinguished by comparing the values to an expected value distribution.

Many of the health tests such as blood tests are characterized by normal distributions. Other categories such as number of children can be classified using discrete distribution. We developed two types of statistic classifiers: Normal Distribution Classifier and Discrete Distribution Classifier. Both classifiers compare the statistical characteristics of column data with known distributions. The Normal Distribution Classifier uses the data's mean and standard deviation while the Discrete Distribution Classifier calculates the data's histogram (for each value, its count and its proportional part). Both calculate the distance between the column's statistic information to known distributions (for example, number of sleeping hours), and selects the category which minimize the distance. This is calculated using Kullback-Leibler Distance (KLD) [8]. For Discrete Distribution we use the KLD method as described in [9].

Figure 3 shows the result of our Statistic Classifier. We created three Discrete Distributions for three categories: number of smoked cigarettes, number of sleeping hours, and number of school years. Figure 3 shows each category's distribution as well as a list of values which are the target of classification (12, 17, 8, 20, 8 …). The result of the statistic classifier – the KL distance between the values and each of the categories – is also shown. We can see that the KL distance of school years is the smallest (0.027), and therefore school years is the selected category.

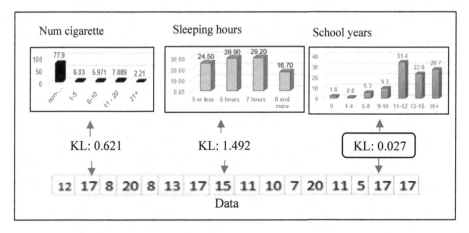

Fig. 3. Applying Kullback-Leibler distance on discrete distribution

4 Summary

The ability to classify correctly multiple sets of values is a crucial step in supporting privacy regulations such as the GDPR. In this paper we present novel approaches that can correctly classify different categories – supporting complex cases where domain values from different categories have been previously indistinguishable. We validate our proposed solutions – one for string pattern categories and one for numeric or discrete categories – on sample data. The initial results are promising. Further work is required to evaluate the approach on larger, industry grade data sets.

References

1. EU GDPR Portal. https://eugdpr.org/
2. Li, Y.C., Yao, Q.Z.: The validation of credit card number on the wired and wireless internet. J. Netw. **6**, 432–437 (2011)
3. du Mouza, C., Métais, E.: Towards an automatic detection of sensitive information in a database. In: Second International Conference on Advances in Databases, Knowledge, and Data Applications, pp. 247–252 (2010)
4. SHiELD. (n.d). https://project-shield.eu/
5. Puckett, C.: The story of the social security number. Soc. Secur. Bull. **69**(2), 55–74 (2018). United States Social Security Administration
6. DeGroot, M.H., Schervish, M.J.: Probability and Statistics. Addison Wesley, Boston (2012)

7. Farinde, A.: Lab Values, Normal Adult (2019)
8. PShlens, J.: Notes on Kullback-Leibler Divergence and Likelihood (2014)
9. Bigi, B.: Using Kullback-Leibler distance for text categorization. In: Sebastiani, F. (ed.) ECIR 2003. LNCS, vol. 2633, pp. 305–319. Springer, Heidelberg (2003). https://doi.org/10.1007/3-540-36618-0_22

Author Index

Printed in the United States
By Bookmasters